A Christian Method of Moral Judgment

J. Philip Wogaman

A Christian Method
of Moral Judgment

———

SCM PRESS LTD

334 01928 1

First published 1976
by SCM Press Ltd
56 Bloomsbury Street, London

© SCM Press Ltd 1976

Printed in Great Britain by
Western Printing Services Ltd
Bristol

To Stephen, Donald, Paul and Jean

Contents

vii

Contents

Preface

As suggested by the title, this volume is concerned with how we arrive at moral judgments. How can Christians and other morally serious people express their central value commitments in decision, judgment, and action?

By speaking of a Christian 'method' of moral judgment two misunderstandings may be raised. First, some may expect to find here a ready-made solution to all of our problems of moral judgment – a more or less 'automatic' method of deciding things. Would that such a method could be found! Since that is out of the question, we shall be concerned rather with approaches to *thinking* about moral issues. That is to say, this volume will not provide ways of avoiding thinking. Secondly, the book is not intended as a systematic treatment of all issues in ethics. For example, one will not find here a rounded discussion of virtue and character-formation. As the first chapter indicates, this side of ethics is presupposed by any discussion of moral judgment. Were there no virtuous people there would be little inclination to raise the question of how such people can go about making up their minds when they face moral dilemmas. But the important matters of character development and analysis of personal virtues are not really the subject matter of the present work.

In the main, this is presented as a Christian moral perspective. One of the issues vigorously debated today among ethical thinkers is whether there is anything uniquely *Christian* about Christian ethics – or, phrased differently, whether Christianity adds anything to ethics. I believe it does, at least when we confront the ultimate meaning of judgments, decisions, and acts. Nevertheless, it must be added immediately that the whole human family occupies common ground in the moral life. The approaches to moral judgment suggested in this book may possibly be useful both to Christians and to non-Christians. Indeed, one of the tests of a method of moral judgment is the degree to which it helps clarify dialogue among persons of diverse background. Among other things, I hope the present volume will help to clarify why it is that some Christians and non-Christians find themselves on the same side in a great social controversy, while other Christians and non-Christians are on the other side. This should not lead us into cynicism about ethics; but it can be a useful goad toward deeper thinking about the sources and methods we employ.

Many (though certainly not all) of the factual illustrations to be found in this volume are drawn from American experience because of its greater familiarity to me. Nevertheless, the vocation of Christian ethics is worldwide in scope. I am particularly grateful that this volume is to be published first in Great Britain, partly because this will put its central ideas to the test in countries other than my own and partly because of the warm associations formed during several months of study and research in Cambridge. Some of the illustrative materials in the volume are, in fact, drawn from British experience, and I apologize in advance for inaccuracies. It needs to be said that in a book of this kind all illustrative materials are designed to help illuminate approaches to ethical thinking. I hope readers will test the major ideas in the light of their own experience and in relation to problems which are not dealt with here specifically.

While I must accept full responsibility for the contents of the volume, much of it has undoubtedly benefited by criticism from various readers and lecture audiences. This has included my own students at Wesley Theological Seminary and in the Washington Theological Consortium, several university and college lecture settings, and a number of ministers' conferences and lay study groups. My colleagues, L. Harold DeWolf, Haskell M. Miller, and Larry L. Rasmussen have supplied particularly valuable support and criticism. I gratefully acknowledge this assistance along with similarly helpful comments from publisher's critics who must, perforce, remain unknown to me. I wish also to acknowledge with gratitude the secretarial assistance of Mrs Carolyn Schneider and Mrs Dorothy Mills Parker. Substantial portions of Chapter 8 were first published in my article in *Toward a Discipline of Social Ethics: Essays in Honor of Walter George Muelder*, ed., Paul Deats, Jr, Boston University Press 1972, and are reprinted by kind permission.

We live at an awkward but exciting juncture of human history. None of us should claim too much for our own wisdom. All of us should confront our responsibilities humbly and diligently, hoping that by our faithfulness the next generation will have more to work with and a better society to live in. It is in that spirit that I dedicate this book to my children and to the members of their generation.

Wesley Theological Seminary   J. Philip Wogaman
Washington, D.C.

I

Moral Commitment and Ethical Uncertainty

> Love without knowledge goes astray.
> Knowledge without love puffs up.
> Love with knowledge builds up.
>
> St Augustine

When it is said that the road to hell is paved with good intentions, the point is not that there is anything wrong with good intentions. The point is that there is a difference between good intentions and intelligently good actions. Good intentions are often misdirected. 'Love without knowledge goes astray.' Even in a world populated entirely by good people this would remain a problem as long as those people were capable of making honest mistakes. Good and honest people are often puzzled by the dilemmas they face in the real world.

This is particularly true in our time. As I write these pages, Christians in Ireland agonize over their responsibilities in the face of violence and confusion. Young people in Rhodesia wonder whether they should put their faith in negotiations or join a guerrilla movement. The British government, along with other Western countries, faces troublesome economic dilemmas, and the trade union movement wonders what kind of wage increases to settle for. An investigation of the US Central Intelligence Agency raises the question of the necessity and propriety of covert operations of various kinds. The governments of such countries as India and Bangladesh contemplate ruinous population growth rates and problems of economic development. Thoughtful people in many parts of the world debate the relative merits of Marxism, democratic socialism, and capitalism as they face an uncertain economic future. Young people everywhere face personal dilemmas involving sexuality, education, and career decision-making in a rapidly changing world. Older people wonder how to interpret and contribute to that same world.

Why is the task of moral understanding and decision-making so difficult? The usual answer is that this is, after all, a complex and rapidly-changing world – and that is certainly true. But the problem is deeper even than the facts of this particular time in history. Our age is plagued by so much uncertainty that we too easily forget that there has always been a gap between moral commitment and moral judgment. There has always been the possibility of the unintended mistake. The reason for this is that there is a fundamental difference between the will and the mind. It is a nice thing when good people are also intelligent and wise, but that is an illusive combination. Sometimes, as St Paul reminds us, we understand the good but we do not have the will to do it. At other times, we have the will but lack the understanding. Sometimes good and loving people do evil things unintentionally. Sometimes evil people do good things by accident or for the wrong reasons. Most of us are a little bit of both and do a little of both.[1]

This volume, however, is primarily concerned with the moral intelligence. It assumes that there is such a thing as good will. It addresses the question of how good people can come to recognize the good amidst the complexities of life.

This volume is explicitly Christian in its fundamental value assumptions, which means that in some way it presupposes a Christian definition of the object of moral commitment. There is a sense in which all ethics is ultimately religious in nature. A non-religious or 'secular' ethics is capable of dealing with the form of moral commitment and judgment, establishing regulative norms and criteria. But it remains uncommitted to any ultimate reference for valuation. Without such a context, ethical judgments remain suspended in a vacuum. As H. Richard Niebuhr has pointed out,[2] all of our values are held in relation to a centre of value. In order to arrive at moral judgments concerning particular values we must see them in relation to this centre of value. Our religious faith is founded on this centre of value; and inasmuch as substantive ethics has to do with values and their ultimate significance, we can scarcely avoid regarding ethics as a religious enterprise. A discussion of moral judgment which seeks to be more than purely formal must therefore be as explicit as possible about its religious commitments.

To be sure, in identifying the commitment of this volume as Christian, I cannot overlook the fact that many people may accept most of its main contentions without regarding themselves as Christians. Others, on the other hand, who do think of themselves as Christians may find it impossible to accept what they read here as being consistent with their faith. Christian faith means many things to many people, and not all of these meanings are consistent with each other. Moreover, Christian faith has affected and been affected by viewpoints which are not explicitly Christian. These ambiguities will have to be explored below with some care even though, in the final analysis, our understanding of what is Christian can yield to no *purely* objective criteria.

Still, the Christian character of our commitment permits a reformulation of the problem of the book: The basic question is, what are the implications of Christian faith for our actual moral judgments? What should be the Christian attitude toward sex, war, race relations, poverty, drug use, development economics, revolution, abortion, population control, political corruption, or any of the other areas where we confront dilemmas and confusions? Put as a question of judgment, it is still an objective matter. The subjective question is whether I will commit myself entirely to whatever it is that Christian faith implies. The objective question is what Christian faith does in fact imply in relation to the circumstances of life. The subjectively committed Christian must ask as an objective question what he should do about his commitment. The commitment may indeed falter in face of the implications of his objective judgment, and in fact this faltering often weakens the objectivity of our judgments themselves. But the question of judgment remains distinct from the question of commitment.

We are led thus to a fundamental problem in the relationship between commitment and judgment. Commitment can be expressed categorically as an either/or. Whether we do or do not commit ourselves without reservation we know we ought to. But ethical *judgment* operates in a climate of uncertainty. This point will become more evident as we proceed, but it can be noted here that even the most optimistic view of the possibilities of human knowledge must concede that there is less immediacy to our knowledge of the factual world than there is immediacy to our own will. Our will is the most immediate aspect of our experience. Formally speaking, we are capable of making a definite choice. But how definitely are we able to know whether or not our choice will in fact be the good that we intend? The objects of our judgment, unlike our commitment, are not immediate to us. First we have to go out and look at the world and think about it and then arrive at a judgment. Even if we believe that we will one day arrive at total certainty in our moral judgments, the first thing that the committed will confronts is uncertainty as to what it should do. This difference is obscured by the fact that we often arrive at judgments without thinking about them. We assume that they are, of course, the judgments which best express our commitment. But it is objectively uncertain whether they do or not. Ethical uncertainty is present even where the moral person is convinced that he or she can depend upon some fixed human authority, such as a church or a respected counsellor – a matter which we shall explore further. The point is that when one confronts a new problem one must go to the church or to the counsellor to find out what should be done as an expression of that moral commitment and one must also wonder whether the moral instruction has been properly understood.

We must confront this objective uncertainty in our moral judgments whether we choose to think of the moral life prescriptively (as a matter of obedience to law) or teleologically (as a matter of creative efforts to achieve good ends) or relationally (as

4

a matter of loving relationships with others). We face this uncertainty whether we view morality as a matter of doing God's will in some definite sense (as though God's will calls for some one best form of obedience, or *telos*, or relationship) or as a matter of our own free creative response to a multiplicity of possible ways of expressing our good will. All of these ways of conceptualizing the moral life depend upon a distinction between the good and that which frustrates the good, and thus all require us to arrive at judgments from a situation of uncertainty in the actual world. Prescriptive, teleological, and relational approaches to ethics are doubtless complementary rather than mutually exclusive,[3] but that is beside the point in establishing that there is a difference between moral commitment and ethical judgment and that the latter confronts us with uncertainty.

The emerging problem, then, is how are we to go about judging so that our ethical uncertainty will not frustrate our moral commitment. For if we cannot know the good, our commitment – however good subjectively – is incapable of fulfilment in the real world.

A. *The Loss of Moral Authority*

There is a world-wide crisis of confidence in specific sources of moral authority in our time. Individuals and societies have always faced some uncertainty in arriving at moral judgments. But for a number of reasons, twentieth-century humanity has lost confidence in the social and cultural authorities which have traditionally provided guidance in making specific decisions. Christians have not escaped the general problem; indeed, their own crisis may be particularly acute. Previous generations of Christians have often been able to follow four interrelated sources of moral authority without having to examine them very much. They often struggled with uncertainties and disagreements as to the facts, but basic sources of authority could often be accepted without much question.

First, many generations of Christians were able to accept the Bible quite uncritically. The simple fact that the Ten Commandments or the Sermon on the Mount or Paul's ethical teachings were in the Bible made them almost self-evidently authoritative. There could be spirited disputes as to the meaning of a particular passage of scripture or as to its precise applicability to a problem at hand, but people on both sides of a dispute would accept the common presupposition of the Bible's authority. Nineteenth-century slaveholders and Christian abolitionists disagreed on the meaning of the Bible, but both quoted it as decisive moral authority. But this kind of confidence has now been eroded by more than a century of careful biblical criticism. The internal inconsistencies, the problems of canon and translation, the human authorship and historical situations underlying parts of the Bible have been scrutinized with care. The net result has been to show that, whatever their sources of inspiration, biblical writers were all flesh-and-blood human beings writing in quite human circumstances. Inevitably, the moral authority of the Bible as the unvarnished word of God has come in for re-examination. Appreciation for biblical insight has often been increased by this process, and in many respects the Bible has been made more available for sophisticated theological reflection. But uncritical and specific use of biblical injunctions as moral authority has been weakened.

A second authority was the church. Roman Catholicism, with its Pope and hierarchy, has traditionally held a high conception of ecclesiastical authority, but Protestant Christians have also had much confidence in the moral authority of the church. Among some Protestants this has been a group matter: the 'sense of the meeting' or the judgment of the 'gathered congregation'. Among others it has been more a matter of high respect for the minister's Sunday sermon. Pronouncements and declarations by Protestant church bodies have sometimes enjoyed high prestige as sources of moral teaching. But the moral authority of the church has been weakened by the demonstrated fallibility of church leaders and members. The moral authority of Protestant churches in

American culture was badly weakened by their haste in baptizing Prohibition and World War I as absolute moral causes,[4] by their reluctance to support some obviously humane causes, and by their intensive competitiveness and racism. Roman Catholicism has been shaken by anti-clericalism in many European and Latin American countries over the course of the past century and by recent forces unleashed by Vatican II. (Ironically, this last event, while increasing respect for Catholicism enormously among non-Catholics, undermined faith in church authority among many Catholics by relativizing the role of Pope and hierarchy.) When Pope Paul VI released his encyclical condemning use of artificial contraceptives (*Humanae Vitae*), Roman Catholicism suffered its most acute crisis of confidence in many years, though it is probable that the crisis was more occasioned than caused by the specific issue.

The relativizing of church authority, both Protestant and Catholic, has probably been made irreversible by the social sciences – particularly by sociology and psychology of religion and by anthropology. Such studies have demonstrated the continuities between religious and other kinds of institutions and the similarities between Christian religious institutions and those of other religions. Moreover, the 'religious' motivations of churchgoers have sometimes been exposed as camouflage for status-seeking, economic self-interest, and neurotic illnesses. Much of this may have contributed greatly to the long-run health and integrity of the church, but it has clearly eroded any simple, unthinking respect for the teaching authority of the church.

A third authority was natural law. Natural law is based upon belief in understandable universal moral principles which can be applied definitively to particular issues. It presupposes considerable confidence in human reason and, more to the point, in the proposition that equally rational people will arrive at the same conclusions on the same moral dilemmas. Roman Catholics have generally considered St Thomas Aquinas the best exponent of natural law. St Thomas also had considerable influence among Protestants, though Protestant theologians from Luther to Barth

7

have been more sceptical of the claims of natural law. Many Protestants have, however, given similar status to the 'inalienable rights' of the Enlightenment, to the Kantian categorical imperative, and to such ideologies as *laissez faire* capitalism or socialism or the democratic creed. Where natural law has restricted itself to a purely rational analysis of the moral will, thus affirming that we are bound morally to choose the good and avoid evil, it may be questioned whether it has been affected negatively by twentieth-century experience. But the formal principle of the good will merely poses, without answering, the problem of moral judgment. Where natural law has been used to provide authoritative guidance in forming specific moral judgments, and where it has treated aspects of physical nature as normative, it has also been weakened for modern life. Too many assertedly self-evident natural law judgments have failed to persuade rational people. When St Paul asks, in natural law fashion, 'Does not nature itself teach you that for a man to wear long hair is degrading to him, but if a woman has long hair, it is her pride?' (I Cor. 11.14–15) it is quite clear to many people now that his 'natural law' has fallen captive to transitory custom. Similarly, when Pope Pius XI writes concerning contraception that 'since . . . the conjugal act is destined primarily by nature for the begetting of children, those who in exercising it deliberately frustrate its natural power and purpose sin against nature and commit a deed which is shameful and intrinsically vicious'[5] non-Catholics and increasing numbers of Catholics suspect that something other than the pure gift of reason has intruded to dictate the moral conclusion. What has intruded is the notion that identifiable aspects and processes of physical nature are necessarily a reflection of universal moral principles.

All of this is not necessarily a revolt against nature or against reason. A dawning awareness that we cannot take unlimited liberties with nature has begun seriously to chasten our pride of technological mastery. Nevertheless, our very great control over the natural world has made it impossible to view any specific aspect of the natural world as normative.[6] Far from being a revolt against reason, this kind of scepticism can be shown to have highly rational roots. Our appreciation for nature and our respect for its complexities may be increasing, but it is certainly more difficult for us to use the natural as a specific norm for moral judgment.

A fourth authority was custom or tradition. Patterns of behaviour and attitudes become engrained through the years, and their authority is accepted without question. Some of the customs of Christians have been rooted in scripture and church teaching, though customs derived from other sources may claim the same authority of assured rightness. Attitudes toward beards, card-playing, the 11.00 hour for Protestant worship, clothing styles, etc., though expressed with intense moral fervour, may reflect little more than the authority of custom. This has also been dissolved by the social sciences and by the increased contact of persons from different cultures with one another. Our sense of the unique value of particular customs has been demolished.

The four types of moral authority were usually woven together into some general conception of rightness, and the individual Christian could use them in situations demanding moral judgment. But this sense of self-confidence is now largely gone.

Many Christians have deplored this loss of moral authority. They have, in one way or another, attempted to counteract the relativizing tendencies of modern life – but usually to no avail, for basic attitudes and values cannot be re-established by *tour de force*. Other Christians have attempted to understand these relativizing currents from a deeper perspective.

Many have concluded that the most subtle and powerful undermining of specific moral authorities is implied by Christian theology itself. One way of stating the point is that if God is greater than any human value or understanding or practice, then nothing human can be made into an absolute. To absolutize God is to relativize everything else – including all of the value standards other than God which we use to make our judgments. If God is, to use the phrase of the early Barth, 'wholly other', then our efforts to symbolize the divine in culture and to concretize God's moral demand upon us will always be frustrated by their incompleteness and their uncertainty. This is not really a new thought. It is as old as the Hebrew insistence that we must not worship idols in the place of God. But the application of the commandment against idolatry has always been incomplete because it has been assumed that certain values, principles, or moral standards were expressions of the will of this absolute God. The development of universal monotheism in the Hebrew-Christian tradition did in fact serve to reinforce the authority of specific moral commandments, for they were thus invested with the authority of the universal God himself. Moral authority, thus reinforced, has served not only as a guide to specific moral judgments but as a basis for religious intolerance and persecution.[7] Now there is less theological confidence in human ability to recognize and enact the divine in socio-cultural form. We are more apt to agree with Tennyson that

> Our little systems have their day;
> They have their day and cease to be:
> They are but broken lights of thee,
> And thou, O Lord, art more than they.

We are less confident of the absoluteness of our own values and standards and more likely to see some value in the standards of those who are different from us. Such people also are creatures of God, and God also has access to them in ways we may not fully understand.

In twentieth-century theology these points have been developed in several ways. Karl Barth himself, besides emphasizing the transcendence of God, has based his theological work upon God's self-disclosure to man through his Word, Jesus Christ. Through Jesus Christ we understand that God has said yes to each of us, and in this acceptance of us has released us from captivity to the law (read Hebrew law, natural law, Protestant moralism, or any other form of law which prescribes specific answers to the questions of concrete moral judgment in themselves). We are free to be what God has chosen us to be: loving, creative children of faith in covenant with the Father. *A posteriori*, after realizing our

new freedom in Christ, we also gain insight into the moral significance of nature, but not in a way which can be generalized into
concrete moral maxims. Barth is specifically critical of natural
law, biblical fundamentalism, and ecclesiastical authoritarianism.

Paul Tillich speaks of the 'Protestant principle' which 'contains
the divine and human protest against any absolute claim made for
a relative reality'.[8] This principle 'is the judge of every religious
and cultural reality, including the religion and culture which
classes itself "Protestant" '.[9] (Thus, many Roman Catholics in
effect live by the 'Protestant' principle and many 'Protestants' do
not.) Tillich also extends the meaning of the classical Protestant
doctrine of justification in the following way: 'not only he who is
in sin, but also he who is in doubt is justified through faith.'[10]
Through our doubts, if they are honestly held and presuppose
our earnest desire to find the truth, we are actually brought closer
to God than we would be through complacent acceptance of
customary religious and moral values. Thus, 'you cannot reach
God by the work of right thinking or by a sacrifice of the intellect
or by a submission to strange authorities, such as the doctrines
of the church and the Bible. . . . Neither works of piety nor works
of morality nor works of the intellect establish unity with God.'[11]

Reinhold Niebuhr underscores a theologically-based relativism
with his emphasis upon the limitations of human nature. We are,
in Niebuhr's judgment, capable of grasping truth and expressing
goodness. But our finitude permanently limits our ability to grasp
all the truth, and our sinfulness permanently distorts the truth
that we do grasp and the good that we do express.[12] The cultural
absolutes of previous generations of Christians were based not
only upon their limited vision; to some extent they were also
based upon selfish personal and group interests. Thus, Reinhold
Niebuhr implies that the loss of moral absolutes in our generation
may be necessary for the sake of recovering a higher loyalty to
truth and goodness.

H. Richard Niebuhr has made a significant contribution to this
kind of relativism in his concept of 'radical monotheism'.[13]
According to Niebuhr's analysis, religious life is based upon the

ultimate object or objects of worship – our centre of value. The centre of value is that which determines all our lesser values and loyalties. He believes there to be three basic forms of religious life, corresponding to three kinds of centre of value: polytheism, which involves worship of many 'gods' or centres of value; henotheism, the worship of one's own group or nation – or even humanity itself; and radical monotheism, which involves worship of the God-beyond-the-gods. The God of monotheistic worship is both the source of reality and the source of value. Every other form of worship sets up some *part* of reality to be worshipped. Thus, every cultural absolute (which makes a god out of some cultural object) involves either polytheism or henotheism. Of course, specific cultural values are themselves valued in their relationship to God. But since all specific values are related to God as the centre of value there is not yet here a principle of differentiation between specific values to serve as a basis for specific moral judgments. Only radical monotheism – worship of the transcendent God – adequately expresses the Christian faith. But we are again left with a radical gap between the transcendent God and the specific aspects of human existence.

Other recent theological movements have had similarly relativizing effects. The 'death of God' movement was unclear in its ethical implications and its present influence is rapidly fading. Nevertheless, this movement obviously contributed to the climate of relativism in so far as it had any effect. The secular theology movement, identified with such theologians as Friedrich Gogarten and Dietrich Bonhoeffer, has been more significant. It sought to establish that Christian faith has 'desacralized' culture. Cultural objects, values, and practices are no longer to be treated as sacred in and of themselves. Emphasizing St Paul's declaration that 'all things are lawful' (I Cor. 6.12), Gogarten proclaims that in Jesus Christ human beings are released from bondage to a world infused with sacred values prescribing their thoughts and actions. In Christ, God's grace has broken through to deny the absolute authority of particular laws and values. We need no longer find life's meaning from within the prison of the world for it has been established once and for all that we are the children of God. Our relationship to the world can now be mature; that is, we can freely *use* the world in accordance with a freedom based upon the security of our relationship with God. To be sure, Gogarten also emphasizes the second part of Paul's declaration: 'all things are lawful, but not all things are helpful' – thus reminding us that our specific judgments matter. But they do not matter in the same way. Ideologies and natural law theories which derive their normativeness from within the world are condemned as 'secularism': they continue human imprisonment within the world, apart from God. 'Secularization', by contrast, involves freedom under God to use the world maturely. Dietrich Bonhoeffer, dealing with some of these same themes in his prison writings, calls for recognition 'that the world and people have come of age'.[14] In this world we are to live for others. We are to plunge into 'the godless world, without attempting to gloss over or explain its ungodliness in some religious way or other'.[15]

Our new freedom – freedom to judge, freedom to decide, freedom to act – is emphasized in one way or another by many of the younger contemporary theologians throughout the world. With most, this freedom is rooted in some understanding of the transcendence of the divine.

Yet this freedom is paradoxical. While it liberates one from many traditional values and authorities, it also seems to lack any particularity. Freedom from cultural absolutes permits wide latitude for creative expression. But now what are we to express, and how are we to express it? Most theologians have strongly asserted that culture matters. Without culture, there is no medium in and through which we can respond faithfully to God's good gift of grace. But in what *particular* ways does culture matter? This brings us back to our dilemma: our loss of guidelines may permit us to judge *everything* for ourselves. But then what is the basis on which we are to judge *anything*?

The loss of moral authority in the contemporary world is thus a paradoxical loss – which is to say that it is also partly a gain. The *basis* of Christian moral authority has been affirmed and purified of earth-bound idolatries. But it is a transcendent basis. It is not immediately evident how it is to be related to the particular aspects of experience without a return to the old cultural idolatries (or to new cultural idolatries). We have cut down the old tree for the sake of its roots, and now it may be a question whether there can be a new tree. The issue is unavoidable for, as Gabriel Vahanian has said, 'without a cultural vocation there can be, insofar as Christianity is concerned, no faith in God'.[16] Unless faith in God can find specific cultural expression it is literally nonsense. The issue is not merely whether or not Christian faith can help us with our moral decisions; it is whether there can be such a thing as Christian faith.

B. *The Response of Situation Ethics*

The problem of ethical method resulting from this theological situation has been posed strikingly by what is loosely termed situation ethics or contextual ethics. This approach has important implications for our method of arriving at moral judgments. A seemingly clear negative answer is offered; i.e., we are *not* to make our judgments on the basis of any moral rules which assume the intrinsic goodness or evil of particular kinds of acts, practices, or institutions. Joseph Fletcher has made the point characteristically: '. . . in Christian situation ethics nothing is worth anything in and of itself. It gains or acquires value only because it happens to help persons (thus being good) or to hurt persons (thus being bad).'[17] The only intrinsically good thing, in his view, is love itself: 'No law or principle or value is good as such – not life or truth or chastity or property or marriage or anything but love. *Only one thing is intrinsically good, namely, love: nothing else at all.*'[18] Paul Lehmann, whose position we shall examine shortly, is also at pains to establish that no moral rule is intrinsically valid and thus universally applicable apart from the rule-transcending theological basis of morality. He thus disputes the Kantian claim that it is universally and necessarily wrong to tell a lie. While Fletcher and

Lehmann are sharply different in their formulation of the basic norm of Christian ethics, they and other situational ethicists agree upon the negative proposition: namely, that there are no universally applicable rules which provide a basis for moral judgment.

How then are we to decide? Here the term 'situation ethics' is itself a bit misleading – at least so far as the intention of Fletcher and Lehmann are concerned. More is involved in the making of an ethical judgment than the situation itself. Situation ethics is not sheer relativism or it would not be ethics but a denial of the moral life. Nor is it a brash hedonism of the 'playboy philosophy' sort. More is involved than the situation and our pure subjective inclinations. Joseph Fletcher carefully insists that his ethics can make use of principles of rational calculation (he speaks, for example, of a coalition between Christian situation ethics and Utilitarianism in acceptance of the principle of 'greatest good for the largest number'), and he speaks appreciatively of the collective moral wisdom of this and previous generations as a resource to enlighten our judgments.[19] Still, we ourselves must judge; and if necessary we must know when to set aside all the rules.

What precisely then do the rules mean? This is a difficult question with Fletcher and it suggests that a whole level of analysis has, perhaps inevitably, been neglected. This is the level of accounting for the relationship between *agape*, the only intrinsic good, and the specific ends sought in relation to the world of nature and of human institutions. Surely these ends are not validated morally solely as 'a function of human decisions' made in love.[20] How is love to know what difference any decision makes? It helps but little to say, as Fletcher does, that the decision is good if it increases the sum total of lovingkindness[21] because we still do not know the relationship between the structures of human existence and lovingkindness. The collective wisdom of mankind is helpful, to be sure; but an appeal to *consensus gentium* in the form of inherited tradition or summary rules only pushes the problem back one step, particularly since the consensus may be set aside if necessary for the sake of love. What relationship has humankind, through its moral traditions and summary rules, perceived between love and the structures of existence? If there is not any objectivity to the structures which stand over against love, then notwithstanding Fletcher's protestations to the contrary, he has surely surrendered to antinomianism.

Fletcher might have gone far toward solving this problem had he made use of the method of Emil Brunner, whom he salutes approvingly as a fellow situationalist. Brunner, while insisting upon the sole primacy of love, develops also the category of human need as it is found in and through nature and society. While need does not establish a self-validating moral claim, it can be discussed as an *objective* claim to which love can at least be related somewhat more dependably. If it is love's intention to serve the neighbour, it is a long step toward fulfilling this intention if we can know what the neighbour's objective needs are likely to be. Brunner in fact goes further in arguing that God has, through creation, established complementarity of natural and social needs as a support for the unity of humanity in love.[22] Natural and social structures may not be intrinsically good, but they add something of objective moral significance to subjective loving.

As it is, Fletcher's ethics contributes a striking reaffirmation of the importance of moral (i.e., loving) commitment, but we are not greatly helped with our ethical uncertainties. As Paul Ramsey has shrewdly observed,[23] even in his own illustrative cases Fletcher demonstrates the inability of his method to provide insight. Ramsey calls attention to two of Fletcher's cases with almost exactly contradictory forms of moral judgment, both of which are offered as possible illustrations of *agape* at work in the situation. In one, the Scott expedition in Antarctica, a heroic group of explorers refused to abandon a badly disabled member of the party even though this slowed them down dangerously and probably contributed to the deaths of all members of the expedition. This was love at work in 'an authentic *kairos*'.[24] The other case is that of the 1841 shipwreck of the *William Brown*, in the aftermath of which a ship's officer ordered a number of men to be thrown out of a perilously overloaded longboat. These men had to be sacrificed unsentimentally so that the remainder, including women and children, could survive. This *also* is offered as a possible instance of *agape* at work. Without pausing to argue the merits of the two cases, it is evident that *agape* is at work only as a possible *motive* – not as a source of insight into *what* should be done if love is well directed. These difficulties are compounded in Fletcher's ethics by the imprecision with which the two chief terms, love and situation, are employed. The question of the definition of love is germaine to the problem of ultimate norm; the question of situation is germaine to the specific problems of judgment. It is difficult to escape the conclusion that so far as judgment is concerned we have been left with a basically intuitive ethics.[25]

Paul Lehmann also rejects any universal claims for moral rules, and in this respect his position is similar to that of Joseph Fletcher. His rationale is, however, strikingly distinct. The fundamental problem of Christian ethics is not, according to Lehmann, how to comprehend the good to be sought through our actions. Rather it is that of analysing the new life, the new maturity of those who have been transformed by God's action in Jesus Christ: 'the main concern throughout these pages is with the concrete ethical reality of a transformed human being and a transformed humanity owing to the specific action of God in Jesus Christ, an action and transformation of which the reality of the Christian *koinonia* is a foretaste.'[26] Christian ethics, therefore, is to be considered indicative, not imperative. The question is not what I *ought* to do but rather what I *am* to do.[27]

Lehmann's meaning can easily be misunderstood. He does not deny that all people, including Christians, confront alternative action possibilities and that it matters, ethically, which of the actions are chosen. He confesses that there is 'an imperative pressure exerted by an indicative situation' and that 'the "ought" factor cannot be ignored in ethical theory'.[28] But this ' "ought" factor is not the primary ethical reality'. 'The primary ethical reality,' he continues, 'is the human factor, the *human* indicative, in every situation involving the interrelationships and the decisions of men.' One may restate this argument along somewhat Kantian lines by acknowledging that it is the will that is decisive, not the specific choice. The ethical problem is in the will, not in the alternatives.[29] There would be no moral issue in any situation of choosing were there not a moral will involved; and thus, the specific analysis of the situation of choosing must be subordinated to analysis of the person who does the choosing. The 'ought' therefore has to do with what a person ought *to be*: he 'ought' to be good. The *further* question of his specific actions becomes (if he *is* good) not an imperative but an indicative question: that is, a question of what a good person will *in fact* do. He does not, in the moment of choosing, decide then whether or not to be good – that question is already, as it were, settled. Since it is settled already, the only remaining question is which of the possible actions best expresses the goodness that he is. That question can be regarded as indicative.[30]

But Lehmann attempts to show why a formal Kantian ethic is not satisfactory. A formal ethic cannot tell us *why* we 'ought' to be a moral person, nor indeed *how* we can be what we ought to be. The will of a formal ethic is an abstract, non-human will. The question of what we are, ultimately, is a theological question. It is settled for the Christian by faith in God's action in Jesus Christ, which has established in human history a 'new order of humanity, in which and by which the Christian lives . . .'.[31] The essential nature of humanity is revealed in Jesus Christ. In the church – the *koinonia* of faith – there is a foretaste of the fulfilment of this new humanity. In a formal sense, the Christian ethic involves doing the will of God. But the will of God is revealed only in what God himself has done and is doing in human history 'to make and keep human life *human* in the world'.[32] Christians grow in maturity as they live in this reality in the *koinonia*. Their actions, then, are simply an expression of their mature humanity. They are to do what they are: 'To do what I am is to act in every situation in accordance with what it has been given to me to be. Doing the will of God is doing what I am.'[33]

Setting aside the question whether Lehmann has adequately

expressed the theological frame of reference in which we are to understand the moral will itself, we must now inquire as to the effect of his position on the problem of actual judgment. Here we reach a bit of an impasse. If a Christian is simply to do what he is, and if his knowledge of what he is is borne to him in and through the *koinonia,* then does this mean that the real Christian will simply know intuitively what he is to do? If this is so, then the Christian who even raises the question may be in something of a bind. The very fact that he has raised the question of *how* he is to know what is to be done would seem to indicate that he is not sufficiently attuned to God's humanizing activity. If he were genuinely mature, he would not need to ask. 'Understandably,' Lehmann writes, 'such an ethic will be puzzling, even ridiculous, to those who have no eyes to see the signs of the times, who do not know what belongs to their peace. Such knowledge comes by insight, not by calculation. It is the gift of faith available to those who are willing to take seriously what faith knows about the doing of God's will in the world.'[34] To be sure, Lehmann acknowledges at the same time the 'complexity of the actual human situation' which 'is always compounded of an intricate network of circumstance and human interrelationships'. He does not pretend that concrete questions of judgment will be easy. Indeed, it is because of their very difficulty that the Christian cannot take the easier but inauthentic route of an absolutist ethic: 'Absolutist ethics declares that the proper answer to the question "What am I to do?" is supplied by an "absolute". And what is an "absolute"? Ethically speaking, an "absolute" is a standard of conduct which can be and must be applied to all people in all situations in exactly the same way.'[35]

In rejecting such an absolutist ethic, Lehmann never really tells us what concrete resources we might have, other than mature insight to help us in actual, complex situations. We may agree with him in rejecting an absolutist ethic, as he has defined it, while still feeling that more must be said than he has said about what it is with which we face situations of judgment and decision. The present writer confesses that he does not simply *know* what is to be done in relation to modern war, the environmental problems, racial tension, allocation of economic priorities, abortion, or any number of other complex issues humankind faces. Intuitive judgments are more likely to reflect Christian faith accurately in the immediate face-to-face relationships characteristic of small groups or communities – though even there sheer intuition often fails. The truth is that Christian ethics, while presupposing much of what Lehmann has said concerning Christian motivation and God's activity to humanize humanity, must involve more personal and collective *thinking* about the implications of this faith in the world of decision-making. When Christians find themselves espousing opposite sides in public policy debates, the differences of insight cannot be attributed simply to differences in maturity of faith or of intuitive perception of God's actions in human history. We need some basis for rational assessment of situations. Rational assessment, for Christians, must involve faithfulness to basic theological insights and recognition of regularities and continuities in God's humanizing action. It also involves the possibility of meaningful communication among Christians concerning the implications of their faith.

By asserting that intuition is not enough we should not think of it as being unnecessary. That flash of insight which we label intuition is bound to play an important role in most actual moral judgment, partly because we often have to make decisions in a hurry and partly because the complexities of actual moral problems are often too great to organize with conscious rationality. In real life we cannot be rational deliberating machines – human computers – coldly dissecting and reconstructing the moral dilemmas we face as systems of ethics sometimes curiously imply we should do. Still, a rational method of moral judgment can at least serve us before and after the fact of intuition. Before, it can prepare us for more faithful, loving, dependable intuitions, so that when we move instinctively it will be instinctively in the right direction. Afterwards, it can help us analyse our intuitions, assessing their adequacy, correcting our errors. Situation ethics does not provide us with a sufficient basis for either of these important functions of ethical reflection, just as it does not afford a more-than-intuitive approach to decision-making in the situation itself.

C. *Beyond Situation Ethics*

A number of Christian thinkers are uncomfortable with the intuitive method of situation ethics, even while remaining fully cognizant of the difficulties of ethical legalism and of most of the traditional sources of moral authority when these are treated as absolutes. Situation ethics has performed a notable service in providing a more distinct frame of reference in which to approach a renewed search for principles to guide Christian moral judgment.

John C. Bennett has wrestled with this problem for many years. Committed to a Christian realism which seeks to maximize the possible good in any concrete moment of decision, Bennett has nevertheless sought to understand the continuities between such moments. His concern is twofold. On the one hand, he wishes to find a rational basis, transcending the immediate situation, on which to apply the Christian faith. On the other hand, he wishes to be able to state moral judgments in such a way as to further the moral co-operation and dialogue of Christians with non-Christians. The first concern has led him to a restatement of the concept of 'middle axioms' as a way of expressing the demands of the gospel in universal terms without making them absolute for all time. The second leads him to a restatement of natural law.

The term 'middle axioms', originating with the ecumenical movement at the time of the Oxford Conference on Life and Work in 1937, had never been defined with great precision. J. H. Oldham at that time defined middle axioms as 'an attempt to define the directions in which, in a particular state of society, Christian faith must express itself'. Such middle axioms 'are not binding for all time, but are provisional definitions of the type of behaviour required of Christians at a given period and in given circumstances'.[36] Picking up this term in 1946, Bennett defined a middle axiom as being 'more concrete than a universal ethical principle and less specific than a program that includes legislation and political strategy'.[37] While 'the Kingdom of God in its fullness lies beyond our best achievements in the world', Bennett argues that 'God does have purposes for us that can be realized'. These purposes 'are not absolute and all-inclusive goals but the next steps that our own generation must take'.[38]

Bennett suggested several middle axioms for the immediate post-war world to illustrate the method. These included the imperative of creating a United Nations political framework, national responsibility for full employment, prevention of private centres of economic power from becoming stronger than government, doing away with racial inequalities of opportunity, and achieving democracy with majority rule, universal suffrage, and constitutional protection for individuals and minorities. None of these middle axioms was offered as a universal moral principle, binding for all time. Yet clearly they could be related to universal principles and they were obviously relevant to large areas of concrete decision-making.[39]

But what is the source of Bennett's universal principles? It is here that his restatement of natural law doctrine is expressed. While he regards Christian faith as crucial to the moral life and judgment of Christians at all levels of analysis, he nevertheless wishes to state moral principles in such a way that they can become the basis for common action and dialogue beyond the confines of the church. In his book *Christian Ethics and Social Policy* he attempted to summarize his views of the relationship between Christian ethics and natural law as follows:

1. There is a moral order in the world that can be known with varying degrees of clarity apart from revelation.

2. The knowledge of this moral order is not as a matter of fact universal but it has a much broader basis than the Christian faith.

3. Some of the perceptions of moral truth doubtless depend upon the direct or indirect influence of Christianity, but when once they are seen they can be supported by facts of experience that can be known apart from Christian faith.

4. There is great contemporary support apart from Christian faith

for the following moral convictions: that the human race is one in the sense that there are no permanently superior and inferior human groups, one in origin, one in essential nature, one in the fact that mutual relations of friendship do now cross all actual social barriers, one in fateful interdependence; that society should be open to free criticism from within; that men and nations should be true to their pledged word; that justice on the corrective side should be administered with impartiality and that on the side of the distribution of wealth it should be so administered as to promote equal opportunity for all children to develop their capacities . . . these principles . . . furnish an extensive moral law that has a basis in experience which is independent of Christian faith. . . .

5. The vivid understanding of the claim and of the range of these moral principles, especially the realization that they are binding on oneself or one's own group, is immeasurably strengthened by the influence of Christian faith within a given culture.[40]

The interaction between natural law and Christian faith is thus seen to occur on two levels: on the first, Christian insight first discovers some moral truths which subsequently are known, *a posteriori*, apart from specific Christian teaching; on the second, Christian faith strengthens commitment to moral principles even though these principles are knowable apart from Christian faith.

Paul Ramsey has also been concerned to incorporate moral principles in Christian ethical reflection, although he has done so from a more specifically theological point of view. Interestingly, in his earlier writings Ramsey's position was not dissimilar to that of Joseph Fletcher on the question of use of principles in the situation. For example, in his important early work *Basic Christian Ethics*,[41] Ramsey wrote that

. . . Christian love takes on the aspect of a quite indeterminate norm when compared with any and all forms of legalistic social ethic. The Christian man is lord of all and subject to none of the rule-morality. Set free on account of his so great responsibility, he must therefore be constantly engaged in 'building up' an adequate social ethic realistically adjusted not to precedents in law or existing conventions of society, but to concrete and changing neighbor need. Searching for a social policy Christian love may make *use* of, say, the ethical insights summed up in the so-called 'natural law', but its *base* of operations never shifts over onto the ground of the rational moral law.[42]

Christian love and the neighbour's need were taken to dominate the Christian's every moral judgment, and every social institution or code of conduct was to be criticized on that basis and, if need be, discarded: 'Even the humblest Christian man must rapidly become willing to have the structures and customs of his world otherwise than they now are. These will not stand long in any case. Why not bend them more to love's desiring?'[43] For the past decade or so, however, Ramsey's ethic has done a sharp about-face toward a new appreciation for moral principles. The substantive basis for his position has not changed, contrary to the interpretation of some of Ramsey's critics. *Agape*, or Christian love, is still the ultimate norm of Christian ethics. What has changed is the appreciation for principle as a method of generalizing in and between situations of moral judgment. Now he is anxious to establish the need for Christians to obey moral principles which embody love even when to do so may require one not to do what appears to be an immediate demand of love. An act of love in an immediate situation may undermine customs, laws, or institutions which embody love.

In his essay 'Two Concepts of General Rules in Christian Ethics',[44] Ramsey suggests three ways in which rules can express and implement Christian love. First is through summary rules – rules which are a summary of previous experiences of attempting to judge and act on the basis of love. '*Summary rules* are reports that cases of a certain sort have been found to be most love-fulfilling.'[45] Summary rules are more than an expression of individual experience. They can embody the wisdom accumulated through centuries in the traditions of a community which has attempted to live on the basis of Christian love. Nevertheless, the status of summary rules is only provisional. They are rules of thumb which can be set aside for the sake of a more direct expression of love whenever the situation demands. The user of summary rules 'still believes that *all* (and not only *some* or *many* or *most*) rules or principles threaten to constrain or constrict love. While he uses principles to guide conduct, still he gets himself ready to violate those same principles in situations in which to follow them would conflict with what love dictates in that situation.'[46]

To Ramsey this is not enough. A Christian, he believes, ought not to reject 'the possibility that Christian faith and love affords mankind more than *probable knowledge* into ethics'.[47] The basic theological ground for this possibility is in the faith that God has in love bound himself absolutely to man. God's binding covenant is the basis for all (binding) covenants among human beings. Therefore, 'love seems to have only a dissolving or relativizing power when the *freedom of agape* is taken to mean love's *inability* to bind itself one way and not another or in no way except in acts that are the immediate response of one person's depth to another's depth'.[48] There are, he concludes, 'some things that are as unconditionally wrong as love is unconditionally right'.[49] The unconditional rightness of love can be embodied in rules as well as in acts at least in the negative sense that some things may be defined as generally (always) unloving. It follows that there are general rules which are more than summary rules. Can such rules be known? Ramsey's position would seem to be that they can *become* known. Whether or not any particular supposedly general rule (such as the rule of promise-keeping or rules against cruelty or rape) is in fact properly so regarded is an important part of the subject matter of ethical reflection. That is, it is the business of Christian ethics to seek out such general rules which embody Christian love. The difficulty of this task is insufficient ground for saying with the situationist that Christian rule morality can go no further than summary rules or 'rules of thumb'. Ramsey insists that such possible general rules are not a form of legalism. It is an altogether different thing to speak of rules for the sake of love than it is to speak of rules for the sake of the rules themselves.

But following John Rawls,[50] he also suggests yet another basis for love-embodying rules in what are called 'rules of practice'. A 'practice' can be understood as a societal rule, or custom, or institution – it is a system of mutual human expectations governing behaviour. If one is involved in the system, it is expected that he will observe the rules of the system – just as the participant in a game must observe the rules of the game. The question whether one will observe the practice and the rules of the practice are not separable. By violating one of the rules, a person simultaneously rejects the practice in which the rule is embodied. Thus, if promise-keeping is accepted as a social practice, one cannot break any of one's own promises without also weakening that general practice of promise-keeping. Similarly, marriage as a generally accepted social practice or institution is weakened by infidelity, regardless of the specific claims of Christian *agape* which may be made in a particular situation to justify the deviation. If some practices (or institutions or customs) embody love so that Christian love has a stake in the continuation and strengthening of the practices, then it is an act against love to violate a rule implicit in such practices. 'Rules of practice,' he argues, 'necessarily involve the abdication of full liberty to guide one's action case by case by making immediate appeals to what love (or utility) requires in each particular case. The point of a practice is to annul anyone's title to act, on his individual judgment, in accordance with ultimate utilitarian or prudential considerations, or from considerations of Christian love in that one instance alone.'[51]

The point is not as conservative as it might appear to be. Practices can themselves be challenged for the sake of love. But 'there cannot be exceptions (to practices) that depart from them by direct general appeals to *agape* overriding the rules in particular cases in which the agent does not take the weighty responsibility of criticizing the practice as a whole and attempting to replace it with another. *Agape* justifies no exception within a practice. One must rather undertake to reform the accepted practice as a whole in some fundamental respect which, he ventures to say, would render it generally a more loving practice.'[52] The point can be revolutionary as well as conservative in tendency if, in fact, it is one's judgment that existing practices or institutions violate rather than embody love. But one cannot sever the connection between particular actions and their relationship to the broader co-ordination of human actions and expectations and do this in the name of particular case-by-case decisions as to what is the loving thing to do.

It is questionable whether either Bennett or Ramsey has finally solved the basic underlying problem of moral judgment. It is one thing to affirm the existence or value of middle axioms, general rules or general practices; it is quite another to identify *particular* axioms, rules or practices which assuredly *do* embody love or goodness. It is still another thing to relate the axioms, rules, or practices to the actual facts at hand. At both these latter points, neither Bennett nor Ramsey has provided us with a sufficient basis of judgment. What both have done is to help locate the thing to be judged and, in particular, to see that the problem of judgment cannot be merely a matter of case-by-case intuition. Life *is* interconnected. There *are* regularities in human social and historical experience. Generalizations *can* be made about what it means to love in society in a broader historical frame of reference than that suggested by the situationalists. But this level of insight does not offer us as much methodological help as we need.

It may be questioned, moreover, whether either Bennett or Ramsey has in fact gone beyond a summary rule ethic. To do so it would be necessary to validate a rule-claim on some basis other than the experience of oneself or of one's community or of tradition. It is particularly evident that Bennett's middle axioms and Ramsey's practices would in most cases be validated in respect to human experience. It is not so clear, however, with respect to Ramsey's love-embodying pure general rules. Here the question is whether or not it is the case that some rules can be found which categorically express love's demand on the basis, not of a summary of particular experiences, but on the basis of an analysis of what it means to be human. Are there some general rules pointing to things that love cannot *ever* permit to be done? Ramsey suggests in passing that some things, like cruelty and rape, 'are inherently wrong, wrong in themselves, because of the lovelessness that is *always* in them'.[53] Similarly, he suggests that 'promise-breaking' might be considered to be wrong by definition. But such asserted general rules are not to be classified as classes of acts alone but as classes of acts undertaken from unloving motivation. It is not, for instance, physical suffering *per se* that is objectionable to Ramsey when he speaks of cruelty as something which is so inherently unloving that it can be proscribed by a general rule. It is suffering deliberately caused. It is not intrinsically immoral, in Ramsey's estimation, to cause suffering in war. Even innocent bystanders can be made to suffer if the suffering was not intended and was only a consequence of necessary and justified measures to conduct a justified war.[54] But if it is the motivation that justifies calling a given act 'cruelty', then we have only a truism on our hands (however helpful the truism may be) – i.e., the truism that unloving acts are intrinsically and generally loveless.

Still, it cannot be excluded that more than the sheer individual commitment of the will in loving obedience to God belongs to what is implied in Christian faith. The question posed by Ramsey's view of general rules is whether or not certain concrete choices are prefigured in the Christian's moral commitment *per se* and by that which has brought this commitment into being – namely God's own commitment to us. In a sense, the answer to this question must be yes. But still a margin of uncertainty remains to plague the application of any ethic – for there must be a relating of commitment (however many general rules can be derived from it) to the empirical world (which is always first of all unknown). How are we to know the empirical world so as to relate it fittingly to whatever ethical principles we feel we can derive directly from Christian faith? And if, as one may suspect, our knowing of the empirical world and therefore our knowing of the relationship between that world and Christian faith is always somewhat problematic (just as our perception of God is, because of our finitude and sin, problematic), how are we to deal simultaneously with the truth that is present to us and the truth which is absent behind our ignorance?

In summary, Paul Ramsey's major contributions to the resolution of the problem of relating moral commitment to intellectual uncertainty appear to be twofold. He has first insisted that the work of ethical judgment is in a world of continuities: of relationships, of institutions, of historical connections between past, present, and future. No one can simply begin to judge the merits of a case when the case is upon him. Whatever goodness there is, it is not merely a goodness of individuals in their face-to-face interaction 'then and there'. It is a goodness for all humanity and for future as well as for present time. It is a goodness which is present or absent in institutions and civil law and social custom. The analysis of such things is not a matter of love deciding 'then and there', as Fletcher maintains, for 'then and there' is also every time and every place. Ramsey's second contribution is to point toward the possibility of deriving ethical content from the Christian faith itself in addition to the simple and obvious motivation to love. It may be questioned whether this ethical content is as immediately dependable a guide for action as Ramsey seems to suppose it is, but this is a point which must be tested in succeeding chapters as we face the same problems. In addition to these points, Ramsey has contributed a useful analysis of the meaning and possibilities of summary rules.

A third significant contemporary thinker who has attempted to find and apply ethical principles is Walter G. Muelder. The starting point of Muelder's ethics is the moral law formulation first developed by Edgar S. Brightman and later refined substantially by L. Harold DeWolf and by Muelder himself. The 'moral laws' developed in this tradition are based upon philosophical analysis, not specifically upon Christian faith claims. The moral laws can therefore be understood as a reformulation of natural law. The table of laws themselves is intricately developed, and it is beyond our purposes to discuss them in detail here.[55] Several things about this formulation are, however, significant. It is, in the first place, structured on a Kantian analysis of the moral will. The moral will is universal and therefore free of self-contradiction. As the will confronts the real world, it always relates to it through affirming the good as it can best be understood. One must accept as binding one's own ideal values and regulate all particular value experience on the basis of what one considers to be the universal good. In the real world, our conception of the universal good may often be frustrated. But if we are to avoid self-contradiction we cannot settle for less than the 'best possible' good in the situation. The total range of consequences of projected actions must be calculated as far as possible and, in this sense, we have here a prudential ethic. But it is important to note also that no conceivable consequence could justify self-contradiction or a violation of the ideal values on the basis of which consequences are themselves evaluated. That would be literal nonsense.

The original Brightman formulation of this system defined the material good in terms of personality. It is our ideal of what we and other persons ought to be and to become which ultimately defines the nature of the good. Subsequent formulation by L. Harold DeWolf emphasized the importance of human interaction in community and of our understanding of the metaphysical unity of reality. Both DeWolf and Muelder stress that Christian theology establishes, for the Christian, the content of the regulative terms person, community, and metaphysical reality. For the non-Christian, the moral laws are equally binding, but for them the particular content will be different. Thus, an attempt has been made here to restate the natural law on a Kantian and personalistic rather than Thomistic basis and to define the relationship between this ethic and the Christian faith which supplies it with concrete meaning. As the moral laws themselves stand (apart from the theological content utilized by particular Christian thinkers), they have the appeal of almost self-evident logical clarity. As a formal analysis of the integrity of the will – which we have also asserted to be the starting point of all ethics – their claim of validity can scarcely be challenged without self-contradiction. It is unthinkable to say that we may do anything less than the 'best possible' or that our acts ought not to be relevant to the context of action or that we ought not to be concerned about the consequences of actions. Moreover, one can defend the centrality of the categories of 'personhood' and 'community' and of the problem of understanding the metaphysical context in which moral action is ultimately to find its meaning. But our problem is how we are to locate this meaning in other than formal terms, on the one hand, and how we are to discover in the real empirical world what it means to be an actually existent person or to have an actually existent community, on the other.

It is here that Muelder's peculiar contribution takes shape in his understanding that social ethics is an intersectional discipline, mediating between normative disciplines (such as theology and philosophy) and empirical disciplines (including the natural and social sciences). What can the one know about the other? Since all disciplines are constantly developing, there is no possibility of a final, once-for-all synthesis. There is rather the prospect of what Muelder calls 'emergent coherence': a constantly developing state of synthesis as the different divisions of human knowledge themselves develop and interact in dialogue.[56] More than the other thinkers we have considered thus far, Muelder therefore takes seriously the contributions of the sciences as providing a basis of dependable knowledge about the actual world. His position can only superficially be dismissed by assertions that science cannot, after all, be the source of values or norms or that living experience is more than what can be discovered through abstract scientific methodologies. The first of these assertions neglects the dialogical character of the interaction between science and normative disciplines. The second mistakes the nature of science itself. The natural and social sciences are not, after all, substitutes for living experience; rather they are an attempt to organize and systematize insights gained from living experience. From time to time the various branches of science have regrettably made claims tantamount to the assertion that this or that science should be regarded as the key to all knowledge or philosophy. But this is scientism, not science – a poor substitute for philosophy.

The question posed by science to the moralist is whether or not our approach to both natural and social phenomena will be casual and impressionistic (and intuitive) or whether it will be orderly, thoughtful and disciplined. How shall we understand, for instance, the rules of practice of which Ramsey speaks? Can a disciplined examination of the family or economic life or particular forms of government contribute anything to our understanding of morality in the real world? Clearly we cannot say that analysis of facts alone is the same thing as moral judgment, for unless there is a potential tension between facts and norms there is literally no such thing as *moral* judgment. But if the facts enter into moral judgment, as surely they must, then a more refined understanding of what the facts really *are* contributes significantly to the accuracy of moral judgment. Among the not inconsequential results of taking social sciences seriously is an increased appreciation of the factual interdependency of all life and of the great complexity of so loose a term as 'situation' or 'context'.

But of course the emergent coherence of which Muelder speaks does not relieve us of the difficulties and uncertainties of judgment. As with Bennett and Ramsey, we still must face the problem of how we are to act with conviction despite our knowledge that we shall never know for certain that our actions and judgments are truly the faithful expression of goodness we intend them to be. It is unlikely that we shall be able to think our way out of this basic problem to a position of certainty. Christian moral judgment can at best do the work of clarification so that we may at least know the basis upon which we judge and act and so that our methods of judging and acting can be open to correction.

D. *A New Evangelical Perfectionism*

All of this may seem too limited and too relativistic to a vital new group of Christian thinkers who have sought to translate the gospel more directly into relevant social decision-making. A new evangelical perfectionism has emerged in recent years to challenge the marriage of conservative theology to conservative politics and, at the same time, to challenge what it perceives to be the sterility of the combination of liberal theology and liberal politics. In one way or another, these thinkers are convinced that the gospel of Jesus Christ provides direct, unambiguous moral guidance. They are also conservative in their use of the Bible, although they do not necessarily believe that every moral injunction in the Bible is of equal significance.

John Howard Yoder is a particularly striking leader in this new movement. In his *The Politics of Jesus*,[57] Yoder argues that Jesus is himself the norm for Christian ethics and that the perfection in love enjoined by the life and teaching of Jesus is fully relevant to human existence. We should therefore reject the false choice between compromising Jesus as the true norm of our actions in order to be 'effective' in the social world and the withdrawal from the world in order to preserve our Christian perfection. Yoder regards Troeltsch's famous 'church-type' and 'sect-type' as equally unacceptable options:

> In the tradition of Ernst Troeltsch, Western theological ethics assumes that the choice of options is fixed in logic and for all times and places by the way the Constantinian heritage dealt with the question. Either one accepts, without serious qualification, the responsibility of politics, i.e. of governing, with whatever means that takes, or one chooses a withdrawn position of either personal-monastic-vocational or sectarian character, which is 'apolitical'.[58]

The choice between these two options is a false one, however, if one considers Jesus to be the Messiah of God. To say that Jesus is Messiah is to say that Jesus' approach to the realities of social and political life is the approach which ultimately has God behind it. We do not need to take responsibility for managing history; ultimately that is God's responsibility, not ours. Nevertheless, we can be sure that in obedience to Jesus' way we shall be most relevant to the historical process, not in retreat from it.

It may be accurate to say that Yoder answers the problem of this book only at the negative end. That is to say that we can be sure in our moral judgments in so far as they involve a rejection of use of evil means, such as violence. In every case where we are presented with the prospect of such moral compromise we are to reject it: about that we can be very clear, and to that extent Yoder would likely deny that there need be uncertainty in our judgments. From this he does not conclude that 'for any question of social ethics a direct solution can be sought in the casuistic teachings of the New Testament'.[59] In order to arrive at judgments concerning the complex ethical dilemmas of modern society we could not do without 'broader generalizations, a longer hermeneutic path, and insights from other sources'. Yoder is not a biblical perfectionist in the sense of affirming 'a specific biblical ethical content for modern questions' – except in the renunciation of violence and other uses of what we ourselves know to be evil. When we cannot reasonably predict 'success' as an outcome of this kind of radical obedience to Jesus we should remember that our obedience is to something deeper than immediate success and that Jesus, as God's Messiah, is Lord of history.

The other prominent thinker to whom reference should be made under this heading of evangelical perfectionism is the French social critic and lay theologian, Jacques Ellul. In a series of writings Ellul has declared his own kind of war against contemporary technology, urban civilization, and political institutions. His often quixotic conclusions on such subjects do not need to concern us here, but his evangelical methodology, particularly as it concerns the question of violence, is unique and interesting.[60] Taking his cue from Pauline ethics, Ellul argues that apart from the freedom which we can have alone in the grace of Jesus Christ, we are inextricably caught in the order of necessity. He does not condemn violence in any specific sense as 'immoral'. Apart from our liberation in Christ we can scarcely avoid violence; it is a necessary part of our social interaction. It is a law of our pre-Christian existence. At the same time, the 'laws of violence' indicate to Ellul that violence never achieves the ends justifying its use.[61] There is no difference between 'justified' and 'unjustified' violence. Violence begets nothing more than violence in endless vicious circles. Ellul does not condemn people who use violence, particularly in revolutionary situations where they are striving to overcome concrete forms of injustice. Christians, indeed, may sometimes be drawn into participation with revolutionaries. But they should never forget that this belongs to the order of necessity and that it finally achieves nothing whatsoever. It emerges from this that Ellul, like Yoder, has a concrete historical absolute but it is linked to his conception of how we can be liberated from the necessity of violence – it is not a matter of what kinds of commitment or obedience should direct our judgment. And Ellul's form of perfectionism, if it can be called that, is to be found in his total rejection of violence.

It is thus characteristic of both Yoder and Ellul, as of most evangelical perfectionists, that there is greater clarity in the negative than in the positive side of social judgment. Certain things are rejected, more or less absolutely. But there may be some continuing uncertainty among the various positive options. Neither Yoder nor Ellul gives us absolute guidelines for moral judgment in situations where we have to choose between alternative positive strategies of witness and action. Taking Ellul's work as a whole, he probably develops more detailed solutions to social dilemmas and more concrete renunciations of present institutional structures than Yoder would ever want to venture. But it remains true that Ellul's methodology does not save us from some continuing uncertainties of judgment even after we have, through grace, escaped from the realms of necessity.

In a later section of the book, we shall return to Yoder and Ellul to examine their views on the question of compromising with evil. But for present purposes, it is evident that they have not provided us with a final solution to the problems of translating love into intelligent action.

E. *The Problem of Ethical Methodology*

We should remember again that the twentieth century has itself placed a heavy strain upon our search for clarity in judgment. The great wars, instant communication techniques linking previously insulated cultures, the rise of Communism, the struggles for the independence of colonial peoples, racial strife, space travel, technological expansion into automation and cybernation, the environmental crises, the population explosion, the nuclear stalemate and nuclear proliferation, the emergent prospect of the collective suicide of the human race – such things tax the maturity of our ethical judgments to the limit. 'New occasions teach new duties, time makes ancient good uncouth.' Surely this is not so of the centre-point of ethics, the good will. Love does not become obsolete. But it is an accurate statement of the problem each new generation, and particularly this one, encounters in trying to locate the good in the real world. If, as we have seen, we are not likely to discover a method of arriving at certainty in our moral judgments, we may at least hope to clarify the bases of those judgments. A method of moral judgment must at least help us to minimize the morally weakening effects of uncertainty. It must permit us to act with *certitude* if not with certainty.

This discussion may be concluded by suggesting certain summary criteria for an adequate Christian ethical methodology:

1. It must be *tentative* with respect to particular moral judgments. It must remember that no one's perceptions of God (and therefore of the full meaning of the good) are ever complete. We are all finite beings. Even were this not so, our judgments would continue to be distorted by our own self-centredness. And even were that not the case, our perceptions of the actual world would remain incomplete. The data are never all in. An adequate methodology of Christian moral judgment must therefore always be open to the possibility that particular judgments arrived at with the best of intentions may be mistaken.

2. It must be *faithful* to the central affirmations of Christian faith. A methodology of Christian moral judgment is rooted in Christian faith. That is its starting point. The centre of value, the ultimate source of norms, cannot be derived from other sources. Christians may and do differ widely in their interpretation of what Christian faith really means. But a methodology of Christian moral judgment will always be some kind of interpretation of what it means to act in faithfulness to the Christian faith commitment.

3. It must provide a basis for investing judgments and actions with *wholehearted commitment and seriousness without abandoning tentativeness*. Commitment itself cannot be tentative, though the particular directions to which commitment is directed must be tentative. Our problem is how to act and judge in the real world so as to preserve the wholeheartedness of commitment without closing off the intellectual openness required by our actual uncer-

tainties. How can we judge tentatively in such a way that the tentativeness of our judgment does not paralyse the will? How can we act with 'singleness of heart', even though we know that our actions may be mistaken? An adequate methodology of Christian moral judgment must provide a way of doing so.

4. It must provide a basis for *clarifying moral dialogue* as to why particular actions have been chosen. We may never have certainty, but it would be a useful service to Christians if better forms of moral communication could be discovered. If the debates raging within the churches over the American involvement in the Vietnam war or regarding economic and racial dilemmas could have clarified the *Christian* grounds for the particular stances taken, this would have been a noteworthy service in and of itself. Moreover, as Christians relate themselves to non-Christians and to policy-makers (who may or may not be Christians) there is need for greater clarity of statement as to why it is that a given Christian or Christian group supports or opposes a particular position. Clarity in moral dialogue is not in itself a sufficient end for ethics, but it is an important service to those who are honestly groping for new insight.

2

The Concept of Methodological Presumption

There is a tendency in ethics to deal with moral judgments in one or the other of two opposite ways. Ethical perfectionists of various kinds may treat a moral problem as though we can know the one correct solution with certainty. A given moral tradition supplies the right answers. A casuistry may need to be developed to clarify the implications of that moral tradition for cases not clearly anticipated in the tradition itself. But we may have confidence that moral judgments can be made without uncertainty. The ethical perfectionist is, in fact, likely to regard uncertainty as evidence of moral, not intellectual failure. We have already seen the impossibility of this as a general stance. The actual content of our judgments simply is not immediate to us. Ethical perfectionism has the virtue of preserving the seriousness of moral commitment in the face of the judgments we are called upon to make in the real world. But it has the drawback of possible self-deception. By holding fast to perfectionist standards or pre-judgments with intellectual rigidity we may unwittingly cause great evil, and the purity of our moral commitment may itself become clouded with self-righteousness.

On the other hand, situationalists and realists have a tendency to weigh the available evidence in moral decision-making without sufficient pre-commitment as to probably the best course to follow. To Joseph Fletcher, love must decide 'then and there' what is to be done from among the existing alternatives. There is no such thing as a moral exception or a necessary evil,[1] for such concepts imply that there may be something suspect about what one must do in obedience to love alone. Or to Reinhold Niebuhr, moral judgment is the sorting out of the most realistic means to attain the most defensible proximate ends – without precommitment to some means as inherently more moral than others. Both situationalists and realists are committed only to what the preponderance of the evidence seems to require. Both have the virtue of openness and a certain quality of humility. Both have the drawback of neglecting to enter prior moral commitments, other than to love itself, into the methodology of judgment. A preponderance of evidence approach to moral judgment tends to treat different *kinds* of evidence without sufficient discrimination.

These points must be examined further and illustrated. By distinguishing rather sharply between ends and means, a situationalist or realist ethics of calculation is forced to treat all means as in themselves morally neutral. Means are evaluated solely on the basis of the ends they produce. Means are morally neutral, while ends are morally significant. Such an ethics of calculation is not necessarily unproductive, for means are indeed to be evaluated on the basis of the effects they produce. But a methodology which neglects a *prior* examination of the moral effects typically associated with certain means goes into each new situation, as it were, only half armed. For example, Joseph Fletcher's case of a German woman who was released from a post-World War II Soviet prison camp by becoming pregnant by a Russian guard may well illustrate a morally intelligent woman arriving at an accurate judgment as to the appropriate expression of *agape* in a particularly difficult situation. But as he has recounted the case, it is nowhere marked off that this judgment should be regarded as a definite exception because of the means used to attain the desired end. Love simply had to decide 'then and there'. Among the means to be used to get out of prison and be restored to her husband and children, the woman apparently did not have any preliminary scruples about sexual intercourse with the guard. That was simply one more alternative to be weighed without any particular bias against it.

Or, in the case of the Niebuhrians (some of whom would illustrate this tendency much more than Reinhold Niebuhr himself), a decision for or against war can be weighed on the basis of a total cost-benefit analysis in which war is considered alongside other alternative means of attaining a desirable end. To be sure, the negative aspects of war would be weighed alongside the positive ones, but without any preliminary bias against war as a usually evil means. We might agree that a particular war is, in the final analysis, a tragic moral necessity. But the usefulness of preliminary moral distinctions concerning certain kinds of means is largely lost to this methodological approach.

To be of greatest use, a Christian method of moral judgment must steer between perfectionism on the one hand and situationalism on the other. It must seek to combine the moral seriousness of the one with the flexibility of the other.

A. *The Moral Burden of Proof*

I believe that the most productive way to do this is by frankly admitting certain initial biases or 'presumptions' into our decision-making. Among the available options, we should look first to the ones with strongest apparent support in our ultimate value commitments and give them our tentative approval. The others should be required to bear the burden of proof. We may call this approach *methodological presumption*. It is the method of arriving at a judgment despite uncertainties by making an initial presumption of the superiority of one set of conclusions and then testing that presumption by examining contradictory evidence. If, after examining the contradictory evidence, substantial doubt or uncertainty remains we decide the matter on the basis of the initial presumption. Methodological presumption seems peculiarly useful in approaching moral judgments in the face of continuing uncertainty. If we can establish in advance what is *probably* the best line of decision in the light of our most basic moral traditions, then we have a clear basis for proceeding – even though this method will by no means banish uncertainty altogether. Such a method gives us more guidance than sheer impulse or intuition. It offers more help than calculation of consequences from scratch without a strong initial preference for certain means over others.

Methodological presumption is important in two areas of human decision-making. In both these areas people have learned to live with uncertainties and still to arrive at the kind of judgments which permit unambiguous action.

The first area is jurisprudence. In the legal process matters are constantly in dispute, and doubt often exists about the facts of a case or the relevant interpretation of the law. The concept of legal presumption has been developed, not to settle matters infallibly, but to organize the process of decision-making along the lines of greater or lesser probability so as to safeguard the most basic community values. A good illustration is the principle of Anglo-Saxon jurisprudence that the accused is presumed to be innocent until proved guilty. The state must prove the guilt of the accused beyond a 'reasonable' doubt or acquittal will result. This principle assumes that all citizens are law-abiding. It protects them from arbitrary detention and frivolous or malicious accusations. The presumption of innocence establishes the method by which both sides will proceed. The state must construct a plausible interpretation of the facts to show that a violation of law has been committed by the defendant. The defendant's lawyer, on the other hand, need only show that the state has failed to make its case. If a reasonable doubt persists, the state loses and the defendant is acquitted. (This possibility was startlingly illustrated in the famous case of the 'Harrisburg Seven' in 1971-72. The defendants, who had been accused of conspiring to kidnap Henry Kissinger and to blow up part of the heating system in the nation's capital, heard an elaborate but insubstantial case presented by the government. Most observers thought that a presentation of their defence would take weeks of testimony, but after the government finished its presentation of evidence the defence chose to rest its case on the grounds that the prosecution had failed to demonstrate that the alleged conspiracy had occurred. The judge agreed, and all of the charges except for one minor one against two of the defendants were dismissed.) Doubt itself has not been abolished by this kind of procedure, but a method of handling doubt has been put into practice.

A similar illustration, with ancient roots, is the legal principle that the actual possessor of property is to be presumed to hold his property rightfully. The burden of proof rests with any challenger to show that the property was gained unlawfully.

Fixing the burden of proof does not end the juridical process. Indeed, the burden may shift in an appellate proceeding. For instance, a defendant who has been found guilty will find that in his appeal to a higher court the latter tends to presume the legal propriety of the lower court's proceedings – hence, the burden of proof is now his to bear. Similarly, a higher court will presume the legality of an act of legislature or Congress or chief executive and require those challenging the constitutionality of legislative enactments and executive policies to bear the burden of proof. Such presumptions help to structure the decision-making process and to make it easier to cope with uncertainty. Such a process makes it possible for society to define in advance the kind of conclusions which, on the whole, can best form the basis of resolution of disputes in the event a full review of the evidence still leaves considerable doubt. In law, as elsewhere, we have such approaches to decision-making in mind when we speak of the 'benefit of the doubt'.

The second area where the method is illustrated is that of decision-making by executives. An executive in modern society is a generalist. He often confronts doubt or uncertainty about the policies he must pursue. He must depend upon expert advice from many specialists who know far more about the various aspects of the problem than he does. He cannot hope to become an expert in all the areas of factual judgment relevant to his decision. Whom is he to trust? He also must establish certain presumptions. Many of his presumptions may be theoretical or traditional in some sense, but others will relate to the kinds of persons whose information or advice he feels he can depend upon. He will tend to place the burden of proof against those whom he regards as laymen or amateurs. Faced with a new kind of problem, a competent executive will normally cast about for the generally recognized experts in the field. He may end up disregarding their advice if, upon closer scrutiny, he finds flaws. But he will tend to take their word first. Of course, he is also likely to place the burden of proof against those particular 'experts' who have let him or others down previously. President John F. Kennedy accepted the advice of the Central Intelligence Agency and the Joint Chiefs of Staff to authorize a previously planned invasion of Cuba at the Bay of Pigs – even despite his own considerable doubts. In doing so he placed the burden of proof against his own judgment and that of others on his staff (such as Arthur M. Schlesinger, Jr) who were not military or intelligence specialists. After the resulting debâcle, he is reported to have developed a considerable mistrust of the judgment of such specialists and to have relied upon them subsequently for only narrow opinions within the confines of their specialized expertise. A year later, during the Cuban missile crisis, he more fortuitously refused the advice of military leaders to bomb the offending missile bases and instead worked out a more general political solution on the basis of the advice of generalists.[2] But the executive cannot avoid the question of what sources of expertise and advice he is to accord a presumptive rightness.

I believe that we all actually tend to do our thinking on the basis of methodological presumptions, though we often do it quite unconsciously and therefore unclearly. We have instinctive points of reference that constitute our initial presumptions. Many of our presumptions have been instilled in us very early in life, though this is not always the case. The point is that we place a conscious or unconscious burden of proof against apparent deviations from what seems to be right. Our presumptions are our basic prejudices; and to say this, in the light of the most usual connotation of the word 'prejudice', is to take note of the fact that our presumptions can be quite evil in effect. Racial prejudice, with its attendant evils, is a matter of placing the burden of proof against the full moral humanity of persons of a different race. A specific person of the other race may meet that burden by outstanding personal qualities; then, if we are really prejudiced, we will carefully mark that person off as an exception to the usual rule! We may place the burden of proof against the intelligence of a poor person or in favour of the competence of the rich. A new book or a new idea from an unknown person is likely to confront a much heavier burden of proof than the same from a person of established reputation. This is what prejudice means: it is a prejudgment of the facts. But despite the evil possibilities in prejudice, it is possibly inevitable that we form and judge things on the basis of presumptions.

This is as true of our moral judgments as it is of factual ones. To illustrate, many people tend to think about political issues with a moral presumption in favour of political democracy. They may agree that in some circumstances (such as in the incipient anarchy of the period following the break-up of most colonialism in Africa) political democracy is not the best immediate answer. But they tend to retain democracy as the moral standard for political organization. Any deviations from democracy must bear the burden of proof. Similarly, in the Western world some persons have a strong initial presumption in favour of *laissez faire* capitalism. Any form of state involvement in economic matters must bear the burden of proof. Consequently, there is a strong initial presumption (by such persons) against public health insurance or socialized medicine or public ownership of the railroads. Vehement initial reactions by some against a guaranteed income system in America surely owed much to such a presumption. Those strongly opposed to such a welfare reform placed an overwhelming burden of proof against 'giving' people what they hadn't 'earned'. But there have also been people who have placed the burden of proof against further extensions of private enterprise or of government measures to subsidize private corporations. During the 1960s considerable opposition was mounted against Federal assistance to the communications industry by placing telestars in orbit or to the aircraft industry through financing part of the development of a supersonic transport plane or to saving particular corporations. Economist Milton Friedman clearly places the burden of proof against any public economic activity[3] while John Kenneth Galbraith tends to place the burden of proof against increased reliance upon the private sector.[4] Moral presumptions are clearly operative in areas touched by human sexuality. Presumptions in favour of monogamy, the nuclear family, and against extra-marital sexual relations and homosexuality continue to influence moral judgments powerfully in most contemporary human societies.

To illustrate further, some of us tend to place the burden of proof against change while others place it against the *status quo*. To the conservative, things should be left as they are unless it can be shown beyond reasonable doubt that changes are needed. To the revolutionary the situation should be changed unless it is shown that change will bring a worse situation.[5]

Thus our prejudices and presumptions. The real question is not whether we have them but whether we are able to clarify and modify our initial presumptions on the basis of our ultimate value commitments. Do our presumptions reflect our deepest moral integrity, or are they rather an evidence of a morally split personality? For the Christian, the issue is whether our presumptions are or can be in any authentic sense *Christian* moral presumptions.

Christian thinkers have indeed illustrated the use of methodological presumption. Sometimes they have done so quite consciously; at other times they have seemed to be unaware of the sources of their actual judgments or of the fact that these judgments had little relationship to the theological foundations upon which they supposedly rested. An example of the latter that would occur to any student of twentieth-century Protestant ethics is Emil Brunner. While Brunner's theological writings have represented a seminal contribution to Christian ethics, his own judgment of concrete issues (such as woman suffrage – which he opposed) sometimes seemed more a product of Swiss conservative culture than of his basic theological position. Or one could take the case of Paul Ramsey, whose published judgments on foreign policy issues have rather consistently supported American military commitments and interests despite considerable change in his ethical methodology over the past thirty years.[6] To some extent this is doubtless true of everybody who has written in ethics. All of us are influenced by background impressions or loyalties of which we may not be fully aware. This does not mean that moral thinking is after all only a rationalization of inherited interests and prejudices. If it were, then we would have no rational basis for exposing any rationalizations. But we are more likely to make good judgments if we are *conscious* of our initial presumptions and if we apply them rationally and clearly.

Christian moralists have often attempted to do this. A very old example is the just war tradition. In essence this tradition represents the effort of successive generations of Christian thinkers, from Augustine on, to define the circumstances under which a Christian could properly approve of war. The immediate impression created by this way of thinking (and by the nomenclature of a 'just' war) is that it is a militant, non-pacifist viewpoint. Indeed, it did represent a major shift from the predominantly pacifist stance of much of the pre-Constantinian church for Christians to accept the notion that any war *could* be justified. Nevertheless, as stated by Augustine and as refined by later Catholic thinkers, the just war tradition was based upon a strong Christian presumption *against* war. It could almost be termed a crypto-pacifist position. Just war doctrine has said, in effect, that *only* under certain exceptional conditions (specified and refined by thinkers dealing with the problem) could a Christian approve of war. Peace, on the other hand is to be regarded as normal. The burden of proof must accordingly be borne by every particular war. In case of continuing doubt as to whether a war is justified, the Christian must continue to withhold his approval and participation.

Another Roman Catholic illustration of methodological presumption is the doctrine of subsidiarity, a principle which has been developed in a number of twentieth-century papal encyclicals. The doctrine was stated by Pope Pius XI in the encyclical *Quadragesimo Anno* in the following way:

. . . it is a fundamental principle of social philosophy, fixed and unchangeable, that one should not withdraw from individuals and commit to the community what they can accomplish by their own enterprise and industry. So, too, it is an injustice and at the same time a grave evil and a disturbance of right order, to transfer to the larger and higher collectivity functions which can be performed and provided for by lesser and subordinate bodies.[7]

According to this principle, the more inclusive or universal levels of social organization would have to bear the burden of proof in relation to the more immediate or local levels. Putting aside the question whether this is good doctrine, we may note that it is a clear attempt to define a methodological presumption. In his later encyclical, *Pacem in Terris*, Pope John XXIII made use of the same principle in calling for a strengthening of 'the public authority of the world community' in view of the fact that lower levels of collectivity are not able to deal with urgent problems now facing humankind as a whole.[8] He held, thus, that the burden of proof posed by the principle of subsidiarity had been met by those calling for a strengthening of international institutions in view of the actual relations of modern nation states.

Catholic moral theologians of various schools through the past centuries have also refined several alternative 'rules of prudence' to guide the conscience when it is in doubt. These rules can also be understood as forms of methodological presumption. Probabilism, equi-probabilism, and probabiliorism attempt to define degrees of latitude which may prudently be claimed by the free conscience when there is doubt as to the applicability of a moral law. Probabilism is the doctrine claiming that a doubtful obligation (a moral law which may not be applicable) must bear the burden of proof. It is a kind of presumption in favour of the freedom of the conscience, for it holds that the free conscience should decide for itself where a moral law has not been shown to apply conclusively. Probabiliorism, on the other hand, holds that any moral law with even slightly greater 'probable' weight than its contrary should be presumed to be binding. Again, a methodological presumption seems to be in effect – this time in favour of the probable law as over against the free conscience. Equi-probabilism holds

47

that neither moral law nor extra-legal freedom should be accorded an initial presumption, but rather that the conscience should be bounded by which ever has the stronger support. Except for equi-probabilism, then, these rules of prudence seem to be good illustrations of a presumptive method, whether or not we approve of the highly prescriptive approach to ethics which they seem to presuppose.

Roman Catholic moral theology has doubtless wrestled with such methodological issues more carefully, by and large, than has Protestant ethical thought. This may be a result of the former's more typically prescriptive approach, although methodological presumption is quite as appropriate to other ways of posing ethical problems as we shall hope to demonstrate. Nevertheless, Protestant moral thought has occasionally provided illustrations of more or less conscious statements of methodological presumption. An example would be Walter Rauschenbusch's view that moral judgment should be weighted in favour of the disinherited. He put the argument in the following way:

> The strong have ample means of defending all their just interests and usually enough power left to guard their unjust interests too. Those who have been deprived of intelligence, education, and property need such championship as the ministers of Jesus Christ can give them, and any desire to pardon and excuse should be exercised on their behalf. . . . Unless a minister consciously puts himself into contact with the working classes by attending their meetings and reading their literature, he will assume that he is judging fairly, whereas he has never heard more than one side.[9]

Somewhat similarly, the Message of the First Assembly of the World Council of Churches (Amsterdam, 1948) asserts that 'we have to make of the Church in every place a voice for those who have no voice . . .'. Those 'who have no voice' are presumed to have the strongest moral claim upon the active support by the church – that is, the church should be biased in favour of such people. The question of the rightness of such an 'under-dog' presumption will occupy us later. For now we may simply note that this is a case of methodological presumption at work.

Another World Council of Churches statement which is some-

what parallel to the Roman Catholic principle of subsidiarity is
the declaration by one of the sections of the Second Assembly
(Evanston, 1954) that 'the state must do those things for the
economy that private industry cannot do properly . . .'.[10] The
presumption here is that private industry should do whatever it
can for the economy, and the state the rest. The point is not
unambiguously stated, but its implication seems to be that the
burden of proof must be borne by proponents of state action.

Many further illustrations of the use of methodological presumption could be brought forth. This is not really some
startlingly new approach to moral judgment. But it is a method
which needs further analysis and development in the light of
Christian ethics so that it can be of maximum use as Christians
approach their moral decisions.

B. *The Testing of Moral Presumptions*

The concept of methodological presumption implies the combination of commitment to an initial viewpoint with an openness
to changes or exceptions. But a practical problem emerges in the
actual process of judgment. It is that while we may be willing
enough to clarify and follow our initial presumptions, few of us
will go out of our way to give the possible exceptions their day in
court. We are convinced that the basic presumption is right and
that any exceptions ought to have to bear the burden of proof.
Therefore, is it not the responsibility of those who favour the
exception to convince us that in at least this or that one case we
should deviate from our presumptions? The practical problem is
that we may not be willing enough to expose ourselves to the
contrary evidence. Why should we?

Often, of course, we can simply follow our initial presumptions
with a high degree of confidence when they are under no apparently serious challenge. Presumptions in favour of peace or
faithfulness in marriage or truth-telling can simply guide us
where there is no substantial uncertainty. The moral life largely

49

consists of the attempt to build one's whole life-style around faithfulness to such presumptions, and one surely need not feel troubled or closed-minded about such faithfulness.

But serious truth-seeking does force us to be honest with our doubts as well as with our convictions. It requires us to examine serious alternatives to our presumptions. On occasion it may even require us to go out of our way to test our presumptions against possible alternatives. Another legal analogy may be useful. While in a criminal prosecution the accused is presumed to be innocent until proved guilty, he *is* brought to trial if there is probable cause to believe that he may have committed a crime. The burden of proof is upon the prosecution to show that a probable cause does exist, but the state has the responsibility to bring this to a test in court if a serious complaint of law violation has been lodged with it backed up by substantial evidence. The court room thus is a testing of methodological presumption (for innocence) versus probable cause (of guilt). Normally a preliminary hearing before a lesser magistrate or grand jury will be required to establish that there is enough probability to justify a full legal inquiry. Trivial matters can be dismissed at this stage as can cases which could not, on the face of it, bear the burden of proof. Something like this establishment of probable cause must also occur in the factual situation of moral judgment. It may become apparent that simple adherence to our presumptions will be impossible or, if not impossible, that it will yield obviously undesirable consequences. In an actual situation it may also appear that some of our basic presumptions are in conflict and thus that some kind of exceptions may be advisable.

Of course many people may be unwilling to examine their basic presumptions (or prejudices) at all; their thinking is clearly not accessible to influence on moral matters. But this is evidence of a lack of genuine moral seriousness or of a sufficiently humble awareness of the actual limitations in our moral understanding. It is possible to discuss this kind of problem in communication as a matter of tactics, but the problem itself does not lessen the potential usefulness of methodological presumption.

C. *Criteria of Exception*

The actual process of determining whether the contradictory of a presumption is able to bear the burden of proof requires some clarity in determining what the burden of proof could mean. The problem is one of defining what kind of reasons are sufficiently weight to justify a moral exception.

The just war tradition provides a useful model of the possibilities. Depending upon the particular formulation, that tradition specifies six or eight factual conditions which must be met if we are to consider a breaking of the peace to be justified.[11] These conditions represent the criteria of exception; all of them must be met if the exception is to be approved. All but one of the traditional rules (the principle of discrimination, which prohibits any direct breaking of the moral law in war) can be described as summary rules. They embody a summary of previous human experience with war and an attempt to relate that experience to the good as it is ultimately understood. No attempt to define meaningful criteria of exception can evade this task of reflecting upon actual experience in the area of human life concerned. This is so because the *need* for exceptions is itself only borne out in actual experience.

One general criterion is involved in all thought about exceptions. This is that more good will ultimately be gained by making an exception than by remaining faithful to the presumption itself. For example, in his interpretation of the doctrine of 'strange love' of Martin Luther, Paul Tillich speaks of love taking negative forms in order to preserve the true intention of love itself: 'it is the strange work of love to destroy what is against love. . . . Love, in order to exercise its proper works, namely charity and forgiveness, must provide for a place on which this can be done, through its strange work of judging and punishing.'[12] The ethical issues raised by a doctrine of 'the lesser evil' are serious and will occupy us in subsequent chapters. But for now it must be marked off that if there are sound reasons for holding a particular presumption then an exception to the presumption, a criterion for setting it aside, is the prospect that more good will thereby follow.

Secondary criteria can be developed out of experience relevant to the presumption. For instance, a presumption in favour of economic equality (if such a presumption could be shown to be good) might be set aside by a finding that economic equality greatly undermines productivity (if *that* can also be shown to be good). One criterion of exception could thus read that exceptions to the moral presumption of economic equality can be made in cases where economic equality will undermine production to an unacceptable degree. The burden of proof would fall upon opposition to economic equality and deviation from the presumption for equality could not be greater than that justified by the probable threat to productivity.

Sometimes apparent exceptions to a moral presumption must be made for the sake of the presumption itself. Thus, for the sake of economic equality certain *apparent* inequalities might have to be tolerated. Persons with greater objective need (such as a difficult medical condition) must have more income in order to be equal to people who do not have as much need. An apparent exception in this case would not be a real one, although the burden of proof would still apply to those attempting to show that it is not a real exception. Criteria of exception can be expressed either on the level of setting aside the presumption for the sake of that which ultimately justifies the presumption or on the level of a proper understanding of the meaning of the presumption itself.

D. *Significant Forms of Presumption*

We may conclude this chapter by listing and briefly characterizing some of the main forms of presumption which have significance for the problem of moral judgment. A number of these will be discussed more fully in subsequent chapters, but their mention here may help to fill out an initial understanding of the breadth of meaning of methodological presumption.

Procedural presumptions represent a bias in favour of decisions reached as a result of certain procedures rather than others. This is quite apart from the merits of the decisions themselves. We might decide, for example, that a policy adopted within a group by majority vote should be presumed to be right simply because that is how the group reached its decision. The basis of such a presumption could be rather pragmatic, with social peace as the governing norm and with the belief that majority rule is less conducive to disorder than the reverse since when the majority rules it confronts only a minority in opposition. Or its basis could lie in a morally principled view of the meaning of covenant in which one wishes to honour one's prior agreement to abide by the wishes of the majority. Here the sanctity of promise-keeping and the importance of personal integrity would be stressed. For the sake of keeping one's pledge to the group, one would be willing to presume the rightness of the actions of the group even when those actions appear to be quite wrong within one's own mind and conscience. Such considerations are, of course, very important in the social contract theories of the past few centuries.

Paul Ramsey has illustrated this kind of presumption by commenting on the question whether the burden of proof ought to remain against war even after a war has commenced. Ramsey concedes that it is a proper inference from just war theory that the presumption must be for peace, with the burden of proof being placed against war: 'In his capacity as a deciding magistrate participating in the public processes, he (the citizen) must make *a presumption against war*.'[13] This presumption would have to be considered substantive, however, not procedural. Ramsey changes to a procedural presumption in order to describe the moral obligation of the citizen: 'Once the decision is taken, however, and the foreign policy of a nation has undertaken a particular political use of armed force the presumption shifts in favor of the justice of the war that these processes have authorized.' Why should there be such a shift from the substantive to the procedural? 'It shifts,' Ramsey continues, 'because there is a shift to a presumption favoring the established or legitimate political processes by which the decision was made.' In a footnote, he remarks further that 'once war is "initiated" and while a nation's course is set every man is subject to these same deciding public processes and must himself now assume the burden of proof that that course and *this* particular resort to arms is unjust.'[14] Ramsey's argument is that, notwithstanding the seriousness of the Christian's presumptive commitment to peace, there is a point in the movement from peace to war at which a commitment to the procedure becomes the dominant presumption and thus that, in effect, the presumption for peace must now bear the burden of proof. Other Christians might well disagree, arguing that there is a presumption against the rightness of war, even when politically committed to it, and that in a covenantal (democratic) political system one never abdicates one's responsibility as citizen and sovereign to continue to hold morally questionable activities responsible for bearing the burden of proof.

Not all procedural presumptions are based upon a process of consensus-formation. I might decide that I would place the burden of proof in any of my judgments against whatever appears to be against my personal self-interest. This presumption of outright selfishness would be procedural in the sense that it could be adopted prior to any consideration of what my own personal interests in fact are. Or one might adopt a presumption *against* one's own self-interest, perhaps on the theory that one needs to compensate for selfish tendencies in judgment. Or pure chance could be employed in a procedure. When confronted by a particularly difficult decision all of us have, at some time or other, been advised to flip a coin between the alternatives, and then to see whether we are happy with the way the coin landed. What this procedure does in effect is to make a choice for us outside our mental processes, placing the burden of proof against those of our inclinations which are contrary to the choice which is fixed externally by chance. Even such a whimsical method may sometimes help us sort out our mental processes; but the point is, in using such a method one has devised a form of procedural presumption.

Usually, of course, a procedural presumption will itself rest upon other, more basic values. If we ever feel we should choose a procedural presumption over a substantive presumption it can only be because of those more basic values that are at stake. If, for instance, we feel we should accept some unjust policy which has just been adopted by democratic process, it can only be because of some fairly substantial values which are at stake in the preservation of that democratic process. Some of the worst dilemmas in ethical judgment doubtless come about in this way.

Presumptions of principle are substantive, not procedural, but they are also general. They abstract from all human experience certain qualities and values deigned worthy of preservation or enhancement in the organization of life. Morally, their status derives from some understanding of what is ultimately at stake in human life – a point we shall survey more closely in the following chapter. But they are meaningless unless they are capable in some fashion of organizing actual experience. Examples of such presumptions are 'freedom', 'equality', and 'unity'. Obviously such principles are capable of being used in diverse, even opposing ways. But where the meaning of such a presumption of principle has been established clearly, it can be used with methodological effect. Much depends upon who is speaking of 'freedom' or 'equality' and out of what kind of cultural tradition. For a Marxist and a *laissez faire* capitalist to use the term 'freedom' clearly in conversation with each other, each would find it necessary to define the term in relation to what is considered to be the source of freedom.

Ideological presumptions depend upon presumptions of principle, but they also represent a model of the world or of human relationships which we consider to be implied morally by our basic norms. Democracy, fascism, Marxism, capitalism, feudalism, democratic socialism, all represent complex systems of values and perceptions of reality. The terms themselves have been employed so loosely as to diminish their ideological precision. Nevertheless, to cite such terms is to recall that people do employ them with quite specific mental pictures of what it is that they would regard

55

as good social arrangements. These mental pictures become tools for judgment when they organize our weighing of alternatives. We place the burden of proof against deviations from these pictures, regardless of whether our model is of a *status quo* we wish to preserve or of a revolutionary future we wish to hasten. The problem of Christian ideological thinking will occupy us in a subsequent chapter. For now, it may simply be asserted that Christians, along with all other people, do their moral judging with ideological presumptions at least in the background.

An *empirical presumption* is a model of situations as they actually are. It is the only one of this list of presumptions which is not normative, although many people often do judge on the basis of preserving some empirical *status quo*. It is proper to refer to this as a form of presumption, however, because we must also act on the basis of our understanding of the factual situation. We tend to form mental pictures (models) of the nature of situations which reduce their complexities to manageable form. Alternative basic models must then bear the burden of proof.

To illustrate, the urban riots of the summer of 1967 in the United States evoked diverse images in the minds of millions of Americans who sought to understand what had happened and why. Among the different interpretative models used by people to provide a simplified understanding of the disasters, one could discern at least the following:

1. The total race-war model: a grim picture of blacks and whites facing each other with irreconcilable interests and unbroken hostility. Those who saw the riots in this light could perceive only hostility in the reactions of members of the other race.

2. The 'immigrant generation' model: a view which interpreted the tensions of the cities as a repetition of the earlier American experience with successive waves of immigrants. This model attributed the tensions to the difficulties of absorbing non-urbanized people (in this case southern blacks) into complex cities in large numbers. It suggests that the children of the first generation, despite present difficulties, may become more easily assimilated.

3. The economic gap model: attributes the disaster to poverty and to the resentments and actual physical deprivation of poor people.

4. The city-planning gap model: suggests that the underlying problems really resulted from ecological and architectural difficulties in the modern urban environment which, once straightened out, could be counted upon to eliminate underlying tensions.

5. The 'fall of Rome' model: regards the disasters as symptomatic of the inner decay of a corrupt civilization which is basically doomed.

These models (and others that could be constructed to interpret those traumatic events) serve as basic presumptions concerning the nature of the events themselves, quite apart from our moral presumptions concerning the values at stake. Facts or interpretations inconsistent with the basic empirical presumptions might actually bear a burden of proof, depending upon the rigidity with which those presumptions were held. But the urban riots and similarly complex social situations require such models or images. The mind is simply incapable of absorbing *all* of the facts and of arranging them into an indubitable presentation of reality itself.

Presumptions of authority can be both normative and empirical. They are the sources of moral guidance and of factual (or expert) information which we consider to be worthy of trust in situations where one cannot make a direct judgment for oneself. Presumptions of authority identify the secondary authorities to which one accords the benefit of the doubt – secondary in the sense that they involve the judgments of other persons or groups. Most religious groups have institutionalized forms of human authority. Doubtless all of us have trusted friends or authority figures of one sort or another to whom we instinctively turn for advice when confronting problems which seem beyond our own resources. Our tendency is also to give the benefit of the doubt to their advice. A subsequent chapter will be devoted to further analysis of this form of methodological presumption.

Presumptions of priority represent our approach to the presumptions when they are in conflict with each other. Doubtless such conflicts do occur. But some presumptions are on a higher level than others. Where conflict occurs we may speak of 'presumptions among presumptions'. For instance, one presumption may be important because it serves another. When there is an apparent conflict, the initial presumption must lie with the higher or more intrinsic presumption, the burden of proof being borne by the lower or more instrumental one. If human equality is regarded as a higher presumption than economic productivity, then, important as productivity may be, it would have to defer to equality unless it could be shown beyond reasonable doubt that loss of productivity would dangerously undermine the very basis and meaning of equality. If, on the other hand, productivity were regarded as the ultimate goal of economic life and equality were treated as a secondary value, then any apparent threat to productivity resulting from egalitarian policies would force the latter to bear the burden of proof.

We could take as another illustration the frequent conflict between presumptions for peace and presumptions for justice. In case of a conflict which should have to bear the burden of proof? Justice might be regarded as the more inclusive category, since justice includes the whole of our normative view of proper human relationships, rights and duties within the community. Peace would then be seen as only a part of the meaning of justice. In an actual case, peace might have to defer to the broader interests of justice in bearing the burden of proof. But the problem could be stated differently as one of selecting those means which are appropriate to the securing of justice, and then the presumption might well be in favour of peaceful or non-violent means. The burden of proof would be upon those asserting that in a given case violent means will better serve the ultimate causes of justice than will non-violent ones.

The preceding discussion may help to clarify the concept of methodological presumption. All people probably do, to some extent, structure their thinking by means of methodological presumptions. But the usefulness of the method depends upon our ability to identify basic presumptions which are rooted in our ultimate moral perspectives. To this task we now turn.

3

Positive Moral Presumptions
of Christian Faith

Is it possible to derive methodological presumptions from the Christian faith itself? Are there moral presumptions which can meaningfully be described as 'Christian' and which can also serve as helpful guides to moral judgment?

It must be admitted at the outset that it is very difficult even to say what 'Christian' means. The definition of Christian faith, when pushed to its sources, poses very complex methodological problems. Is Christian faith what Christians say it is? Then how are we to adjudicate the irreconcilable interpretations which admittedly exist among individuals and groups all calling themselves Christian? The very question of who are the *real* Christians is tied up in the definition. Is it a question of belief in the Lord Jesus Christ as God and saviour, or some such formula? Again, interpretations of christology vary widely. Or, is Christian faith what the Bible (with particular emphasis upon the New Testament) says it is? But the Bible is itself a diverse set of materials, with many levels and nuances of meaning. To identify the Bible as source of an adequate understanding of Christian faith is simply to pose the hermeneutical problem – the question of how we are to locate the essence of the biblical message wherewith to interpret the whole. Or should the meaning of Christianity be resolved on the basis of what the church has said it is? If so, what part of the church? Which groups, which traditions, which thinkers are decisive?

Despite the centrality of the question, it may be best not to press it too sharply as though some definite, final answer could be reached. Whatever it is in objective substance, in form Christian faith is a relationship between Christians and their understanding of reality itself. Since reality always transcends our understanding, this relationship cannot be expressed in exact terminology. The nature of the divine can be symbolized; it cannot be stated exactly. A Christian understanding of reality is not unique in this respect. Everyone's view of ultimate reality similarly depends upon the limited ability of symbols to convey meanings. (This is particularly true of atheistic views, for atheism is simply the denial of the validity of affirmative symbols. As such it does not even take the limited step toward truth implied in the affirmation of a positive symbol.)

These remarks are only the preface to an obvious conclusion: *any* view of the nature of Christian faith is interpretative. It is an interpretation of the meaning of a complex but definite, objective tradition (including the scriptures and the whole remembered expressions of people calling themselves Christians through the centuries). In the long run, those who call themselves Christian can be expected to interpret Christian faith in the light of their profoundest experiences of reality. When the Christian tradition no longer suffices as a vehicle for understanding reality, one can be expected to abandon it altogether. But it is typical of the life experience of Christians that they continue to find profounder levels of meaning in the Christian tradition the longer and more penetrating their experience. There is thus a dialectical relationship between the believer's life experience and the tradition through which the believer interprets that experience.[1]

A statement of the theological basis of Christian moral presumptions must therefore be rooted in experience on the one hand and in the Christian tradition on the other. It is not pure subjectivism or relativism because it refers to a definite tradition and to objective reality. But it is subjective to the degree that it must be as an attempt by a limited individual to understand and express the meaning of infinite (though objective) reality. Is this a weak reed on which to rest the whole of Christian ethics? Perhaps it is. But it is no weaker than the seriousness of a person's attempt to express the very basis of his or her existence. Nor is it just one person's witness, because every serious statement of Christian faith is largely dependent upon the witness of many generations of Christians.

A. *The Theological Basis of Christian Moral Presumptions*

In turning directly to the problem of the theological basis of Christian moral presumptions we should recall that moral life belongs to the *essence* of the Christian faith. We do not go far wrong in asserting that the gospel is *about* moral life. But in order to say this we must also reconstruct our understanding of the meaning of moral life. Christian faith is a moral interpretation of the meaning of reality. A statement of this sort can lead to misunderstandings because moral life is so often dealt with on a moralistic plane, whereas a Christian understanding of moral life identifies it in the nature of reality itself. This point may become clearer as we proceed. Christian faith can be described as moral because it is essentially relational. It is an interpretation of reality through which one sees oneself in relationship with the ultimate, not as an objective observer, but as an interacting, personal being.

For this reason Christians cannot finally dispense with God. God is at the centre of the faith of Christians because without God we are utterly incapable of having a 'yes' said to our being by an otherwise blind, impersonal, objective reality. Efforts to reconstruct a Christian faith apart from God, such as those of Ludwig Feuerbach and the 'death of God' theologies of the 1960s, generally emphasize the self-sufficiency of justification by faith and the primacy of love.[2] But apart from God, human relationship with reality remains curiously both subjective (because values can only be one's own creation) and impersonal (because there is no personal answering from across the void). If the gospel narratives are to be trusted at all, faith in a personal God (*abba*) was at the centre of the faith of Jesus himself. To the earliest disciples and Fathers of the church, Christ was divine precisely because in the life and faith of Jesus they found manifest the nature of God. They believed this to have been confirmed finally in the resurrection. God could now be understood as the God and Father of our Lord Jesus Christ. At last, in Jesus Christ, is revealed 'the plan of the mystery hidden for ages in God who created all things' (Eph. 3.9b).

Of course it remains very difficult to speak meaningfully of God in most contemporary ethical discourse. The point is that to abandon the attempt is probably to abandon Christian ethics *per se*. Christian ethics is not simply about *agape* until in some fashion we define *agape* theologically.[3] It is not a matter of rightly obeying the Ten Commandments, or the injunctions of the Sermon on the Mount, or the prescriptions of Paul, or even in rightly living out the implications of grace in creative Christian freedom – until such things are placed in their setting within the relationship between man and God. It is that relationship that is definitive.

In the Hebrew-Christian faith tradition (if we may speak broadly), the divine-human relationship is expressed early in the idea of covenant. As portrayed in the biblical narrative, it was God's covenant with the Hebrews that formed them into a community – the nation Israel. God was to be the Lord of Israel, to protect them, to bring them to the promised land, to give them a destiny. God *chose* Israel. Israel was to respond by loving and obeying God. With only the smallest exceptions, it is this basic covenantal relationship which organizes the world-view maintained by the writers of the Old Testament. The great prophets, such as Amos, Hosea, Micah, Isaiah, Jeremiah, and Deutero-Isaiah, confronted the profoundest experiences of Israel's unfolding life-history in the light of the covenant. Inevitably, their interpretations of the covenant in response to Israel's tumultuous history broadened and deepened its meaning. It is arguable that among the greatest of the prophets the covenant conception broke loose from its narrower mooring to a single chosen nation and that Israel's own proper destiny came to be seen as one of bearing witness to the saving reality of this covenant for the whole of humanity. Among the greatest prophets, steadfast love (*chesed*) is understood to be basic to the covenantal relationship and to the interrelationships of human beings within the community which the covenant has brought into existence.

Some interpretations of Christian faith (particularly the docetic views which were branded as heretical by the early church) stressed the absolute discontinuity between Hebrew and Christian faith. But the far more characteristic view has been that Jesus Christ in some decisive way reveals what was already implicit (or at least anticipated) in Hebrew experience. God was already at work among the Hebrews. In some sense this was anticipation or preparation. In Jesus Christ it is decisively and fully revealed that God has said yes to humankind, both individually and collectively. On the one hand we are saved from meaningless existence, and on the other hand we are spared the frustration of the demand of absolute moral perfection. The power which lies beyond all other powers is revealed, in Jesus Christ, to be loving. We are not alien beings in the universe, nor need we fear the covenantal relationship through which alone our lives can be saved from ultimate alienation. We are free now to live the life of the spirit, confident that the life of the flesh – which exists under the law of sin and death – is not the sum of human meaning.

These themes are developed with countless richnesses of nuance in the basic scriptures and traditions of Christian faith. Obviously they cannot be fully explored here, if ever they could be fully explored anywhere. Our problem is the more modest one of locating the points where the content of the faith has critical relevance to the methodological problems of moral judgment. A certain short-hand is called for, though it must be remembered that such abstractions can never do justice to the full richness of meaning in Christian faith.

An immediate problem poses itself: How are we to make the leap, as it were, from the pure 'spiritual' or relational realities of the Christian life to the concrete objective world? Many of the crucial terms in the Christian tradition, such as 'covenant', 'life in the spirit', 'salvation', 'justification', 'sanctification', 'love', etc., can be expressed, so to speak, 'above the world'. It can be said that since it is our covenantal relationship with God that is decisive, the concrete realities of our existence in the world matter but little. So far as our relations with other persons is concerned, is it not also now a matter of spiritual love only – even despite whatever adversities of circumstances we are subjected to in this vale of tears? The point is that much of the language of Christian faith can occur on this plane because whatever else we may say about the concrete realities of an earth-bound existence such concrete realities are not the source of the *meaning* of human life. Every pastor of a Christian congregation who has chanced to preach upon themes injurious to the material interests of part of the membership has doubtless been reminded that Christianity is, after all, a 'spiritual' faith and that he would be well-advised to restrict his preaching to that sphere. In one sense this is right. Interpersonal relationships are non-material, or rather they are material-transcending and spiritual. And Christian faith is, as we have seen, essentially a matter of interpersonal relationship.

Compounding this problem of relating the material world to spiritual reality is the problem of relating this present age to the anticipated consummation of God's intentions for human history – the eschatological problem. This problem can also be posed in such a way as to leave practical moral judgment in a vacuum. If God alone can bring the kingdom in his own time; if we are living in the 'time between the times' in which God's kingdom is not yet manifested among us; if we live only in hopeful expectation of that entirely future consummation – then the issue is sharply before us whether and why the concrete judgments of the here and now ultimately *matter*.

To be relevant to moral judgment, theology must provide us with some account of what is at stake in the structures of human existence and during the time in which judgment must be made by the faithful Christian. It is regrettable that there is what can be called a rhetorical gap at this point in some theological literature. In its zeal to emphasize the otherness of the faith and the fulness of God's own eschatological responsibility, the impression can easily be left by this literature that nothing ultimately is at stake at all in the moral judgments made by people. This should be called a rhetorical gap because it is often a result of oversight or overstatement rather than intention – a point often confirmed by the concrete moral judgments offered by the same theologians. To repeat, what we are looking for is some conception of how it is that the inconsequential things (the things which are not themselves ultimate) gain consequence in the light of Christian faith.

Easy answers to the problem are available both on the 'left' and the 'right'. On the 'left' among those most zealous to emphasize the importance of what we do in the actual world, there has sometimes been a tendency to designate the actual world as the locus of God's whole intention and to speak of man's definitive role in bringing that intention to entire fulfilment. A certain social gospel perspective, not to be identified with major figures like Washington Gladden and Walter Rauschenbusch, spoke loosely of our task to 'build the kingdom of God'. By healing the sick, feeding the hungry, and establishing just economic and social relationships, we are bringing in the kingdom. The kingdom is thus conceived as a directly achievable possibility. In somewhat different cultural attire, some current rhetoric of liberation theology or theology of revolution conveys this same impression.[4] But of course, those who speak loosely of the kingdom or of liberation in human society must never forget that loving relationships and ultimate meanings can never be derived simply from concrete historical accomplishments.

On the 'right' are those who seek to establish an absolute discontinuity between the physical world and the real world of the spirit. Their tendency has been toward complacency concerning the physical distress and injustices which activated the social gospellers. If anything, their solution has been less relevant and less faithful to the gospel than that of unsophisticated social activists. The latter are at least prompted by an instinctive belief that physical needs and social justice are important in the light of Christian faith. Moreover, the latter have the weight of Christian scripture on their side.

Dietrich Bonhoeffer's concept of the penultimate furnishes us with at least a provisional approach to the problem. The penultimate is understood in relation to the ultimate. For Bonhoeffer the ultimate includes a full theological conception of the redemption of man through grace which is a new possibility as a result of the saving work of Jesus Christ. The full content of his meaning does not need to detain us at this point other than to note that the 'ultimate' is not identified with the structures of our this-worldly existence as such. Rather, it is the reconciliation of man with God through Christ and the final consummation of God's purposes beyond history. What then is the penultimate? It is, he writes, 'everything that precedes the ultimate, everything that precedes the justification of the sinner by grace alone, everything that is to be regarded as leading up to the last thing when the last thing has been found'.[5] The penultimate is not self-validating. It depends for its meaning upon the ultimate. In this sense it 'follows the ultimate'. Nevertheless, it also precedes the ultimate. It is what prepares the way. While the material, social, economic, political structures of this world are in no way to be regarded *as* the ultimate, they represent the conditions upon which the ultimate depends.

Bonhoeffer illustrates the conception concretely: 'If, for example, a human life is deprived of the conditions which are proper to it, then the justification of such a life by grace and faith, if it is not rendered impossible, is at least seriously impeded.'[6] 'The hungry man needs bread and the homeless man needs a roof; the dispossessed need justice and the lonely need fellowship; the undisciplined need order and the slave needs freedom. To allow the hungry man to remain hungry would be blasphemy against God and one's neighbour. . . .'[7] Again, dealing with hunger and injustice remains in the penultimate realm. The conditions of human existence are not, in themselves, ultimate. Nevertheless, writes Bonhoeffer, 'for him who does these things for the sake of the ultimate, and in the knowledge of the ultimate, this penultimate does bear a relation to the ultimate. It is pen*ultimate*. The coming of grace is the ultimate. But we must speak of the preparing of the way. . . .'[8] The way in which these penultimate problems are dealt with by human beings can make a large difference: it can either aid or impede the full manifestation of the transcendent ultimate.

Bonhoeffer thus lays the basis for an understanding of what is at stake in judgments about the altogether material world. It is 'the ultimate' that is at stake, not because the world itself is ultimate but because worldly structures, events, and decisions *affect* that which is ultimate. Through his concept of the 'mandates' Bonhoeffer organizes his own views of the directions in which God calls us to act as his deputies in dealing with penultimate things.[9] The specifics could be discussed in a variety of ways and from divergent perspectives. What is important is the general conception that the specific aspects of life (which form the content of our moral judgment-making) are to be regarded as aiding or impeding God's full, though transcendent, intention.

In theological terms, the doctrine of creation may finally prove decisive in laying the foundations for a methodology of Christian moral judgment. This is so because it is through a doctrine of creation that we express our understanding of how it is that God himself is related to the structures and events of this world. Terms such as 'covenant' or 'justification' or 'redemption' express a theological understanding of how it is that God relates himself to human life. Creation expresses our understanding of how God relates to human life in the actual setting of concrete existence.

Karl Barth's formulation of this problem has proved especially productive. Barth speaks of 'creation as the external basis of the covenant' and of 'the covenant as the internal basis of creation'.[10] If one understands by 'the covenant' the full gospel proclamation concerning God's gracious redemptive relationship with man, which alone affords meaning to human life, one may also understand by 'creation' the biblical idea that God is also the creator of man and his world and that this prior act of creation is a necessary (but not sufficient) condition of there being a covenant at all: '. . . God's first work, the positing of the distinct reality of man and his world, is indelibly marked off from every other source or beginning by the fact that it precedes and prepares for the second work, God's gracious dealing within the sphere of this reality.'[11] The two, creation and covenant, are inseparable. We may say that the first is instrumental with the respect to the second:

> Creation is the external – and only the external – basis of the covenant. It can be said that it makes it technically possible; that it prepares and establishes the sphere in which the institution and history of the covenant takes place; that it makes possible the subject which is to be God's partner in this history, in short the nature which the grace of God is to adopt and to which it is to turn in this history. As the love of God could not be satisfied with the eternal covenant as such; as it willed to execute it and give it form outside the divine sphere, it made itself the external ground of the covenant, i.e., it made necessary the existence and being of the creature and therefore of creation. It is, however, only its external basis.[12]

Without creation, all that we mean by Christian faith could exist only as an idea in the mind of God. In any event, it is known that we do not exist as ethereal spirits of some sort, floating in a material vacuum. Any presentation of Christian faith which tacitly assumes such a conception of the 'spiritual' lacks foundation, either in reality or in basic Christian faith.

On the other hand, while the 'spirit' clearly exists in a world of nature, the natural world is understood in Christian faith to be created. To speak of nature as 'creation' is to make clear that nature is not self-originating. Nor can the meaning of nature derive from nature itself. To speak of nature as creation is to say that it is created by that which is not nature and that it has its source and destiny in the intention of God. A theological interpretation of creation thus must address itself to the question how, specifically, in the context of the created world God's intentions can be brought to fulfilment in and through human activity. A purely natural law approach to ethics is right at least in that it locates moral issues in the context of the natural order; but it is wrong in so far as it considers nature itself to be the source of the good. The Barthian approach to creation affirms the value of the natural and also locates moral value in the specifics of the created world. But it avoids the naturalistic fallacy by viewing the whole of the created world as instrumental with respect to the transcendent covenantal reality revealed most ultimately in the person of Christ.

B. *Positive Moral Presumptions*

We are prepared, then, to take up the question whether there may be positive moral presumptions in the basic content of the Christian faith which can serve to guide our judgments in the world of existence.

I wish to propose four basic presumptions which I believe can be derived from the Christian faith. These four presumptions are affirmative. They state positive expectations or assumptions to serve as a basis for initial attitudes. They will later be contrasted with certain 'negative presumptions' which point to limitations in the human situation and to some extent modify the full force and applicability of the positive presumptions. Such positive and negative presumptions can be restated in different linguistic or typological form. Indeed, the four positive presumptions overlap one another to a considerable degree. They are different angles of vision into the same reality, although they will prove useful in bringing different aspects of that reality to bear upon the judgment-making situation.

(i) *The Goodness of Created Existence*
It is implied in all that we have been saying about creation that it is good. Creation has its source in the activity of the same good God who intends good for humanity. Creation is to be viewed as intended by God to help in the fulfilment of love in the divine-human covenant. The goodness of creation is affirmed throughout the biblical tradition, beginning with the very first chapter in Genesis: 'And God saw everything that he had made, and behold it was very good.' The creation narratives of Genesis and the great nature psalms specifically celebrate the goodness of creation. Elsewhere in the Old Testament there is a notable frankness about the necessity and goodness of the material conditions of life, and

justice is largely understood as equitable provision for each person to share in those conditions.

The theme of the goodness of creation is not developed in a particularly polemical spirit in the Old Testament. The ancient Hebrews show little awareness of theological or philosophical alternatives to their optimistic attitudes toward nature. What polemic there is of this sort is mainly directed against the absurdities of polytheism in the face of the monotheistic conception, as in Isaiah 40, for example.

The New Testament is no less affirmative about God's creative role, but at points the development of the Christian scriptures show the effects of a death-struggle against a spiritualistic dualism. It will be recalled that early gnosticism pictured the actual physical world as evil. Christians with gnostic tendencies (such as the second-century Marcion) tended to repudiate the Old Testament heritage and to speak of a spirit-God and a spirit-Christ at war with the alien material world. The world was sometimes pictured as the source of evil. Early docetism sought to preserve the figure of Christ himself from any real connection with (or contamination by) the physical world. He was viewed as an appearance only. He was not actually born; he did not actually suffer; he did not actually die; he did not actually taste and touch and experience pain. In the New Testament there is evidence of struggle against this view that creation is evil or illusionary and that Christ had nothing to do with the created physical world. The epistle to the Colossians states in the strongest language that God is not merely spiritual. The created world is to be attributed, not to the powers of darkness, but to the loving activity of God himself. In one particularly striking passage, Christ is vigorously identified with God on the one hand and with creation on the other:

> He is the image of the invisible God, the first-born of all creation; for in him all things were created, in heaven and on earth, visible and invisible, whether thrones or dominions or principalities or authorities – all things were created through him and for him. He is before all things, and in him all things hold together (Col. 1.15–17).

In the same way, the pastoral epistles reject a false asceticism with

71

the exclamation that 'everything created by God is good, and nothing is to be rejected if it is received with thanksgiving . . .' (I Tim. 4.4).

To be sure, both the biblical witness and subsequent Christian tradition are also well aware of the existence of evil within the created world. Moreover, it cannot be said that there is any one dominant Christian understanding of the precise nature of evil. The problem of sin (human rebelliousness against God's intention) intersects the problem of evil. It is arguable that there is no intrinsic evil in the created world apart from some sinful human will. It is also arguable that frustrations arising from natural causes (such as earthquakes, volcanic eruptions, disease epidemics, birth defects, etc.) can properly be called natural evil – though a doctrine of natural evil needs to confront the question whether a world in which accidents could not occur would really be so good. Clearly a doctrine of natural evil which went so far as to regard nature as *essentially* evil would be a reversion to gnostic dualism. A view of evil which attributes it to the fall has certain symbolic possibilities which we shall examine in greater detail in the next chapter. However it should be said here that even the doctrine of the fall implies that the original intention of the creator in and through the creation was good and not evil. Moreover, the fall is not really to be understood as the fall of creation so much as it is the mythical or symbolic representation of the tendency of human beings, *in their freedom* and not through creation, to sin. The profoundest grappling with evil is at the point of human sin. Everything that exists on the physical plane as a frustration to the fulfilment of God's intended human life on earth properly challenges us to vigorous, creative action whenever possible. But when such frustrations arise from entirely physical causes, the word evil cannot unambiguously be used to describe them. The word evil might better be reserved for frustrations of the good which derive from malevolent wills. Natural forces are not intrinsically evil, although if we are to live with our vulnerable bodies in such a world we are liable to be injured or destroyed if we chance to be in the wrong place at the wrong time or if our bodies become the carriers of harmful viruses or genetic distortions. But if we were not thus vulnerable during our earthly pilgrimages could we be sensitive? Could we experience the physical as an avenue of awareness and as a basis for creative activity in God's intended covenant?

Everyone who has known and seen suffering and has lost loved ones through the final earthly calamity of death will not be too glib about the problem of natural evil; and yet the article of faith, the presumption, remains: God has created the world and the creation is good. How, exactly, can such a faith claim serve as a methodological presumption to help guide Christians in their moral judgments?

In a general sense, the answer to this is that in any issue of judgment where the postulated goodness of creation is itself the matter in question, our presumption should always lie with actions reaffirming that goodness. Potential suicide is an obvious illustration. Excluding deliberate acts of martyrdom or heroism, which are not really suicidal, taking one's own life always suggests that existence has become intolerable. The psychology of suicide is complex, and we cannot explore it here. Nevertheless, the presumption of the goodness of creation necessarily places a burden of proof against such a desperate act. To put this differently, our initial presumption must be that suicide is incompatible with Christian faith since such an act always suggests that for the individual involved existence is no longer good.

Some forms of alleged suicide may be excluded from this assessment because they are in no sense based upon suicidal intent (or upon the conclusion that existence is no longer good). In war there have been reported instances of soldiers hurling themselves on live grenades in order to absorb the lethal impact of the explosion, thus saving the lives of comrades. This kind of act is suicidal in the limited sense that the one who did it could be almost certain of death as a result of his own actions. Nevertheless, his *intent* is not to cause his own death but rather to preserve the lives of his comrades. Presumably he would be overjoyed if the grenade, by some happy accident, were not to explode. The act is not based upon loss of faith in the goodness of creation. Exactly the opposite, it is motivated by a generous desire that others should continue to enjoy that goodness. (Of course, 'unselfish' acts of heroism in war can sometimes be unconscious expressions of self-destructiveness, in which case they do represent that loss of faith in the goodness of creation which Christian faith does not accept.) The word suicide ought to be reserved for those actions which have the termination of one's own existence as their primary end – and not for those actions which, while inevitably self-destructive in effect, are designed to save the lives of others.

Still, the burden of proof ought to be against even generous actions which will inevitably result in personal loss of life. Among those who love life, who find created existence good, this presumption functions automatically and can only be overcome when some greater good than one's own continued physical existence is at stake. The burden of proof may then have been met. A tragic incident which occurred in California during the mid-1960s can illustrate the problem. A small aircraft crashed into the home of a minister who lived near an airport and exploded into flames. Miraculously, this man escaped uninjured through the front door. Without his knowledge, his wife and mother escaped through the back door, also uninjured. Frantically looking about for his loved ones, he dashed back into the burning house to save them. As a result of this unnecessary act of bravery he received severe burns from which he later died. What should be said concerning such an instinctive act of self-sacrifice? Surely one could not fault this kind of sacrificial courage. Nor could one say that the man should have waited until the facts were more clear since there was virtually no time. If his wife and mother *had* still been in the house, only that quick impulsive act might have saved them. It might be said that the burden of proof justifying this exceptionally perilous act had been met. However, the objectively needless waste of this good man's life should remind us that heroic self-sacrifice where there is virtually no hope of achieving the good sought must have a burden of proof placed against it. The instinctive feeling of one who is driven to a hopeless act *may* be that life would not be worth living without this or that loved one, and against this the presumption

74

stands that existence will continue to be good, even despite the tragic loss. This is why more cool-headed bystanders do well physically to prevent hopeless and dangerous acts of heroism.

Euthanasia poses similar questions. How are we to judge in the case of persons whose existence apparently is *not* good, either to themselves or to society? How are we to assess an act terminating the life of somebody known medically to have no hope for anything other than a slow, painful death?

As generally proposed, euthanasia would involve the patient's consent (thus entailing a suicidal factor), though it would be an act in which society would also participate responsibly. Of course some kinds of suffering can be excruciating and, in terminal illness, hopeless. They can involve virtual disintegration of personality. In face of this, are we to say that for such people creation continues to be good, and are we then to forbid release from existence? Answers to this question cannot be given casually by those who have never experienced such suffering. I would not wish to exclude euthanasia categorically, but the burden of proof should be strongly against it. As long as a person retains consciousness, there are some *aspects* of his existence which may be regarded as good. Despite suffering, his physical existence still provides the condition necessary for his continued interaction with loved ones – and that possibility of interaction, as such, is to be presumed good. He may find it possible to formulate and achieve some creative purposes as his own contribution to the improvement of existence – and that possibility, too, must be presumed good. I once served as pastor to an elderly woman who was suffering from a terminal cancer. She did outlive by some months her doctors' prognosis, but in a wasted-away condition accompanied by great suffering. Nevertheless, despite her suffering and her inability to do anything physically other than communicate, this woman's radiant spirit was obviously a great force for good within that close circle of her family and friends. The question of euthanasia must be posed in the light of that kind of radiant spirit first, because it is that spirit which is authentically attuned to what the Christian means by the goodness of creation.

But what is one to say to a father who knows he is suffering a terminal disease and who knows that continuing treatment will eat up the financial resources his wife and children need to have after his death? Would he be justified in terminating his own life? Would a compassionate physician be justified in helping him? Of course it is an intolerable piece of social irresponsibility that permits a family to face such a dilemma alone. Extremely costly forms of treatment, if justified at all, should be borne by the whole community, and a just community does not neglect its widows and orphans. The Health Service in Britain and comparable programmes in a few other countries show that this kind of basic social decency is not at all inconceivable. Nevertheless, in our imperfect world fathers (and mothers) can face such cruel dilemmas. Surely the burden of proof must continue to be placed against suicide or euthanasia. If a family is bound together by genuine ties of love, it will be worth a great deal of subsequent economic deprivation to know that everything possible was done; and, moreover, the continued existence of the terminally ill patient would be considered an intrinsic good. It should also be emphasized that a considerable subsequent family sacrifice in terms of standard of living would be justified. In American society at least, it is rarely the case that financial hardship is so great for survivors that a family is broken up, the children are unable to be educated, or other drastic effects. The burden of proof could not be met by establishing only that a family's standard of living would be relatively lessened, for one cannot balance relatively desirable economic goods against the final yes or no of physical existence itself.

Even in the case of what medical practice terms the 'withholding of support', euthanasia should have to bear the burden of proof. Where the possibility of life support remains, the presumption should lie with efforts to preserve life. Even in cases where a human organism has been reduced to vegetable existence, with no apparent possibility of revival of consciousness, the burden of proof should show that the situation really is hopeless. But where the appropriate tests, including electroencephelograph and the lapse of a sufficient period of time, indicate the overwhelming improbability of a recovery of consciousness, the normal presumption for medical efforts to maintain life might well be set aside. The presumption for life does not mean that in every instance persons ought not to be permitted to die.[13]

Another important illustration of the presumption of the goodness of creation is presented by sexual life. Sex is a powerful force, and every civilization has greater or lesser difficulties in regulating it. Now and again in Christian history, attempts to regulate sexuality have gone to the extreme of portraying sex itself as evil. This is a pronounced tendency in Augustinian thought (in part perhaps because of St Augustine's reaction against his own rather promiscuous early years). Even some of St Paul's writings convey a negative view toward sex ('It is well for a man not to touch a woman.' I Cor. 7.1b), although St Paul also explicitly taught that sex in marriage is no sin and that husband and wife should 'not refuse one another except perhaps by agreement for a season . . .' (I Cor. 7.5a). One of the important vows of most monastic orders was the vow of chastity, and it is difficult to escape the implication that the life of chastity is regarded as being on a higher plane morally. Some interpretations of the doctrine of original sin have conveyed the impression that sex is somehow responsible for its transmission. The Roman Catholic position on use of artificial contraceptives and a strong residual element of Victorianism in Protestant culture alike suggest that sex, *per se*, is at least suspect from the moral standpoint.

And yet, despite all this, a clear implication of faith in the goodness of existence is the positive value of sex. It is not a question of sex being a necessary evil which must regrettably be tolerated since this is the only way the species can be propagated. The burden of proof is not to be placed against sex. As an important aspect of our creaturely existence, sex is good. Of course the regulation of proper use of sex is another matter. Here the relationship between sex and covenantal good faith must be considered, and the fact that sex is good does not mean that it should not be disciplined in some way. But the point to be made now is that any moral judgment concerning sex which begins with the presumption that sex is essentially evil must bear the burden of proof. It is likely to be a wrong judgment, for it is based on a faulty premise. The same point can be made concerning every asceticism which suggests that the normal life of the senses is evil. Quite the contrary. The Christian presumption is that the life of the senses can be affirmed as a God-intended condition or basis for the spiritual life. The spiritual life is not to be opposed to the physical as though it could only occur through the defeat of our physical nature. Physical nature is not the same thing as spiritual life. It is not the *meaning* of our existence; it cannot be made an end in itself. Nevertheless, it is a good.

The goodness of creation is also to be affirmed in a presumption against the disruption of nature. In recent years, environmentalists have reminded us that man's freedom to dominate nature has distinct limits. It is even possible that man, in his arrogance, might succeed only in destroying the conditions necessary for his continued survival. Frederick Elder has pointed to two strands of ancient Hebrew tradition concerning man's relationship to nature.[14] According to the first, man is viewed as lord of nature; he is responsible for filling the earth and subduing it. This strand gives rise to a human-centred view of nature, with nature existing only to serve human interests. This strand, according to Elder, has led to a highly exploitative view of nature. According to the second tradition, on the other hand, human beings exist *in* nature and as a part of it. While nature extends certain facilities and opportunities to us, we do not have unlimited dominion over it. This distinction, suggested by Elder, is an illuminating one, although even the first stand of tradition in the Old Testament may not be so much human-centred as it is God-centred. Man has dominion, to be sure, but only in the form of a stewardship or responsibility given him by God. We are responsible for the exercise of this stewardship to God. So really in both traditions the presumption should be against any reckless dealing with nature. We need not be opposed to the economic development of the earth, nor do we need to apologize for viewing humanity as a higher level of creation than other aspects of nature. But nature is to be respected. Accordingly, a proper understanding of the goodness of creation should lead us to a strong presumption in favour of conservation. Wasteful dealing with nature and its resources should always have to bear the burden of proof.

This section ought not to be concluded without noting that humanity today has, for the first time, the power to destroy the planet earth as a fit habitation for man or beast. Quite apart from other things we shall say subsequently about war, it should be noted here that nuclear war poses an awesome potential threat to the future of the world. A strong presumption for the goodness of creation should stand also as a strong presumption against actual preparation for nuclear war. A casual attitude toward nuclear war can only reveal a low regard for the goodness of creation. Erich Fromm, in making essentially the same point, cites a Congressional hearing on the effects of nuclear war in which Professor Herman Kahn was questioned as to the possible quality of life in a society which has lost tens of millions of people through bombing. Kahn is quoted as remarking that 'war is horrible. There is no question about it. But so is peace. And it is proper, with the kind of calculations we are making today, to compare the horror of war and the horror of peace and see how much worse it is.' In response to a reporter's later questions, Kahn explained this remark by saying that 'I meant that the quality of life after a thermonuclear attack would not be much different than before. And who the hell is happy and normal right now? We'd be just about the same after a war – and we'd still be economically useful.'[15] These dismal pronouncements, made in 1959, illustrate precisely the attitude against which the Christian presumption of the goodness of created existence must stand.

To summarize: it is not possible for a Christian to base a judgment on the proposition that God's created physical world really does not, after all, matter very much. It matters very much indeed. It is intended as the material basis of God's covenant with human beings and may have further purposes which we cannot fathom.

79

(ii) *The Value of Individual Life*

Western civilization has a habit of speaking rather casually about the 'sacred' or 'infinite' worth of the individual. It has become a cliché, even among people whose economic or political practices betray anything but concern for the worth of individual human beings. Christian faith is not opposed to this habit; indeed, it is to a considerable degree the source of it. However, we should remember that personal or individual life is not self-validating. The dignity and worth of individual life cannot be derived from analysis of individual life itself. Man is not 'the measure of all things'. Whatever value human beings have is strictly transitory unless it is in our relationship to some ultimate source of value outside ourselves.

Christian faith understands human value as being established by our relationship with God – a relationship created and given by God himself. It is because we have our being from God and sustained by God that we can meaningfully affirm the value of individual human life. Christian scripture and tradition have always made this affirmation, even when insisting upon human unworthiness and sinfulness. The essence of this faith is that despite our sinfulness God has chosen to relate to us as a father to his children. We may be miserable worms (as one old gospel hymn suggests), but if so we are still *God*'s miserable worms, and that makes a considerable difference. We do not need to reopen here the question of the *imago dei* by asking whether the image of God in us is placed there through creation or as a 'reflection' in us from God's gracious relationship to us. Nor do we need to imply that somehow the image of God in us makes us equal with God. The crucial ethical question is whether by virtue of God's love of individual human beings we should properly regard each other as having boundless value. The answer of Christian faith is that what God loves, no person should despise.

Nor can we treat human value as though it were predicated only of mankind as a whole. While the social dimension of human existence requires equal stress (as we shall note in the following section), the Christian faith concerns also the radical worth of the individual person. Each one must, as Luther said, do his own believing just as he must do his own dying. What Luther meant is that regardless of whatever else we must say about our social nature, justification by faith means that *each* person is the beneficiary of God's gracious love. Nor does this mean simply the value of each *Christian's* life, as though non-Christians are not yet to be treated as the children of God. The parables of Jesus which emphasize God's loving concern for even the least of the lost sinners and Paul's insistence that God's grace is a gift to us notwithstanding our total undeserving both underscore that the relationship with God which is the source of all our value as individual human beings is prior to our own responsiveness. To be sure, the effect or fulfilment of personal value may be lost upon people who have no faith in the source of their own worth as individuals. But this does not mean that that value is itself the result of what people do. God's creation and grace, which are the basis of our value, are prior to our response (or our works, as Pauline theology put it). Viewed from this perspective, faith is itself a coming to awareness of God's immeasurable gifts. Faith is a release, on the one hand, from frantic efforts to create some transitory illusion of value and, on the other hand, from callous disregard for the value of each of our fellows.

When it is really understood, the presumption for the value of individual human lives runs directly against the grain of much contemporary culture. Actions and policies have often been taken quite for granted which should rather have had to bear the burden of proof because of their callous disregard for human life. The century of total war, of nuclear armament, of genocide, of concentration camps, of racism, of political repression, has often reversed the order of presumptions. The 'majority report' of this century may well have been expressed in Bertrand Russell's arresting words: 'Brief and powerless is man's life; on him and all his race the slow, sure doom falls pitiless and dark.'[16] But if so Christian judgment must reverse this majority report and insist rather that each individual life is of infinite value. It must insist that no life can be disregarded as unimportant. Whenever it is apparently necessary to treat persons as objects to be used or to be removed, the burden of proof must be met that such an exceptional action is clearly necessary for the sake of God's whole human enterprise. Even when persons must be 'used' the Christian will try to do so in such a way that the person's worth continues to be affirmed.

Thus, the burden of proof falls against any action or policy or social movement which has as its rationale the alleged unimportance or disvalue of any individual lives. Grosser illustrations, which leap to mind, need not detain us. Obviously genocide or chattel slavery or the use of unsuspecting individuals in dangerous medical experiments can be excluded by Christian judgment on the face of it. Other kinds of problems may pose more difficulty for sensitive Christian consciences in our time. There is, for instance, the problem of capital punishment. While the historical momentum in many countries is clearly running against capital punishment and it has been outlawed in a number of places, there are Christians who still strongly believe in it and who wish to see this momentum reversed. I believe that such Christians should reflect more deeply upon the meaning of the presumption of the value of each life. The Christian moral presumption ought to be against capital punishment even when it is punishment for the crime of murder. I find it conceivable that under extreme historical circumstances some form of capital punishment might be necessary as a deterrent. The burden of proof should still be against it. It should not be used unless there is very strong evidence that it is necessary as a way of saving lives and as a way of affirming the sanctity and security of all life in community. (Actual evidence to that effect is lacking in most areas of the world.) Nobody claims that capital punishment is capable of bringing back the life of a murder victim; it is only a question of what should be done with the murderer. Apart from practical questions of deterrence or disablement of a criminal so he cannot repeat the crime, capital punishment rests on the postulate that the criminal is no longer fit to live. It is this postulate that has to be rejected. Even the perpetrator of the most heinous of crimes has a life which is of value to God. The value of life in general cannot be affirmed if the value of *his* life is denied. One suspects that even in purely practical terms, the net effect of capital punishment may often be to decrease society's respect for life and thereby to increase the rate of killing. Suppose, in the case of Adolph Eichmann, the authorities in Israel had found it possible to spare his life in spite of the enormity of the genocide in which he had had a prominent part. Might this not have been a significant witness to the value of life which would have tended more to emphasize than to minimize the enormity of the crime? At any rate, I believe the burden of proof ought to be against capital punishment.

Similarly, it should be against disregard for life in war. The question of whether war itself can ever be justified is involved here, and it is worth noting that the classical just war criteria emphasized regard for the worth of life as a major consideration in deciding whether war should be commenced at all. Assuming the possible justification of war itself, however, the burden of proof would still need to be placed against any particular taking of life even within the war. Nobody can be written off simply as the enemy. Even the enemy remains a person who also has his life from God. It is reported that the President of the United States decided to use the first atomic bomb on Hiroshima and Nagasaki because this would save countless American lives.[17] Possibly the bombs did have this result, and conceivably the net result was also to save more Japanese lives as well. But one could not as a Christian decide the question on the basis indicated. Life as such was morally at stake, not just American life. During both the world wars, the mass media in most of the participating countries betrayed a striking tendency to portray their respective enemies in sub-human terms, thus helping to legitimize the increasingly vicious methods of extermination.

Regard for the value of personal life also entails a strong presumption for personal freedom. Freedom has become an increasingly ambiguous term in the modern world since many people claim the freedom to infringe upon the freedom of others. But freedom to exploit others, to discriminate racially, or otherwise to injure one's fellows is not the freedom of the Christian presumption. Unfortunately, the association of the term freedom with injustice has helped confuse discussion of a truly central human value. For without some kinds of freedom to be and to express one's selfhood, talk of the value of individual life is meaningless. Religious liberty is perhaps the most basic of all forms of freedom since it involves expression of the individual's relationship to the transcendent ground of all life. Religious freedom implies a basis for personal being which lies beyond social conformity and civil obligation.[18] It includes respect for freedom of communication and creative expression and freedom from being required to express loyalties and beliefs which one does not hold. All of the forms of what we term 'civil liberties' are involved: freedom of the press, freedom of speech, freedom from arbitrary search and arrest – including, in our time, freedom from electronic forms of eavesdropping, freedom for peaceful assembly. A strong presumption in favour of such freedoms must be fixed in law and custom, as indeed it is wherever bills of rights are respected. The current brutal disregard for freedom of the press and freedom of speech in such countries as Czechoslovakia, Korea, the USSR, and Chile is rightly condemned on the basis of Christian moral presumption.

Freedom is, in fact, a problem in most countries. Dominant majorities often conclude that the freedom of despised minorities to express unpopular views is not morally required.[19] But the burden of proof ought to be borne by those who think that this or that form of communication or aesthetic expression cannot be tolerated. Among some Christian groups this burden of proof should be accepted more seriously even in cases of alleged pornography. There may be forms of communication that are, as the courts sometimes put it, so devoid of redeeming social value as to merit no legal protection. Indeed, a case can be made that some of this may be exploitative, particularly as regards young and impressionable minds, and thereby a limitation of the freedom of others. But the burden of proof should be against censorship even so, and it is difficult to think of any good faith expression of ideas that should be forcibly suppressed even when the ideas themselves are thoroughly repugnant to most people.

The presumption in favour of the personhood and freedom of each individual clearly extends to a presumption against violence or coercion of all kinds. The problem of war will occupy us later. But it is well to bear in mind that violence and coercion can occur in more commonplace terms in daily life – even within the family, where corporal punishment and other forms of violence can be meted out altogether too casually and where the burden of proof should be placed against them more rigorously. It is difficult to see how such things can be avoided altogether in the raising of children from infancy to maturity, but it is a sound rule that wherever possible the use of sanctions should be clearly related to behaviour to be corrected. Placing the burden of proof against ordinary arbitrary force may lead us to explore more creative alternatives in correcting deviant behaviour.

In evaluating the plethora of conflicting social movements and organizations, all bidding for support from unaligned persons, a Christian confronts especially complex problems of judgment. But the presumption for the value of every person presents us with at least one important criterion. In so far as a group depends for its rationale upon the proposition that some categories of persons can be disregarded altogether, the Christian must require that group to bear the burden of proof before supporting it. In the social ferment of the late 1960s some movements and organizations thrived on portraits of their enemies as 'pigs' or 'Communists' or 'fascists' or 'hippies-and-yippies'. Movements at both ends and the middle of the ideological spectrum neatly divided the world among the good people and the bad people. A Christian can vigorously support or oppose a movement, but he can never dismiss the humanity of his opponents. His presumption is for the worth of *all* people, even those to whom he is vigorously opposed.

(iii) *The Unity of the Human Family in God*
If Christian faith entails a strong presumption for individual worth, it also implies that life cannot be lived in isolation. The two

presumptions cannot really be separated. That relationship with God which establishes our value as individuals is at the same time the basis of our unity, our fellow humanity. The epistle to the Ephesians expresses this unity of the human family in God by speaking of the way in which Christ 'has broken down the dividing wall of hostility' that previously had separated members of the community of Israel from the rest of mankind. Prior to Christ, the Gentiles were considered 'alienated from the commonwealth of Israel, and strangers to the covenants of promise, having no hope and without God in the world'. The significance of Christ is that he has reconciled man to God and thereby reconciled both Gentile and Hebrew 'to God in one body through the cross, thereby bringing the hostility to an end'. It is through our unity with God that our unity with one another is established. The divine-human covenant has created a covenant community. Israel always understood this covenant as the basis of its own national unity; now, in Christ, it is to be understood that the whole of mankind is the covenant community. This theme, which is treated explicitly in Ephesians, is implied elsewhere in the New Testament. Even in those passages which seem to exclude some from the unity of the human family it is because of their own rebellion against that unity and its basis in God. In principle the whole of mankind is included.

L. Harold DeWolf has pointed out that love itself needs to be understood as the affirmation of our basic unity in God and that a regrettable tendency of much discussion of love in Christian ethics has been to imply a curious insularity.[20] Even *agape* can imply a kind of atomistic individualism. This characteristic word for love in New Testament Greek has been taken by contemporary theology to mean a total, unselfish form of love which utterly disregards its response. The problem is that such an understanding of love implies that it is entirely a matter of what I do to or for somebody else 'out there'. DeWolf argues that Christian love cannot be individualized in this way. Love, rather, is a sharing of experience, an expression of our recognition of our underlying kinship in God. In this understanding, love is neither a matter of seeking an object (*eros*) or of altruistic self-giving (*agape*); rather it is an expression of mutuality in which the giving and the receiving are united. DeWolf regards the New Testament term *koinonia* (common) as a better linguistic clue to the meaning of Christian love since it suggests the fellowship-creating and fellowship-fulfilling character of Christian love. The point is well taken. Etymological analysis of terms for love in New Testament Greek is a particularly complex undertaking, and our understanding of love ought not to hinge simply on such analysis. Ancient as well as modern theologians use the same words with variant meanings, and it is impossible to establish fixed meanings to words when it is precisely the work of theology to establish more profoundly what certain terms *really* mean. But the decisive test is whether a given understanding of love accords well with the overall meaning of Christian faith. And here DeWolf properly reminds us that Christian love is a sharing in the gift which God has given alike to all of us. We love because he first loved us. Our love is an expression of our God-given unity.

Paul Lehmann and Joseph Haroutunian are among other theologians who have also emphasized the importance of social unity as an implication of Christian faith. Lehmann speaks of the 'fellowship-creating reality of Christ's presence in the world' manifest in the *koinonia* and contrasts this with the 'individualistic error' which has crept into many interpretations of the thought of St Paul.[21] While acknowledging Jesus' own concern for the individual, Lehmann insists that his messianic identity 'is unintelligible apart from the covenant community, the corporate structure of God's activity in the world'. Haroutunian likewise notes the importance of the individual and individualism but points out that we do not exist as human individuals: 'We do not know our "nature" except in our transactions with our fellowmen. We do our speaking and thinking, our purposing and acting, in the process of our mutual transactions.'[22] To be truly human is to be a 'fellowman', not a rugged, selfish individualist. Compare such theological reflections with the theme of rugged individualism in much Western culture – as exemplified, for instance, in the words of Ayn Rand, 'I swear by my life and my love of it that I will never live for the sake of another man, nor ask another man to live for mine'. It is difficult to see how this kind of individualism could possibly be reconciled with a Christian conception of unity in love.

The effect of such an understanding of Christian love is indeed to make every question of moral judgment a family question. It is no longer possible to treat another human being as though he or she were an alien – no matter how high our regard for aliens. Our love for the other is no longer based simply upon his or her value, much as we do continue to affirm the value of every child of God. Now it is based upon our own prior involvement in his or her life. We cannot, of course, become acquainted personally with more than a small fraction of the population of the world. Yet by faith we affirm our unity with all. In any situation of decision, those human beings who are affected by our judgment – whether or not they have previously been total strangers to us – are to be regarded as brothers and sisters in the human family. Each new person we chance to meet is not to be considered alien; even before we know the person's name we know that he or she is one with us. We need not be sentimental about this unity. It is in fact only as we come to recognize this unity as an objective reality that we are saved from undue sentimentality in love. As in a human family kinship dominates decisions despite the ebb and flow of emotional feelings, so the Christian's understanding of the objective kinship of all mankind in God dominates decisions. Love thus is given a steady, objective character. It is not without feeling, but its roots are deeper than feeling.

Such a conception of the unity of humankind would, if general, create a Copernican revolution in society. No longer would it be possible to treat life as a competitive struggle between alien beings struggling for the prize. No longer would it be possible to treat some part of humanity as a moral universe in itself, excluding all others. The fact that this sense of the unity of the human family is not generally accepted and the fact that it is clouded by selfishness in all of us may require compensating negative actions apparently in sharp conflict with unity. This point will be explored more carefully in the next chapter. Nevertheless, the unity of the human family functions as a methodological presumption of the first importance. The presumption is always for the most direct expression of human unity. The burden of proof must always be borne by every apparent disruption of the unity we have in God. Every barrier which owes its existence to deliberate human action must bear the burden of proof. Some barriers may, for a time at least, succeed in bearing this burden, but only if it can be established clearly that the barrier is itself necessary for the sake of a profounder fulfilment of God's intended covenant community. Few human barriers can meet that test.

It must be granted that certain forms of human exclusion are necessary. These are not to be considered in the same way as being a result of deliberate human action, although they may seem so. Every concrete relationship between two human beings is, in a sense, exclusive. The choice to spend these hours in interaction with these persons, and not with others, is exclusive. In marriage a covenant exclusiveness is established for life. (Even a totally promiscuous approach to sexual life is exclusive in the sense that most people will still be excluded, although some have attempted to exclude as few as possible!) But such forms of exclusion have their basis, not in a denial of the fellow humanity of another, but in the factual limitations of our temporal existence. The exclusive character of marriage can be understood as having its roots in the facts of biological existence. As Karl Barth reminds us, our created sexuality is the material basis for the profoundest human expression of covenant relationship. Our decision to marry this one person and only this one person and to make to him or her the pledge of covenant faithfulness is not predicated upon the belief that *only* this one person is worthy of such a covenant. *All* persons are worthy of such a covenant (though some may be incapable of its physical fulfilment), but the marriage *form* of covenant is such that having chosen one mate we may not choose another. That form has its basis in our created sexuality, not in a denial of human unity. Indeed, it is precisely in our recognition of the underlying unity of the whole human family that we best understand the foolishness of sentimental interpretations of the exclusiveness of marital love. The notion that for every person there is, somewhere, only one intended life mate (the Hollywood myth) is sentimental nonsense. It is based upon a love exclusion in *principle*, and it is often enough demonstrated that such a sentimental basis for marriage is incapable of maintaining its stability over time. What we recognize as the physical basis for a factual exclusiveness in marital covenant is in principle similar to other physical limitations. We cannot choose to interact with every other human being all the time. Our created social nature is such that the full exploration of human mutuality requires the cultivation of friendship, and friendship implies exclusion. Even within the family, certain members 'hit it off' with other members to a unique degree. Still, the exclusiveness of friendship, if it is an expression of the underlying unity of humankind, cannot be such that other relationships become impossible. We should find it possible in principle to cultivate specific relationships with *any* other human beings, particularly if we perceive and can respond to their peculiar need. We do not cultivate old relationships or create new ones as something we are doing for some other person; instead, we recognize and bring to fulfilment a kinship which already exists since we both already exist in union in God.

These points are made to counteract the idea that since some relationships must be exclusive it follows that exclusion is a more basic presumption than unity. For exclusion finally means that we have excluded ourself from fulfilment in God's intended covenant community which is the basis for our humanity.

In our own time, the presumption for unity has perhaps been tested most severely in the confrontation with racism. Racism is a world-wide phenomenon, with particularly deep roots in the United States and southern Africa. Basic to racism is the view that persons of different racial groups may not interact fully and deeply as fellow human beings. While racists sometimes say that we should all be united 'spiritually', they deny that that spiritual unity should ever be made concrete in actual relationships in the real world.

Against this conclusion, an ecumenical conference reported in 1954 that

> The great majority of Christian churches affiliated with the World Council have declared that physical separation within the Church on grounds of race is a denial of spiritual unity, and of the brotherhood of man. Yet such separations persist within these very churches, and we often seek to justify them on other grounds than race, because in our own hearts we know that separation solely on the grounds of race is abhorrent in the eyes of God.[23]

Racial discrimination, segregation, and apartheid transform (often arbitrarily) certain biological characteristics into the basis of exclusion in human relationship. The biological characteristics chosen are generally quite superficial, and not infrequently even imaginary. Racism amounts therefore to the creation of social barriers against the fulfilment of the unity of the whole human family. Racism is utterly inconsistent in principle with Christian faith.

The drive toward racial integration in the twentieth century is solidly rooted in the presumption for human unity. In recent years, however, those who have most seriously supported this drive have had to face a dilemma. On the one hand, they have understood that integration is in the long run the only possible solution to the moral question of how persons with different racial[24] characteristics ought to relate to each other. Race should pose no barrier at all, even in relation to marriage. But on the other hand, they have confronted a strong separatist drive coming not simply from the white racist but from within the black community itself. In part, this separatist drive can be understood as a psychological defence mechanism – an assertion of the equal value of black or brown skin, etc. – or as an attempt to be sure that important cultural values within the minority group will not be demolished in the name of some melting pot. In part, however, the separatist drive has asserted the need for real social separation. The development of minority group economic and political institutions and caucuses may partly represent temporary tactical expedients, designed to establish a more favourable bargaining position and to sensitize consciousness within both minority and dominant groups. But this development may also mean to some a more or less permanent model of how groups should interact in a pluralistic society. The integrationist, regardless of his or her own racial characteristics, has been placed on the defensive. In so far as, for example, the movement toward black separatism has represented a self-conscious effort to develop racial pride and self-respect in order to make it possible for black people subsequently to enter into full relationships with white people on a basis of self-respect, the objective could hardly be questioned. The presumption for unity cannot be fulfilled without mutuality of self-respect. Any 'integration' which in fact represents covert dominance of black people by white liberals must be rejected out of hand. Any 'integration' requiring black people to forego or apologize for their own cultural heritages in order to unite with white people on the basis of some middle-class white cultural heritage is also to be dismissed. True integration involves mutuality of respect for all persons and all cultural heritages – recognizing, of course, that there are good, bad, and neutral elements in every culture from the standpoint of Christian faith. Anything less than this mutuality of respect cannot be the basis for integration.

Still, in racial matters, a presumption for integration is implied by belief in the unity of the human family. This means that the burden of proof must be placed against racial separatism or segregation, even if only of a temporary kind. This also means that the burden of proof must be placed against a pluralistic model of racial interaction which contemplates the interaction of racial groups as groups but rejects the interaction of individual persons of different racial and ethnic groups. Personality is a fundamental moral category, but race is not. Despite pressures for separation from either the 'right' or the 'left', the Christian must require those who support separatism to make an overpowering case. Any residual doubt should be resolved by supporting integration. Even where one's own support for integration is met by rebuff, one must remember that the objective reality affirmed by faith is of a unity or kinship between oneself and those who resist relationship. In many parts of the world, including America, white people must learn something from the rebuffs. Perhaps only through rebuff can they purify the integrity of their own understanding of integration. Perhaps only through rebuff can they learn the meaning of the humiliation that black people have had to bear for generations. Nevertheless, the burden of proof must continue to be against racial separatism.[25] In most cases that burden will not be met successfully. This is particularly true in the American and the South African contexts for two reasons: In the first place, the sheer magnitude of existing social and economic relationships precludes real separation on a large scale. Even persons living in the great urban ghettoes have constant interaction with many outsiders. In the second place, separatism is unlikely to achieve a restoration of self-respect and dignity. Where relationships have been based upon illusions of superiority and inferiority along racial lines, the illusions have to be routed out in the context of the relationships themselves. A retreat from relationship in order to recover one's sense of dignity is more likely to have exactly the opposite result.[26]

Other kinds of social barriers also confront Christians and require moral assessment. Many outgrowths of nationalism need to be challenged in the light of the presumption of unity. National chauvinism among the more powerful established nations must, in all its expressions, bear the burden of proof. The restrictive immigration policies of, say, the United States and Australia, must be evaluated closely in the light of the need for stable labour relations, educational facilities, and other considerations. Nevertheless, the burden of proof ought to be against any specific restriction of immigration. Similarly, national policies forbidding travel to other countries ought to bear the burden of proof. At this point the Marxist countries have been particularly restrictive. Wherever nationalism builds barriers between peoples the presumption of Christians must be against the barriers and for the visible unity of the whole human family.

Probably the nationalism of the newer, recently colonial societies can present the strongest case. In Africa and Asia (and

93

in a somewhat different sense, Latin America), nationalism really represents two forces which are not in principle contrary to the presumption for unity. The first is the force to overcome exploitation by other countries. Exploitation is itself opposed to unity, and the drive to overcome it is a necessary precondition for the restoration of authentic unity. The second force is the drive to create a unity out of diverse opposing groups (such as competing tribal groups in Africa). Nationalism in that sense can be a unifying phenomenon, just as it was historically in the case of the development of European nation-states out of the feudalistic divisions which existed in the Middle Ages. But even nationalism as a resistance to exploitation and as a drive for regional unity has its dangers. In our era, policies growing out of even the more defensible forms of nationalism must bear the burden of proof where their effect is to maintain barriers.[27]

Fuller consideration of the effect of the presumption of unity requires us to proceed to the final positive presumption.

(iv) *The Equality of Persons in God*

The presumption of equality can be related to the preceding ones. Equality is implied in the value individual persons have through their relationship to God. When we say that individuals are valued 'infinitely' or 'totally' by God and that their life's meaning is entirely based upon this relationship of love, we assert that the essence of human life is beyond gradation. 'Infinite' value is value without qualification or limitation. Only limited objects can be differentiated and related to each other unequally. It is proper to speak of human limitations, of course. Man is a finite creature whose earthly career is bounded in time and space. But in value he is beyond these limitations because his value is based upon the valuing of God, who *is* infinite. Those philosophers who challenge any inherent worth or property of man as a ground for the equality of persons are not incorrect.[28] Human value is not a property of man *qua* man. In Christian perspective, it is solely a gift of the Father's love. Apart from faith in a source of human worth transcending human life itself, it is dubious whether either human value or human equality can be demonstrated philosophically. But the faith of the Christian in God's total love of each person is at the same time an acknowledgment of the equality of persons. A person who is *totally* loved by God cannot be loved any less than another person who is also totally loved. One infinite value cannot be less or more valuable than another infinite value. It is in this ultimate perspective that we are equal.

It is even doubtful whether we ought to speak of the equality of persons 'before God', as though our equality obtained from God's calculating judgment that we who stand 'before' him are equal. Equality is not from God's judgment (although there is also a sense in which we can speak of our equality as sinners before God as judge); rather it is from God's love. God's love is prior to his judgment. His judgment is a function of his love.[29] It is also true that there are apparent differences in human response to God. Whatever universalism theologians may ultimately derive from grace,[30] both scriptural sources and theological traditions assert that some are worse sinners than others. That point seems well-founded empirically! But the distinctive mark of Christian faith is the trust in God's love 'while we were yet sinners'. Gradations in sinfulness, even if we could identify them ourselves with confidence, are irrelevant to the source of human worth. God's love cuts through all the gradations to the core of human being. Were God's love rationed out on the basis of the relative degrees of human worthiness, then it would be precisely accurate to say that God's love is something we must (and therefore may) earn – i.e., that 'works' are prior to 'grace'. The contrary affirmation, that grace is prior to works, cuts the ground from beneath any human pretensions to superiority.

Equality is also implied in the Christian view of unity. There is an immediate sense in which this is true, for the basis of our unity in God is at the same time the basis of our equality. The love which binds us together is the same love which loves us equally and therefore makes us equals in our relations with each other. But unity can be related to equality in other ways as well. Unity in relationship implies mutuality: in relationship with one another

95

we both give and receive our essential being. As we have noted, people do not exist as truly human apart from social relationship. In relationship we receive back from others a confirmation and fulfilment of our humanity. But we cannot receive from inferiors the basis of our superiority. Ironically (perhaps this is the ultimate human irony), the deference which social inferiors pay to their alleged superiors detracts from – rather than adds to – the latter's essential humanity. How could this be so? The one thing that an inferior cannot give to his superior is the human acknowledgment of a fellow being who is in every respect a *fellow* being. Hegel noted this fact in his analysis of how the master-slave relationship undermines that self-consciousness which people must have to be human. When the master refuses to regard the slave as a fellow man, deserving of equal recognition, he deprives himself of recognition by another self-conscious human being.[31] Inequality alienates us, not simply from others, but also from our own humanness.

Nowhere is this more evident historically than in the relationship between the sexes. The created sexual nature of men and women provides the possibility for the deepest kind of mutual affirmation and fulfilment, as Karl Barth has argued so profoundly. It can, as he has noted, serve as a physical symbol of the whole meaning of covenant and of the overcoming of every form of human alienation. Yet it is ironic that the role inferiority of women throughout most of recorded history has tended to deprive both men and women of the deeper fulfilments in sexuality. Unquestionably, some differences of function between men and women have flowed from biological differences. But where these differences have led to inequalities of status and perceived value, the humanness of all has been diminished.

To be sure, not every relationship is a human relationship, i.e., one based upon the premise of equal consideration. The relationships of man with beast, or even the purely functional or utilitarian relationships which involve entirely objective manipulation, are not essentially human. Slavery is, in principle (though not entirely in fact) based upon such manipulative, non-human relationship.

Truly human mutuality has to occur among the slaves and among the free in such a society; that is, it has to occur where people can regard each other essentially as equals. The Christian claim is that wherever there are people there is that essential humanity, and therefore equality. To put all this differently, whatever it is that detracts from our unity helps undermine equality; and whatever vitiates equality also undermines unity. The unity of unequals is not real unity unless the forms of inequality are mutually recognized as unimportant alongside the more fundamental human equality. There can be no fraternity without equality, no equality without fraternity.

If all persons are ultimately equal, then a strong presumption exists for equality of treatment in the concrete relationships and structures of the world. Any inequality in existence is a potential threat to mutual recognition of that equality and unity we have in God – and therefore it is a threat to the fulfilment of our unity with God himself. Equality cannot merely exist on the 'spiritual' plane; existential equality is an important condition of spiritual recognition of equality. It aids the fulfilment of our true humanity while existential inequality impedes it. The burden of proof must therefore be placed against every factual inequality. On the face of it, it is inequality which must be justified. Equality has an immediate presumption of rightness.

Nevertheless, *absolute* equality in existence is both impossible and inadvisable.

It is impossible since even the natural distribution of the conditions of life is uneven. Physical constitution, health, mental capacity etc. differ widely, even though hereditary equality can itself be effected to some extent by greater equality in the distribution of the goods of life. It appears unthinkable that a day might come when all persons would inherit precisely equal physical and mental capacities.

But absolute equality is also *inadvisable* since unequal distribution of facilities and rewards appears, to some extent, necessary for the sake of greater social benefits. The case for unequal distribution of facilities is almost self-evident, both in terms of recognizing differential need and in terms of differential function. A person with eye difficulties may need the unequal, extra something of eyeglasses in order to enjoy equal vision with those who do not have the same difficulties. Some persons require very expensive medical care and remedial facilities even partially to correct nature's inequalities. This would be the moral basis for the provision of specially equipped automobiles for the handicapped at public expense by the British government. Different social tasks or roles likewise require different facilities. Different crafts require different tools. Even intake of food must vary with the strenuousness of functions performed – at least to some extent. It is arguable that some particularly unpleasant or nerve-racking forms of work require unequal recreational facilities or a higher degree of freedom from economic worries. In contemporary education, provision is often made for the variable needs of mentally retarded children, on the one hand, and for the particularly gifted, on the other. Both can be defended as ways of equipping the young to make their fullest contribution to society. Justification of an apparent deviation from the presumption of equality would here take the form of a demonstration of needs which, if not met, would themselves create inequalities.

But it is also arguable that some unequal distribution of social rewards may be advisable as a means of influencing behaviour in society. Here the determinant of unequal treatment is not one of need but of merit, as socially defined. In a perceptive essay, Ralf Dahrendorf argues that a reward system of some kind is implicit in the very notion of society:

> Human society always means that people's behaviour is being removed from the randomness of chance and regulated by established and inescapable expectations. The obligatory character of these expectations or norms is based on the operation of sanctions, i.e. of rewards or punishments for conformist or deviant behaviour. If, however, every society is in this sense a moral community, it follows that there must always be at least that inequality of rank which results from the necessity of sanctioning behaviour according to whether it does or does not conform to established norms. . . . The origin of inequality is thus to be found in the existence in all human societies of norms of behaviour to which sanctions are attached.[32]

It is certainly the case that all known societies have had reward systems of some sort. Complex modern societies have numerous, sometimes conflicting systems of rewards corresponding to the different subgroups and cultures. Much sociological study is, in one way or another, occupied with the analysis of relationships between social norms, social behaviour, and social rewards. Social stratification – the status-system of a society – is partly a matter of social reward for behaviour advancing social norms; it is also a matter of symbolizing and providing support for leadership roles. Inequality of rank and power thus becomes intertwined with the designation and distribution of rewards. It is important to remember that social rewards are not entirely economic. Any scarce values (that is, any objects of desire which do not exist in sufficient quantities to satisfy demand) require a distribution system, and any distribution system will embody different kinds of social reward in accordance with social norms. Economic values, social prestige, and social power are all scarce values and are all likely to be involved in a reward system.

Needless to say, no social reward system is likely to remain very efficient. The problem is that persons of high status have disproportionate power in determining the allocation of future rewards and the norms upon which such allocation will be made. Merit cannot be rewarded in any simple, objective way because those who do the rewarding will themselves have a major stake in the outcome. They will tend to define merit and reward in such fashion that they continue to merit and receive the best rewards themselves. This is a practical difficulty.

From a Christian moral perspective there is an even more serious problem. When a reward is sought in the form of scarce values (that is, when I seek wealth, power, or prestige in order that I may have more of these values than others have), the effect of this desire is spiritual isolation. This is ironic. By seeking fulfilment through a higher status in life, the 'reward' of higher status is precisely the undermining of the only true basis for fulfilment in covenant community with God and fellowman.[33] This is the moral Achilles heel of social reward systems: the reward offered is alienation. The more intensely it is desired and pursued, the greater the alienation. It is primarily internal and subjective. Alienation accompanies the desire for status even when the reward is not pursued successfully. Alienation might not occur among those who receive social rewards without having sought them. The latter point is unimportant for our present analysis because the question is whether social rewards, entailing inequality, ought to be offered with the intention that people should desire them and seek to merit them.

Is society, then, at war with itself? Is the factual precondition of civilized community in conflict with the normative precondition of fellow-humanity? Of course even the fact that all recorded societies have apparently had social reward systems is not sufficient to make this an adequate basis for exception to the presumption of equality. All recorded societies have also been plagued with murder and other social pathologies. It may be that a reward system creating inequalities should be tolerated by Christians only in the same way they tolerate murder: i.e., it is only to be accepted when one does not have any power to do anything about it.

But even within the context of the presumption for equality, some form of social reward system might be able to bear the moral burden of proof. If it is evident that *without* a social reward system, organized society would collapse or economic productivity would fail to meet basic needs, or if equality can only be attained by suppressing basic civil liberties and arousing general social bitterness, etc., then a case could be made and the reward system, inequalities and all, would be considered a price well worth paying. In his study of justice, John Rawls argues that justice begins with the examination of every question of social policy from the standpoint of the least privileged members of society. Only those policies which can be regarded as being in the interest of these least privileged persons can be regarded as just.[34] Inequalities cannot be justified by the benefits accruing to those who already benefit too much. But if a fully rational, less privileged member of society considered the inequality to be in his or her own interest, then the price might indeed be worth paying.

It should never be forgotten that inequality is costly in moral terms. It is undesirable but possibly necessary. I shall say more on this point in the next chapter in connection with the problem of the 'necessary evil'. But here we may note that methodological presumption permits us to accept undesirable realities where every alternative is even more undesirable. The burden of proof is against inequality, but that burden will be met if it can be shown that more evil will result by clinging to equality than by admitting some inequality. It should not be forgotten, moreover, that any society (which may mean *all* societies) which depends upon inequalities for motivational purposes is, to that extent, probably incapable of the fulfilment of real covenant community. There may be a sense in which it is pointless to sacrifice some tolerable justice and social cohesiveness and purpose for the sake of the kingdom of God on earth, if the kingdom of God on earth is not a factual possibility anyway. I do not wish to press this point too hard, for what is at stake is not either/or, but rather degrees of equality and inequality, of fulfilment and alienation. The presumption for equality is a useful method of keeping the pressure on inequality and alienation. In the absence of such tension, we settle too easily for morally undesirable policies and practices. In a very real sense, this does mean that society must be at war within itself. And so it shall be until the final consummation of history.

In discussing the use of unequal distribution of scarce values as a social incentive, an important distinction must be borne in mind. Elsewhere, in the context of an analysis of income incentives, I have suggested that 'absolute' incentives need to be distinguished from 'relative' ones.[35] An absolute incentive is one which turns the fundamental conditions of a person's social existence into rewards or punishments. The reward for approved behaviour is one's social existence itself. The punishment for disapproved behaviour is deprivation of the conditions of social existence. Capital punishment is the prime illustration of the latter; normal security in the community illustrates the former. A relative incentive, on the other hand, is one which offers rewards or threatens punishments which are only relatively desirable or undesirable. A small raise in pay or some small symbolic recognition is a relative incentive.

If inequalities can be justified morally by the Christian, they should be of the relative rather than the absolute kind. An absolute incentive is predicated upon a distinction between those who have the right to exist as members of the community and those who do not. The fundamental, underlying equality of persons is not recognized and the united fellow-humanity of persons in the community is, in principle, denied. The first claim of all people, which precedes all justification of inequalities of privilege, is the claim upon the basic conditions of life. This precedes everything else because nothing else can be justified apart from the social existence which is intended by God. Relative incentives do not in principle deny the premise of equality and fellow-humanity. We must remember, however, that there is a point beyond which relativities of inequality begin to act as severe impediments to fellow-humanity. A society might abolish poverty altogether (in the absolute, objective sense in which poverty means deprivation of the conditions of life and health), but if some were permitted to accumulate wealth and privileges vastly in excess of others, it would be difficult for social relationships to proceed on the basis of mutual recognition and shared experience. This is why even relative incentives should be required to bear the burden of proof: Are they really necessary for the sake of some greater social good? Will they not create such great disparities as to build formidable barriers to human mutuality?

I do not doubt that relative incentives can, in every conceivable society, meet this burden of proof up to a certain point. But requiring such incentive rewards to bear the burden of proof will make it easier to define that point. In most modern societies, not excluding those in the Marxist camp, excessive privilege is to be found alongside deprivation in the economic and/or political and legal conditions of authentic human life.

Meanwhile there is every presumption in favour of social incentives based, not upon selfishness, but upon social fulfilment itself. It is sometimes mistakenly supposed that recognition of the uniqueness of the contributions of individuals and groups is the same thing as recognition of inequality. But uniqueness and inequality are not the same thing. A unique contribution is, to the extent of its uniqueness, literally incomparable; and incomparable things cannot be related to each other either as equal or as unequal. By what intrinsic criterion would we attempt to compare the Mona Lisa with Beethoven's Fifth Symphony? We may be more greatly moved by one than by the other, but these are unique expressions of art. Only in an external, secondary sense can they be compared. Recognition of every person's contribution is a recognition of every person's humanity. It is a celebration of the expression of our human worth at the same time it is gratitude for its value to the community. Social recognition does not have to be accorded by means of reward in scarce values; it is not a matter of what we give to one not being available to give to another. To illustrate this point obliquely, and at the same time to bring the discussion back to Dahrendorf's argument concerning the necessity of society's use of a reward and punishment system, it can be pointed out that the reward for not violating criminal law is available to everybody. In a reasonably just society nobody needs to go to jail. But similarly, everybody in the community can be commended for their contributions and all can rejoice together in the creative and useful treasures which each person can, in his or her own way, bring to the common store.

Even a social stratification system can in principle function in this way – where leadership is not sought as a means of separating oneself from one's 'inferior' fellows, but where it is the contribution which persons with peculiar forms of talent can make. Where leadership positions are sought as a means of self-aggrandizement they are corrupting and unfulfilling. Where leadership is unselfishly offered and received it can help in the fulfilment of the whole community. The kind of leadership structure which serves in this way is not a threat to but a confirmation of the essential equality of persons: 'whoever would be first among you must be slave of all' (Mark 10.44).

· · ·

These, then, are the four positive presumptions of Christian faith: (i) the goodness of created existence, (ii) the value of individual life, (iii) the unity of the human family in God, and (iv) the equality of persons in God. Each of these is derived from the core of Christian faith and they are not entirely distinct from each other. Other statements of presumption could similarly be drawn from Christian faith. The attempt in this chapter has been to illustrate the ways in which Christian faith itself can supply the positive content for our methodological presumptions.

4

Negative Moral Presumptions

A. *Presumptions*

The positive presumptions we have been considering express the goodness that is at stake when moral judgments are made. Were we living in a world in which existence simply demonstrated the power of such presumptions there would be no need to speak of exceptions to the presumptions. Some exceptions are little more than a logical application of the presumptions to somewhat complex problems. These, then, are only apparently exceptions. But other exceptions arise from the genuine negation of the force of our presumptions. They arise from obstacles to the full positive organization of life on the basis of the Christian faith. By speaking of presumptions we indicate that we have made *preliminary* judgments and that any exceptions will have to bear the burden of proof. But the question remains, why should a Christian be willing to speak of moral exceptions at all? Has Christian faith been compromised or abandoned when exceptions to the presumptions implied in Christian faith are admitted?

The weight of this question has been felt by every serious Christian moralist. If deviations from the direct moral implications of Christian faith are capable in principle of bearing the burden of proof, then the theological rationale for such deviations is a central problem. Some moralists in the long tradition of Christian perfectionism deny that such a rationale is possible. Others have sometimes assumed that there must be some deviations or exceptions for 'practical' reasons without wrestling with the implied meaning of this 'practicality' in terms of Christian faith.

As we begin to explore this problem, we do well to remember that there are negative as well as positive implications of Christian faith. A part of Christian understanding is the insight that there are important limitations built into the human condition. Part of this pertains to the realities of sin and evil; part of it to the simple fact that we human beings do not have unlimited intelligence, knowledge, and capabilities. The word 'negative' may not be quite right if it suggests only sin and evil. But this word does indicate points at which we must say 'no' to illusions about human nature and the possibilities of *perfect* goodness and justice being realized in this world. This negative aspect of the Christian view of reality in fact suggests further presumptions which must also be taken into account in the formation of judgments. A burden of proof must also be borne by those who totally neglect *these* presumptions. I propose to state the negative implications of Christian faith in the form of two presumptions.

(i) *Human Finitude*

To be a human being is to be limited. In our short span of life each of us is capable of experiencing only the tiniest fragment of reality. Our best judgments will never be informed by *all* of the relevant facts, nor can we regard our understanding of the meaning of Christian faith itself as completely infallible. To be sure, the meaning of incarnation is that the infinite God has manifested his true nature to finite people in concrete form. Christian faith, including the positive presumptions outlined before, requires confidence in the dependability of this divine self-disclosure of God in Christ. Unless it can be affirmed that the infinite God is also capable of limiting himself through self-disclosure and that he has indeed revealed his essential nature in Christ, then there remains little basis for Christian faith. But a part of the character of that revelation itself is the paradox that through it we come better to understand how it is that in our creatureliness there is much that we cannot understand. As John Dillenberger has put this, following Luther and others,

> both Christian thought and experience imply a concept of a hidden God. It is affirmed, not eliminated, through God's activity. It is not that God is hidden and then discovered. Nor does he simply step out of hiddenness into the sight of man. Revelation, which is always revelation to someone, itself established God as hidden or veiled in imparting himself, and as hidden in the depths of his being. Revelation shows the hidden character of God.[1]

Or to put this differently, it is revealed that while God's goodness in covenant love for human beings is decisive, no one possesses the mind of God. Now we see only in a glass darkly; under the circumstances of our creaturely existence we may not see 'face to face'.

This would be true even if we could justly claim moral perfection, a point which is emphasized scripturally through the doubt expressed by Jesus on the cross and by the agony of his wrestling in prayer. Even philosophers who have a high degree of confidence in the human mind (such as Thomas Aquinas) have recognized that our intellects are connected with the actual world only through physical senses and that the senses are capable of deceiving as well as of informing our conscious experience. This is what, in theological perspective, is meant by being a creature dependent upon a physical body. Kantian epistemology demonstrates unalterably that the mind does not *know* the thing outside the mind *in itself*. One does not have to accept Kant's exact formulation of the categories which the mind imposes upon external data to conclude with him that we do not have immediate (unmediated) contact with the essence of the objects of our experience. Even the experience we do have is sharply limited in time and space, and our ability to act upon what knowledge and wisdom we can accumulate is limited by time, physical location, and finite power.

These points, which were also touched upon in the first chapter, are a reminder, not only of the tenuousness of our own moral judgments but of the tenuousness of the moral judgments of others. They suggest that we can approach every problem secure in the understanding that every participant in the situation is likewise finite. The relevance of this to our judgments will be explored further below.

(ii) Human Sinfulness

Paul, in the book of Romans, writes that 'all have sinned and fall short of the glory of God'. This theme, which looms so prominently in the writings of that first Christian theologian, is really an inescapable part of the biblical drama. We need not be detained here by the details of a doctrine of sin to note what seems essential in this biblical theme for our methodological purposes. The crucial questions are really two: Is there any warrant in the Christian view for regarding *any* persons as sinless? And, even if so, is there any way we can be sure who these sinless people are? The function of the myth of the fall or of the doctrine of original sin is to emphasize the universality of sin. *All* people are sinners. Precisely how this has come to be may be unimportant, although some may need to be assured that this does not depend upon acceptance of the literal factual details of the Garden of Eden story and others may need reassurance that this is not a matter of sin being transmitted through sex. Such reassurances are needed by many contemporary people in order to preserve a sense of the intellectual seriousness of the problem of original sin. Probably no recent theologian has done more to recover this sense of seriousness than Reinhold Niebuhr, who relates the universality of sin to the universality of the anxieties engendered in man by his ability to understand his own finitude and by his tendency to place himself at the centre of the universe which he is able to comprehend.[2] Sin, to Niebuhr, ultimately is man's tendency toward self-seeking pride. It is trying to establish ourselves as God. Biblical religion, according to Niebuhr, provides us with resources to obtain release from the anxieties which give rise to the need for self-centredness. But nobody can be presumed ever to be totally sinless.

There is also another way to approach the problem of the universality of sin – through the universality of moral freedom. In so far as people are free to choose the good the logical corollary is that they are also free to choose evil. By affirming that human beings will always possess this freedom to choose good, we are at the same time asserting that every person in every time and place of moral decision is at least *potentially* capable of sin. So long as people are free, sin is always a possibility. Thus, even if we were to satisfy ourselves that this or that individual or group were in fact now sinless, we could not (as long as we also regard them as free moral beings) be confident of their continuing in that state.

What then of grace? Is it not also a biblical understanding that grace is capable of redeeming humanity from the grasp of sin? This problem has challenged theology almost from the beginning: is grace irresistible? is it at least powerful enough to overcome the power of sin? have we any warrant to establish human sinfulness as a methodological presumption of Christian judgment?

Two things should be said in response. First, as generally developed in the Pauline tradition and in much subsequent theology, grace is understood as having effect despite our continuing struggle with our tendency toward self-centredness. The doctrine of sanctification, which speaks of growth toward holiness or wholeness, clearly implies that we continue to be infected by the tendency toward sinfulness. (Only in one Wesleyan tradition is much claimed for the perfectability of man in this life, and even John Wesley thought this mainly a possibility at the very end of our earthly pilgrimage.) Secondly, if grace is to have authentically human significance, it must be understood as a reality which affirms human freedom, not one which sets it aside. Paul himself speaks of grace as setting us free from the 'law of sin and death'. Grace makes it possible for people to escape the bondage of a self-centred life and of a hopeless prospect toward death. But it also opens up possibilities of genuine choice. Some great Christian theologians, including Augustine, Calvin, and possibly Paul himself, have felt it necessary to picture grace as finally overwhelming every human resistance among the 'elect'. Yet, is this not even more to make man a slave to an external power apart from his own responsive action? Would this not be dehumanizing in the fullest sense of the word? To know, through the grace revealed in Jesus Christ, that one is a child of God is, on the one hand, to realize that one is free to rebel against God but, on the other hand, that one need not do so to fulfil the meaning of one's humanity.

The basic proposition remains that all people are sinners – that all are somewhat disposed toward self-centredness. The methodological significance of this point will be developed below. But it should be added here that even the degrees or relativities of human sinfulness may be of little importance. It is one thing to argue that some people are more sinful than others – a point which is clearly within the biblical tradition. But it is quite another to assert that we can dependably *know* who are the greater and lesser sinners. It is one thing to insist that grace is at work to redeem us from our wretched selfishness; it is quite another to claim the power to judge the extent of that work of grace. Some relative judgments have to be made, after much serious wrestling. But the more ultimate judgments have to be left to God. Moreover, so far as our own judgments of ourselves are concerned, there is a very strong New Testament tradition of the importance of confessing first our own sinfulness. Those who feel most self-righteous are most likely to be, in fact, the most self-centred.

Of course, too great preoccupation with the pervasiveness of sin can lead to cynicism. We may too easily make too much of the presumption of sin and too little of the power of the positive presumptions. False complacency can be created either way. That is either by giving in too readily to the inevitability of sin (and thus expecting too little of people) and by ignoring sin altogether (and thus failing to deal realistically with sin's power to wreak havoc amid God's intended purposes for human life).

B. The Effect of Negative Presumptions

The most immediate effect of the negative presumptions is to call into question any social policy which depends for its justification upon the assumption that some persons *are* infallible or morally perfect. To the extent that proposals or movements depend upon such assumptions they must be presumed to be wrong, or at least to be highly suspect. Since, according to Christian insight, everyone is presumed to be a finite sinner, no one ought to be treated as though he or she were all-wise and perfectly good. Policy proposals or social movements which seem to depend upon such a wrong view of man should be made to bear the burden of proof. Extreme viewpoints of both right and left often need this kind of correction. Marxist movements, for instance, have depended to a considerable extent upon their claim to have discovered the science of human social history. They rather too neatly divide mankind between those who know and those who do not know what is to be done to advance the authentic destinies of humankind. They also tend to absolutize the goodness of the revolutionary class, the evil of exploiting classes, and the goodness of future man whose life will no longer be corrupted or repressed by class exploitation. But how could a Christian depend upon a diagnosis of a particular social problem which depended, for its validity, upon taking such absolute claims at face value? This is not to question the Marxist capability of astuteness in the judgment of particular issues. Rather it is to say that one must expect the overall Marxist assessment to be distorted. One must therefore place the burden of proof against the Marxist assessment *as a whole* while discriminately weighing the particular judgments of Marxists. An illustration of the failure of a Christian writer to be sufficiently cautious at this point is Harry F. Ward's book, *In Place of Profit*,[3] which was published during the 1930s. Taking Soviet claims quite at face value and accepting almost without reservation the Marxist criticism of the non-Communist societies, that volume completely missed the viciously repressive side of Soviet life in the 1930s. It would have ill-prepared the reader for the realities of Stalinism which were more fully exposed by Nikita Khrushchev in 1956. A Christian might have been more alert to the danger signal posed by the absolute moral pretensions. Again, this does not mean that Soviet life was all bad nor that Marxist criticism of the West was devoid of merit. But particular claims, criticisms, and proposals have to be detached from their packaging in pretensions and illusions about human nature.[4]

As another illustration from more recent history, James Forman attracted wide notice with his celebrated 'Black Manifesto' of 1969, which suggested quite broadly that black people 'are the most humane people within the United States' and characterized those who make up the power structure of the United States as 'ruthless, barbaric men' who 'have systematically tried to kill all people and organizations opposed to its imperialism'.[5] Black people who support 'black capitalism' were characterized as 'black power pimps and fraudulent leaders'. Again, danger signs have been raised. The language suggested that some people are absolutely and totally sinful while others are absolutely humane and to be trusted. One need not reject the specific points at which the Manifesto may have well-diagnosed the American racial and economic situation, but the implied doctrine of man might well lead one to place the burden of proof against the document taken as a whole.

The intellectual and moral absolutizing of the left has had its counterpart on the right. For more than half a century Americans have tended to go far beyond mere criticism of Marxist Communism. Communism has become the very incarnation of evil for many people. The Communists' own Manichaean conflict between the powers of oppression and the forces of revolutionary liberation has its Western counterpart in the conflict between 'freedom' and the Red menace. As one militant anti-communist, the Rev. Billy James Hargis, explained the dynamics of his own following,

> They wanted to join something. They wanted to belong to some united group. They loved Jesus, but they also had a great fear. When I told them that this fear was Communism, it was like a revelation. They knew I was right, but they had never known before what that fear was. They felt better, stronger, more secure in the knowledge that at last they knew the real enemy that was threatening their homes and their lives. They came to me and I told them.[6]

Another such leader, Dr Fred Schwarz, attracted quite a following in the early 1960s while describing Communism as a cancer – a term hardly calculated to encourage careful distinctions among the truths and errors of Marxism.⁷ The fault, at bottom, is again the implied doctrine of man: an inability to take into account that we are all finite sinners.

Movements of disadvantaged groups have often had to combat such self-righteousness. One recalls the response of tycoon George F. Baer during the US coal strike of 1902: 'The rights and interests of the laboring man will be protected and cared for, not by the labor agitators, but by the Christian men to whom God in His infinite wisdom, has given control of the property interests of the country.'⁸

Those words were echoed as recently as the late 1960s in the attitudes of California and Florida growers who resisted agricultural unionization. Many a good Christian grower argued that the migrant field workers should trust the growers to pay the best possible wages and to guarantee the best working and living conditions without joining the farm workers' union headed by Caesar Chavez. Many others, who had no immediate stake in the dispute, were inclined to take this position at face value. But how could they? To accept without question the growers' views would have required one to have unlimited faith in both their wisdom and their goodness. In fact, the growers represented only one side in a conflict of interest, and their views corresponded rather directly to their own self-interest. Should one not have been on guard against their demonstrated inability to take their own sinfulness into account? Some aspects of the views of the growers might well have been true; yet the burden of proof needed to be placed against their views as a whole, for no allowance had been made for the fact that the growers also were finite sinners. It was his encounter with similar attitudes among the Henry Fords of the auto industry that gave rise to so many of Reinhold Niebuhr's sharpest insights into the sinfulness of man.

On the basis of a realistic Christian appraisal of human finitude and sinfulness, we could very well speak of two useful compensatory presumptions. The first might well be a presumption against one's own self-interest in any decisions where one's own tendencies toward selfishness might be expected to be expressed. Most of us have a tendency to accept at face value the apparent congruence between universal truth and goodness and our own personal self-interest. One need not become cynical in taking this into account. The process is very largely unconscious with most people. Yet this is just what makes it so great a distortion of reality. People tend to place the burden of proof against whatever challenges their self-interest rather than placing the burden of proof against themselves. Thus, when new taxes are proposed the initial reaction of many people (probably *most* people) is to be strongly opposed unless it can be shown beyond doubt that the taxes are needed. Often we insist that the new tax itself be in our own self-interest. Legislative appropriations for foreign assistance or poverty programmes must bear a heavy burden of initial opposition because such expenditures are considered by many people to be wasteful on the face of it. Or people without school-aged children may object strenuously to taxes designated for state school education. An attempt to correct such myopia by placing a compensatory presumption against oneself may be as useful as it is difficult.

The other compensatory presumption could be called a presumption for the underdog. The negative presumptions of universal human finitude and sin create important reasons why a Christian should seek especially to empower the weak. The strong cannot be presumed to be righteous enough to determine the fate of the weak. In a dispute between the powerful and the weak, the presumption must be for the weak in order to compensate for their powerlessness and for the presumed sin of the strong. This does not mean that the strong are necessarily more sinful than the weak, but only that they have more means whereby to express their sinfulness. Indeed, yesterday's underdog may easily become tomorrow's oppressor. One should be neither surprised nor disillusioned by this. It is rooted in the sinfulness of man. But neither should one neglect to be particularly sensitive to the interests of both yesterday's and tomorrow's weak ones. The interests of the weak will be defended by those concerned for justice even in the full awareness that those who are defended today may have to be fought tomorrow when they come into power. The statement from the Message of the Amsterdam Assembly of the World Council of Churches, quoted above in Chapter 2 ('we have to make of the Church in every place a voice for those who have no voice . . .'), embodies such a presumption for the underdog. So does Walter Rauschenbusch's comment that 'those who have been deprived of intelligence, education, and property need such championship as the ministers of Jesus Christ can give them, and any desire to pardon and excuse should be exercised on their behalf . . .'.[9]

Compensatory presumptions of this kind certainly need to be used with intelligence. The two mentioned here can even come into direct conflict. Suppose one is oneself a member of a weak, repressed group or class. Should one then have a presumption for the underdog position or should one's presumption be against one's own self-interest (which happens to be that same underdog position)? Perhaps the only thing that can be said is that even here a person should be particularly alert to the ways in which his or her own personal self-interest can distort the appraisal of the just interests of his or her own group. The problem can be illustrated in relation to the social change methods of Saul Alinsky.[10] Alinsky's own motives apparently were an outgrowth of his sense of outrage at the injustices inflicted by the strong upon the weak in our society. He often enlisted similarly motivated clergymen and others of good will in his campaigns. But his method of approach was based upon the assumption that the organization of a community (such as a ghetto neighbourhood) can only be effected by appealing to the outraged self-interest of its residents. Such people will presumably be ill-equipped to be at all sensitive to the elements of truth or goodness embodied in their opponents (who were collectively to be treated as the enemy). A community organized along such motivational lines would not seem to be a particularly promising place to recruit selfless champions of other disadvantaged groups. The approach to this problem which is discussed in Chapter 8 in connection with the strategies of Martin

Luther King represents a more promising way to overcome the tension.

Having explored some possible applications of the negative presumptions we must return to a theological problem. The presumption against human infallibility may be easy enough to accept. But it may seem more doubtful whether we should place a similar presumption against the sinlessness of persons and groups. Does such a presumption vitiate our faith in the power of grace? Can we presume against the sinlessness of any particular man or group at the same time as we are acknowledging the power of grace to overcome all human sin?

It is to be remembered that such a presumption of human sinfulness is solidly biblical and in accordance with most human experience. But it is also to be remembered that any social movement or social policy which depends for its appeal upon the alleged perfect goodness of its own supporters or members is not making an isolated judgment about those people alone. It is also comparing itself with other people who support contrary viewpoints, and it is judging these other people to be uniquely sinful. The claim has not been made that humankind is universally good, but only that this or that particular group is good. It is one thing to affirm the power of divine grace to overcome the effects of sinfulness; it is quite another to assert that grace has in fact already done so only with respect to this or that limited group of people. Even the church should never make such a claim. The church has no ground for believing that its members are now all freed from the sinfulness which infects others. Even Augustine, whose high conception of the church helped pave the way for medieval tendencies to identify the visible church with the kingdom of God, was careful not to say that all persons within that visible church have been transformed by grace. Only God can be taken to know ultimately who has and who has not.

It may be more helpful to regard both sin and grace as being at work within every person, and thus to do justice to the destructive, distortive aspects of the one and to the redemptive possibilities of the other. The presumption of the sinfulness of every person is an attempt to take this into account lest we slip into naiveté or self-righteousness.

C.   *The Problem of 'Necessary Evil'*

The problem of moral exceptions or necessary compromises with evil has apparently occupied Christians from the very beginning. Jesus' own consideration of divorce in Matthew includes the view that Moses had permitted the dissolution of marriage only 'for your hardness of heart', i.e., as a lesser but still necessary evil. Jesus in the same passage will permit divorce under the circumstance of unchastity. Paul argues that under present circumstances it would be better for all to be as he was, i.e., living a celibate life, but that marriage and the mutual exchange of conjugal rights can be accepted as a 'concession' (I Cor. 7.6). Early Christian thinkers had to wrestle with the hard realities of slavery, war, the exploitation of the poor by the rich, etc. The underlying problem addressed by these thinkers was how far Christians should go in accommodating themselves to such a world. The earliest writings are strongly perfectionist in tone. This is partly because of their expectation of the end of the age and of Christ's own return to earth, although early Christian perfectionism cannot simply be regarded as an *Interimsethik*, a temporary ethic, which such thinkers would not have believed in apart from their eschatological views. Arguments for pacifism, for instance, would have been just as valid in form were there no expectation of Christ's imminent return. With the passage of time, however, and with the growing influence and power of Christianity (and its finally arriving at official status), Christian thinkers increasingly developed arguments permitting moral exceptions in response to perceived dangers and necessities.

It is worthy of mention that early Christian grappling with this problem was parallel with and influenced by that of the Stoics. Stoic philosophy, like Christianity, was positive and universal. It

117

viewed man and nature as both being governed by rationality and goodness. Such Stoics as Seneca even spoke of a golden age in the past in which mankind lived in unity on the basis of equality: 'Men enjoyed Nature in common, and she that begot them supplied them all as guardian and assured them possession of shared resources.'[11] Rulers 'exercised scrupulous self-control, protected the weak from the strong, urged or dissuaded, explained what was useful and what disadvantageous. . . . To govern was to serve, not to reign.'[12] The Stoic golden age was, in considerable measure, governed by the positive presumptions discussed in the preceding chapter. But 'avarice invaded this happy system, and in its desire to withdraw property to subvert to its own uses it alienated the whole and reduced itself to narrowly delimited instead of undefined resources'.[13] In this fall away from the golden age of reason and goodness, mankind fell under the necessity of coercive laws, selfish property rights, and even the institution of slavery. Given the fall away from goodness, social policy could no longer be expected to function on the basis of a positive natural law alone. A remedial, relative natural law must now be employed to compensate for the effects of the fall and to maintain a tolerable degree of harmony with the pure law of nature.

This general picture found its parallel in the doctrines of the fall employed in later Christian patristic writings and in many of the patristic discussions of property, slavery, and war. Augustine, for example, did not regard slavery and war as being consistent with the gospel except in the sense that they are a necessary remedy for the effects of the human fall into sin. Augustine's discussion of the just war clearly recognizes that war is a tragic evil, to be avoided if at all possible. But, in the light of the fall, he also considers it a sometime necessity if even greater evils are to be prevented. As a last resort, a Christian ruler can go to war to protect the commonwealth from aggression.[14] Subsequent Christian thinkers, including Thomas Aquinas, Martin Luther and many others, have also contributed to this general line of thinking. Even most of those who strongly oppose such an approach to moral judgment would probably agree that this has been the 'majority report' of most Christian thinking through most of the church's two-thousand-year history.

Notwithstanding this, can a Christian legitimately speak of a 'necessary evil'?

Before considering the problem directly, it is necessary to clarify a semantic point. The term 'necessary evil' must not be equated with 'necessary sin'. To say that a given deed is evil in its effects is not the same thing as saying that it is sinful. The term sin is attitudinal and volitional. It must be reserved for attitudes and acts which intentionally violate the good. It is a turning away from goodness, or a condition of being alienated from goodness. Evil, on the other hand, refers to a condition or effect which frustrates the good. In theological perspective, we can refer to evil as a frustration of God's good intentions. The possibility of a 'lesser evil' thus depends upon the relative character of such frustrations. It is *conceivably* an act of moral goodness, and therefore no sin, to choose a lesser evil in a situation where choice is in fact limited to actions or inactions which can only result (one way or the other) in *some* evil.

But the question we must now face is whether such situations *do* exist or whether, when the only actions available to us are evil, it is invariably best to do nothing. Or whether there is always some creative, positive option. Notwithstanding the realities of sin is it indeed desirable to organize our judgments and actions entirely on the basis of positive presumptions?

I know of no more persistent effort to do this than that of Leo Tolstoy. In his spiritual memoirs,[15] Tolstoy reports that his own personal moment of illumination came upon recognizing that pure obedience to the positive ethic of Jesus was not only intended by Jesus but is the only possible way of incorporating the Christian gospel into actual existence. The Sermon on the Mount, in its declaration that we must not resist evil, should be fully, precisely, and literally obeyed. Resistance to evil implies compromise with evil. The Christian must live entirely on the positive plain of love, trusting that his example, like that of Jesus, will prove contagious. And if it does not, the Christian must be willing to abandon himself to suffering, knowing all the while that his life will not have been wasted – as it would have been had he yielded himself to the use of evil. In many of his later writings,[16] Tolstoy expresses the view that if we would cease to rely upon armies and police and prisons (and other supposedly necessary evils), then we might expect those who are presently evil-doers and criminals to turn toward positive goodness since it is the coercive institutions of society which in fact turn people toward evil.

In response to this, we may begin by noting with many of Tolstoy's literary critics that there is a curious sterility in much of his later writing. Perhaps it was to have been expected. The later Tolstoy was captive to the principle of non-resistance, which he took to be the essence of Christianity. The principle, as held in his mind, had two flaws which help to account for the comparatively lifeless way in which he expressed it. First, it tended to reduce Christian faith to an ethical principle, thus substituting a 'works righteousness' for grace. It was a slave ethic, and not an ethic grounded in the gift of life. Second, the particular ethical principle employed required him to reduce man to abstract goodness: if not repressed by society, people are bound to be good. Thus, the late Tolstoyan novel, *Resurrection*, while possessing all the materials for a profound exploration of the capacity of grace to transform human sinfulness and the ambiguities of human existence into the victory over sin and death, in fact turns out to be little more than propaganda for Tolstoy's principle. Human sinfulness and the ambiguities of human life are there. But they are overcome more by moral *tour de force* than by love active through freedom. It is freedom itself which has been violated. Profounder moralists have generally understood that unless human beings are in some sense free to sin human goodness means little. If people are sinful *only* because of the institutions which have conditioned them, then how are we to suppose that goodness is not likewise a product of conditioning? In order to preserve the Christian ethic in a positive, perfectionist form, Tolstoy has been forced to sacrifice man's very humanity.

Tolstoy's position has the indubitable advantage of utter consistency. In contrast with some present-day pacifists, he recognizes that the absolute case for pacifism takes one far beyond simple rejection of war into rejection of all violence and coercion – even that of the local police and certainly even that of the revolutionary (no matter how justified the revolutionary cause). He has honestly faced up to the problem that there is no place to draw the line between outright condemnation of violence in war and the limited acceptance of physical coercion by the local police if violence itself is in principle absolutely wrong. The moment one begins to justify coercive actions taken by the local police to uphold the law, one has begun to imply the existence of criteria under which other uses of violence might possibly be justified. In other words, one has unconsciously exchanged the pure pacifist position for some variation of just war doctrine. Tolstoy certainly has not done that, although his apparent abandonment of human freedom and his overlooking the realities of sin seem desperate prices to pay for such ethical consistency. Is it possible to reject all violence and coercion absolutely without at the same time abandoning belief in human freedom and recognition of the realities of sin? Can it not be argued, even from quite different premises, that the best Christian *response* to the sinful human misuse of freedom is always still a direct, positive, loving application of the gospel?

Two contemporary Christian thinkers have sought to do so, and both raise significant issues which cannot be avoided by any Christian who believes he can justify any use of coercion and violence.

In his discussion of violence[17] Jacques Ellul acknowledges the depth of human sinfulness and makes no claims for the possible effectiveness of non-violence as a technique. He even argues that apart from the gospel, we are driven to respond violently. It is a part of the law of our fallen, sinful nature. But Ellul refuses to condemn people who respond violently, since they can scarcely help doing so. His argument is on a different level. It is simply that even though people *must*, in a sense, respond to violence and frustration violently, violence is *never* good in its effects. Nor can it be a relative good even in the limited sense of treating it as a lesser evil. It is always better, from the standpoint of what a Christian considers to be good, *not* to do violence! Ellul offers a series of laws of violence[18] which suggest that the use of violence always contributes to a vicious circle of more and more violence. The argument against violence is thus not a moralistic one. It is not that violence is contrary to this or that moral principle. It is not that violence is a specific sin which we are to avoid in order to guard our moral purity. Rather, it is Ellul's contention that violence simply does no good and that it always contributes to the further career of evil in this world.

Ellul, like Tolstoy, is consistent in his application of this judgment. He does not suppose that violence is one thing on the level of international war and another thing on the level of coercive local institutions within a society. The tendency of his thought, like that of Tolstoy, therefore is also anarchist. Government is founded upon violence. Without violence government is unthinkable. But violence, in Christian perspective, is always contrary to good. Thus government, inasmuch as it must be founded upon violence, is not really capable of doing good. Ellul does not argue that government could not be positively good, but he does not think any government could be based upon what a Christian would consider to be good in a world of fallen humanity. Ellul also avoids the alternative of sectarianism. Christians, though aware of the necessity and futility of violence, are not to withdraw from contact with the world. They are not to fear 'getting their hands dirty'. They are to identify with the weak and the troubled; they are to maintain prophetic contact with the rich and powerful. In every one of their human contacts they are to bear witness to the saving reality of Jesus Christ, to the authentic freedom from the realms of necessity (such as the necessity of violence) which infect this world. But they are to remember that only through the grace of Jesus Christ is it possible for human beings to find real liberation from the structures of necessity.

Ellul's approach to violence can be extended to other apparent moral compromise. It can also be argued that all lying, all appeal to baser motives, etc., however necessary they may seem to be in a fallen world, are in fact futile in the light of a Christian understanding of the good.

It would be difficult to refute the claim. In order to do so we could not point to the immediately tangible effects of such alleged necessary evil. Despite the apparently desirable consequences of some action involving a 'lesser evil', it usually remains arguable that the ultimate, long-run consequences will involve the perpetuation and deepening of evil. For instance, if it is argued that the dropping of atomic bombs on Hiroshima and Nagasaki shortened World War II and saved millions of lives (itself an uprovable proposition), the moral calculus must be extended beyond that immediate benefit to the effects upon the attitudes and expectations of the whole human race. Was a brutalizing precedent established through those acts of war? Did those bombs contribute to the willingness of countries to build up nuclear armaments, numbing them to the morally unthinkable consequences of actually using such devices? Was an evil genie of barbarism set loose and given a newer, firmer grip upon the human consciousness by the fact that in that time and place men actually did such deeds? In short, did something happen on the cultural level, the level of human values, which quite transcended in seriousness and ultimate peril the supposed gain of even a few million lives?

Moral perfectionism of this kind can lay claim to the indefinite future, regarding present sacrifices made through the neglect of 'realism' as tragic requirements if mankind is ever to become aware of God's loving intentions. The important, all-consuming cause of Christian witness must be the proclamation of the value, unity, and equality of the whole human family, created and redeemed by God, in as direct and pure a fashion as possible. Refutation of this position is nearly impossible because it rests upon grounds which lie beyond any tangible evidence – and also, of course, because positive moral perfectionism has never been practised on a large enough scale or for a sufficiently long period of time to test the question of lasting consequences.

The other contemporary thinker who has proposed a powerful and consistent basis for rejecting a doctrine of necessary evil is

John Howard Yoder.[19] As we have already seen in Chapter 1 Yoder points out that the usual Christian discussion of the possibility of there being a 'necessary evil' in ethics is between two main alternatives – either that we should be willing to use evil means when necessary for the accomplishment of morally desirable objectives or that we should abandon completely the effort to be relevant to human history. In Yoder's view, however, this puts the issue falsely because Christ himself represents a third way. Christ's way combines political relevance with refusal to use or countenance methods involving evil. The two usual alternatives are false 'if Jesus is confessed as Messiah'. For if Jesus is Lord of history, then Christian ethics cannot abandon his approach to political action without at the same time abandoning faith in the meaning of history as this is revealed in Christ.

In an interesting exegesis of the famous hymn on Christ's humility in Philippians ('Have this mind among yourselves, which you have in Christ Jesus, who, though he was in the form of God, did not count equality with God a thing to be grasped . . .' Philippians 2.5–6), Yoder argues that Jesus himself did not seek to invade God's province by attempting to manage the course of history. Jesus' renunciation of any claim to 'equality with God' was an 'acceptance of impotence'. That is, 'Christ renounced the claim to govern history'.[20] Like Christ, we are not to seek to be 'effective' by assuming responsibility for the course of events. We are not to plan the future calculatively. We are not to take responsibility for the government of human history. We are to call into question the whole logic of 'the "strategic" attitude toward ethical decisions' with 'its acceptance of effectiveness itself as a goal'.[21] We must instead face the deeper question 'whether it is our business at all to guide our action by the course we wish history to take'.[22]

But, according to Yoder, this does not mean that we have to sacrifice being relevant. Jesus himself 'gave up every handle on history'[23] but he thereby became more, not less, relevant:

> *Because* Jesus' particular way of rejecting the sword and at the same time condemning those who wielded it *was* politically relevant, both

the Sanhedrin and the Procurator had to deny him the right to live, in the name of both their forms of political responsibility. His alternative was so relevant, so much a threat, that Pilate could afford to free, in exchange for Jesus, the ordinary Guevara-type insurrectionist Barabbas. Jesus' way is not less but more relevant to the question of how society moves than is the struggle for possession of the levers of command; to this Pilate and Caiaphas testify by their judgment on him.[24]

Still, the question would have to be faced whether Caiaphas and Pilate then had the last word: Did Jesus, for all his relevance, simply lose out? If we follow that example, will we similarly be 'relevant', but lose thereby any prospect of really affecting history?

It would be possible to answer this question by pointing toward the many good consequences that have in fact flowed forth from the life of Jesus and his followers throughout subsequent history. But Yoder himself would not claim a full historical vindication for Jesus. There is far too much evil and injustice in the world for us to be able to claim that Jesus' way has been clearly and decisively effective. At the same time, the empirical results of misguided Christian efforts to govern history along the Constantinian pattern show that 'effectiveness' can often mean sabotage of the real meaning of history. But the Christian's relationship to the course of historical events ought not to be pitched on this plane at all. When we link our lives to Jesus, the Lord of history, we can take it on faith that our obedience to his way will in the end be used for God's own purposes in the fulfilment of his kingdom. Ultimately, this is the meaning of the resurrection: God has placed his seal of approval and his guarantee of final triumph upon the life and the obedience of Jesus, and he has designated Jesus as Lord of history. Using the imagery of the 'war of the Lamb' of the book of Revelation, Yoder puts it this way:

> The cross is not a recipe for resurrection. Suffering is not a tool to make people come around, nor a good in itself. But the kind of faithfulness that is willing to accept evident defeat rather than complicity with evil is, by virtue of its conformity with what happens to God when he works among men, aligned with the ultimate triumph of the Lamb.

This vision of ultimate good being determined by faithfulness and not by results is the point where we modern men get off. We confuse the kind of 'triumph of the good', whose sole guarantee is the resurrection and the promise of the eternal glory of the Lamb, with an immediately accessible triumph which can be manipulated, just past the next social action campaign, by getting hold of society as a whole at the top.[25]

To be Christian, then, is to affirm one's faith in this eschatological perspective. It is to renounce evil and at the same time to live obediently and lovingly, knowing that one's life will be fully relevant to the only history that counts.

Yoder deals with an important related issue in his commentary upon Karl Barth's attitude toward war and other 'necessary evils'.[26] That issue is posed by Barth's idea of a *Grenzfall*, an exceptional or extreme case in which it is possible that God himself will command, for his good purposes, actions which involve doing evil. The issue is whether God himself has freedom to set aside the usual norm of obedience to what Christ represents in the way of direct, loving obedience. If God is truly God, in other words, must we not make allowances for the possibility of God's setting aside the whole normative frame of reference outlined by Yoder in his *The Politics of Jesus*? That issue is particularly important in the present discussion, because if such an exception can be admitted that is a long stride toward an approach utilizing methodological presumption – a presumption in favour of avoidance of evil (in obedience to Jesus as Lord of history) but with allowances made where a burden of proof can be borne on behalf of an exception when an exception has apparently been commanded by God. In other words, there would be a possibility of a 'necessary evil' after all, but one disciplined closely in accordance with the approach suggested by the present volume. But Yoder will have none of this. The problem is that we have no reliable guide other than Christ to serve as an indication that God has in fact commanded some exception. Accordingly,

Barth has not constructed in the *Grenzfall* a reliable method of theological ethics in which it would be possible to found either logically or with relation to the revelation of God in Christ the advocacy of certain deviant ways of acting, such as killing when killing is otherwise forbidden. He has simply found a name for the fact that in certain contexts he is convinced of the necessity of not acting according to the way God seems to have spoken in Christ.[27]

In summary, Yoder's position is a powerful one; it is not easily to be dismissed by any faithful Christian. Acceptance of that position would not necessarily destroy the usefulness of methodological presumption as an approach to uncertainties of judgment, but it would undermine the proposition that a part of moral uncertainty is doubt concerning cases where evil is or is not to be used in order that good may be done. That aspect of the problem of Christian ethics would be settled in absolute, not relative terms.

What are we to say to this kind of moral perfectionism? I believe there are two reasons for not accepting it too readily – at least in the forms stated by Tolstoy, Ellul, or Yoder.

The first is that the position tends to understate the importance of objective economic, social, legal, and political *conditions* in the fulfilment of God's loving intentions for humankind. All three of these perfectionists are, of course, specifically concerned about such conditions. All are distressed by poverty and resolutely opposed to every form of legal and social tyranny which humankind is capable of exercising or institutionalizing. But the point is that notwithstanding this concern, each of these thinkers believes that the attempt to deal with dehumanizing *conditions* must be subordinated to the exigencies of a positive Christian witness in *every* case where there is an apparent conflict. In no case can conditions be so bad, so frustrating of God's loving intention, as to justify negative actions. *Nothing* on this earth is worth defending by the sword. Not food and drink for the hungry, not freedom for the enslaved, not the right to vote, to speak, to write, to associate. 'The Christians who preach violence in the name of the poor,' writes Ellul, 'are disciples of Eros and no longer know the Agape of Christ.'[28] Translate: Such Christians are concerned only about their attachment to objects; they no longer are attuned to the life of the spirit which is other than the world of things. They have placed their treasure on earth where moth and rust consume.

Tolstoy, in his admonitions to military officers, flatly asserts that 'it is not true that you are concerned with the maintenance of the existing order: you are concerned only with your own advantages'.[29] Even if this were not so, Tolstoy urged his officer readers to view every institution or order which can only be preserved through killing as being unworthy of being preserved.

But does not this view come into tension with a Christian doctrine of creation? What are God's intentions through creation? Without ascribing intrinsic significance to the things which may be vulnerable to attack on the human plane, is it not so that objective conditions *serve* intrinsic ends and that intrinsic ends can never be actualized in the real world apart from their fulfilment in and through objective conditions? To argue otherwise is to turn the gospel into a neo-docetic spiritualism. Of course human beings do not live by bread or freedom or justice alone. But is it not mere sentimentality to argue that the conditions of existence do not partake of the ultimacy of the ends they serve?

Ironically, the perfectionist argument can even be turned on its head. If the conditions of bodily life are relatively unimportant, then what is so important about killing? Negative actions (even killing) can thus be relativized along with perfectionist inactions (such as permitting others to kill or enslave). The reader will note that I am very seriously opposed to killing. But the point is that those perfectionists who are willing to sacrifice all concern for the conditions of human existence when necessary to guard what they consider to be perfect obedience to the loving command of God may have undermined the basis of their own case by casting doubt upon the whole realm of worldly conditions and bodily well-being. In the specific case of Yoder, it must be said that his eschatology has too greatly dominated his doctrine of creation. God's final triumph and the lordship of Christ would not be too helpful to those people whose lives have been utterly ruined or tragically unfulfilled because of Yoder's unwillingness ever to approve the wielding of the sword for the sake of social justice. What does he think is at stake in relation to the conditions of human existence? Can we so easily disclaim responsibility for the factual course of history? Is there no point at which the Christian is driven to be the instrument of God's factual victory over specific injustices? Is there no time or place for the Christian to exchange the abstract perfection of the ideal for the concrete possibility of human fulfilment?

Still, the 'conditions-worth-fighting-for' must be understood in a relative light. The above arguments should not be taken as neglecting the more ultimate claims of loving relationship. Here, a second objection to moral perfectionism of Tolstoy or Ellul or Yoder must be entered. This is that they are too sharply sceptical about the possibilities of positive Christian witness in the face of negative actions. That is to say, they too greatly doubt the Christian's ability to do negative things in a redemptive way. Admittedly, this is hazardous ground to traverse. How many people, really, can 'kill lovingly'? Probably not many. But can it be done at all? Luther's doctrine of strange love is based upon the possibility; it is the love which is strange because it is in negative form, but which still is love because however negative the action is it is dominated by a positive end. Luther himself would countenance no self-defence for the sake of self. But negative action for the sake of the preservation of others is, he felt, possibly a loving responsibility. It seems to me that it is indeed a possibility, but only when appropriate limiting criteria are met, when negative action is dominated by concern for objectively good ends, and when persistent, creative effort is made to interpret even negative action in the light of good will toward those against whom the action must perforce be directed. Can policemen do this? There is much affirmative evidence to be drawn from many different societies, despite many evidences of police abuses. Can soldiers? This is more difficult in a wartime situation, but expressions of human concern for the enemy have not been unheard of. The vast impersonal mechanisms of modern war pose more difficult arenas in which to symbolize sensitivity for human good. This may tell us, among other things, that it is nearly impossible to reconcile present-day coldly logical capacities of immense destruction with the Christian conscience.

Before adopting the perfectionist position it is well to recall specifically that the whole taxation system in contemporary society rests to a considerable extent upon the ultimate prospect of coercion. To abolish this or put it on a voluntary basis would quickly undermine the universal opportunity of free state education, along with other social welfare benefits of immense scope. It would literally be a life-or-death question for multitudes of people, and for many more it would be a question of whether any meaningful degree of human fulfilment is possible. I question whether the perfectionists have weighed sufficiently the concrete life and possibility of fulfilment of those who would be most vulnerable to any abandonment by Christians of responsibility for the government of human events. It is not enough simply to commend the vulnerable multitudes of human society to God's provident care in some future time. God expects more of us than that.

Nevertheless, the perfectionists have reminded us that negative actions *always* pose problems for the Christian conscience and must never be treated as commonplace virtue. Karl Barth, who was not a pacifist, may have expressed the point well in his own statement on the question of war: 'All affirmative answers to the question are wrong if they do not start with the assumption that the inflexible negative of pacificism has almost infinite arguments in its favour and is almost overpoweringly strong.'[30] In this quotation, the word 'almost' is very important, for it marks off Barth's unwillingness to accept the absolute perfectionism of the pacifists. Yet, the other words are also important, for they point out the positive direction of normal Christian presumption and place the burden of proof powerfully against the negative.

The weight of arguments against *any* negative actions is sufficiently strong to require that they bear a heavy burden of proof – and this is all I wish to claim. The negative presumptions should require us to be open to the possible use of negative means; but we should always be reluctant to do so. We should *not* do so until it has been established beyond reasonable doubt among persons of good will that more in the long- as well as short-run will be gained in terms of faithfulness to God's loving intentions. We need, moreover, to acknowledge that *any* theoretical justification of moral exceptions can readily become the basis of arrogant rationalization. Having admitted that an exception *might* have to be accepted, we will always be tempted to regard every attractive moral short-cut as that acceptable exception. The fact that just war doctrine has been perverted so easily into rationalizations of military policies is largely responsible for its bad name among many sensitive Christians. This should remind us again that Christians themselves partake of the sinful nature against which the moral intelligence must ever be on guard. Methodological presumption is the best way to handle this need for self-critical sensitivity without abandoning responsibility.

5

Polar Moral Presumptions

A. *The Nature of Polar Values*

In the last two chapters we have examined both positive and negative presumptions based upon Christian faith and understanding. They point to the tensions and conflicts which are inescapable in arriving at moral judgments. Many of our more serious decisions are actually quite complex. It is not as if any one of the positive or negative presumptions could by itself structure our decision-making, although each may have much insight to contribute to our judgments. Often we find ourselves having to choose between two goods or between various shadings of evil. The use of methodological presumption helps us to engage our minds more clearly than simple reliance upon intuition, but it is a way of handling risk – not of avoiding risk.

In this chapter we must examine a further complexity in judgments involving competing goods. I shall argue here that there are some apparently competing values which cannot be treated as if they were mutually exclusive. These are polar opposites, values which actually belong to each other even though they are apparently contradictory. Judgments involving polar values must somehow include the good represented by each of the opposite poles. Such judgments cannot be a simple either/or choice between contradictory goods; they are a kind of both-or-neither. Neither pole can continue to exist without some inclusion of the apparent opposite. Some physical analogies may illustrate the point. A world without either men or women is rationally conceivable, though far-fetched.

But 'male' or 'female' would become meaningless without its complementary term. Similarly, 'mass' and 'energy', as physical properties, are necessary to each other. One thinks also of light and darkness, north and south, and other opposites. In a truly polar relationship, the opposites are not really in competition with each other. Each is needed even to define the other.

It is worthy of note in a study of moral judgment that some good things can only be had when their polar opposites are also preserved. Many ideological debates or disputes over public policy treat opposites as if they were mutually exclusive when, in fact, the conflicting values actually depend upon each other. A presumption in favour of *some* maintenance of the balance requires us to place the burden of proof against a policy proposal or ideological appeal which seems to neglect one side altogether. A polar moral presumption cannot tell us exactly *what* relationship should exist between the two poles, but it can require that neither side be used to exclude the other. For instance (in relationships we shall examine more closely later), freedom should not be set over-against responsibility as though one had to choose only one; nor should the individual be opposed to the community. In both these cases of broad generalization, one value cannot be meaningful in the total absence of its apparent opposite.

The literature of ethics, ancient and modern, frequently appeals to this insight, although popular ethical discussion often neglects it. Aristotle's principle of the 'Golden Mean' is an important example. Aristotle did not refer in this to a simple mathematical averaging of conflicting claims. He was rather concerned to protect the legitimate values of each. In Aristotle's world, as in ours, conflicting and mutually exclusive claims were registered between those who saw human fulfilment in terms of gross sensual indulgence and those who advocated asceticism. In his judgment, both were wrong because both neglected the truth contained in the opposite ethical attitude. Aristotle identified the Golden Mean as that judgment or action which lies 'between excess and deficiency'. Too much sensual indulgence is excess, too little is deficiency. One cannot easily state what the right balance is, but it is clear that total excess and total deficiency are to be avoided. We can therefore say that a polar presumption exists against the complete exclusion of some sensual fulfilment and of some sensual control.

Of course there are some kinds of opposites which are not related in this way. Sometimes all of one side is no excess and none of the other is no deficiency. In the conflict between justice and injustice we do not seek a proper balancing so that we shall not have too much justice or too little injustice. We can *never* have too much justice or too little injustice when these terms are properly understood and applied. Nor, in the conflict between honesty and dishonesty, is there any reason for presuming that there must be some dishonesty. There can never be an excess of justice or honesty since these values are aspects of the good in itself. Injustice and dishonesty are never to be sought as values in themselves, although in the real world they must sometimes be tolerated in one form in order to avoid it in other, more serious forms.

L. Harold DeWolf has appealed to certain dialectical values such as 'devotion to the community and affirmation of the individual' and 'loving service to the neighbor and realization of the highest values in the self'.[1] Such pairings truly represent pairings of values which are mutually supportive, even to the point of being dependent upon each other. Neither side can be neglected without something of the other also being diminished. Edward LeRoy Long, Jr, while not employing the dialectical principle, appeals to a similar inclusiveness in his rejection of 'polemical exclusion'. The latter term refers to the use of one approach or 'motif' of Christian ethics to the total exclusion of others. Thus, we may use a prescriptive (deontological) approach to the exclusion of relational or deliberative (teleological) motifs. But ethics requires use of all three dimensions. Long urges a 'comprehensive complementarity' in which we do not neglect the insights of any.[2] It is difficult to say how, exactly, ethics should balance itself so that the truth of each of these motifs (and others pertaining to the implementation of ethical decision) is preserved comprehensively. It is easier to notice when any motif is totally excluded.

One of the dangers in analysing moral judgments in dialectical terms is that in the nice balancing of opposites we may completely vitiate the thrust of judgments. A little-of-this and a little-of-that can add up to not much of either. The on-the-one-hand this but on-the-other-hand that, which is typical of much dialectical thinking, can so easily keep us aloof from concrete engagement with the real issues. Such aloofness is more likely when we attempt to use a polar presumption to locate the precise directions of judgment rather than using them as a corrective of one-sidedness. The stating of polar presumptions is most useful, not in identifying precise judgments but in identifying the boundaries within which precise judgments must lie. We know that there must be some freedom and some responsibility. This judgment has great force where freedom has been crushed or responsibility is openly mocked. But the polar presumption cannot by itself tell us in a given situation how to relate the two; it can only say that neither should be excluded. Where either seems excluded, a burden of proof must be met.

An important instance of this can lie in the attempt to balance over-emphases in moral discourse or in the culture at large. Utilizing the approach of 'burden of proof', one may deliberately wish to compensate for what seem to be one-sided emphases. In a celebrated passage on the 'Golden Mean', Aristotle seems to have this kind of corrective presumption in mind:

> Hence he who aims at the intermediate must first depart from what is most contrary to it. . . . For of the extremes one is more erroneous, one less so; therefore, since to hit the mean is hard in the extreme, we must as a second best, as people say, take the least of the evils; . . . but up to what point and to what extent a man must deviate before he becomes blameworthy it is not easy to determine by reasoning, any more than anything else that is perceived by the senses; such things depend on particular facts, and the decision rests with perception. So much then, is plain, that the intermediate state is in all things to be praised, but that we must incline sometimes towards the excess, sometimes towards the deficiencies; for so shall we most easily hit the mean and what is right.[3]

The point of this is clear if we do not think of this in terms of 'middle-of-the-roadism' or a merely average morality (translated as moral mediocrity and sloth) but rather of avoiding over-emphasis or under-emphasis of important values. It is not moral mediocrity to insist upon the neglected good, even though doing so may appear a relative weakening of the opposite side of a polarity of values. In plainer terms, we must sometimes place a burden of proof against fanaticism. Fanaticism is not wrong, usually, in the values it espouses but only in the one-sidedness with which it espouses them. Those who seek to correct this one-sidedness may be made to appear weak or mediocre, but in reality their judgments are likely to be closer to the mark.

Are there, then, specifically Christian polar presumptions paralleling the positive and negative presumptions of the preceding chapters? There is, in one sense, a certain polar relationship between those positive and negative presumptions themselves, at least so far as a Christian view of human possibilities is concerned. The positive presumptions indicate the positive directions of God's intended goodness, while the negative presumptions mark off the limitations within human nature. I shall discuss the implications of this point more fully below. The polar presumptions now to be outlined can also be understood and accepted quite apart from the Christian faith. Nevertheless, Christian faith both supports each and provides it with an ultimate context of meaning. Without pretending that the list is exhaustive of the possibilities, I wish to suggest five such polar presumptions:

B. *Presumptions*

(i) *Individual/Social Nature of Man*

There has been a striking tendency in the ideological debates of the past two centuries to play off man's individuality against his social nature, and vice versa. Western societies, such as the United States, tend to emphasize individualism. Against this tendency, revolutionary movements and Fascism have often emphasized this or that form of collectivism. The former is illustrated characteristically by economist George J. Stigler:

The supreme goal of the Western World is the development of the individual; the creation for the individual of a maximum area of personal freedom, and with this a corresponding area of personal responsibility. Our very concept of the humane society is one in which individual man is permitted and incited to make the utmost of himself. The self-reliant, responsible, creative citizen – the 'cult of individualism' for every man, if you will – is the very foundation of democracy, of freedom of speech, of every institution that recognizes the dignity of man. I view this goal as an ultimate ethical value.[4]

While this does not go so far as to state that individualism is the *only* ultimate ethical value, it clearly has neglected man's social nature. The other extreme is suggested by some variations of Bolshevism or Maoism or by the fascism of Mussolini's statement that 'the fascist conception of life stresses the importance of the State and accepts the individual only in so far as his interests coincide with those of the State, which stands for the conscience and the universal will of man as a historic entity'.[5] Most military discipline presupposes the same moral one-sidedness: the individual is nothing; the group or the cause is everything. Sometimes this kind of one-sidedness is even characteristic of rhetoric within the church: the church or the kingdom of God (as a cause) is everything, the individual is nothing – despite the fact that concern for the individual belongs to the definition of the meaning of the church and the kingdom of God.

But, as we have already noted in relation to two of the positive presumptions before, it is not possible for a Christian to think of human life in either purely individual or purely social terms. Karl Barth confronted the need for maintaining both:

Might not humanity be a corporate personality of which individuals are only insignificant manifestations or fragmentary parts? Or might not the whole notion of humanity be a fiction, and the reality consist only of a collection of individuals each essentially unrelated to the others and each responsible only for himself? Romans 5.12–21 points in neither of these directions. If we base our thinking on this passage, we can have nothing to do with either collectivism on the one hand or individualism on the other.[6]

What we need to do, he continues, is to see 'the man in humanity and humanity in the man'. The point is that man is neither individual nor social alone, but both at once. The destruction of our individuality undermines genuine human society; the undermining of our social nature for the sake of individualism destroys not only society but our individuality as well. A really human society is made up of creative individuals. A real individual is a person fulfilling his or her personhood in community.

The effect of this presumption is to require any proposal or social movement or ideology which rests upon either absolute individualism or absolute collectivism to bear the burden of proof. If, for instance, a proposal (such as that of Professor Milton Friedman)[7] to return all the national parks and state schools to private ownership seems to rest only upon a one-sided competitive individualism, we may well place the burden of proof against it to show that it takes the social nature of human beings seriously. It may well be that good and sufficient reasons can be found to place the national parks under private ownership (although this seems inconceivable to me), but if the main reason advanced for such a move is a kind of ideological individualism, then we must place the burden of proof against it. Ideological individualism cannot stand alone as an ethical principle without some reference to the complementary pole of social relatedness. Or if, in the name of some conception of corporate good, it should be decided that medical experimentation known to be harmful to the subjects might proceed because of supposed benefits to the whole of society, we must place the burden of proof against it in the name of the value of the individuals involved.

The widely established practice of experimenting upon 'volunteers' from prison inmate populations is a case in point. Why are prison inmates singled out as potential volunteers? Presumably a judgment has been made at some level that such persons are of less value to society and hence are more expendable. Their individual value somehow has less weight when measured against potential good for society as a whole. There may, of course, be ample ethical arguments for giving people an opportunity to volunteer for particularly hazardous experiments or missions, but important questions have to be raised when certain classes of individuals are singled out for such experiments or missions because their lives are regarded as having less worth. Indeed, the burden of proof might well be placed against all social policies requiring the sacrificing of certain individuals for the sake of the greater public good. From time to time every society has to do this in some way or other, but much would seem to hinge on whether the actions are fully voluntary and not predicated upon any invidious judgments of the expendability of some classes of persons. At the least, persons who voluntarily make great sacrifices for the good of society should be honoured in a special way. This is often done in warfare, with praise heaped upon those who lay down their lives in defence of the homeland or for the sake of this or that momentous cause. But it is interesting that almost invariably certain classes have to bear the gravest risks and that a relationship exists between these risks and the supposed expendability of those called upon to make them. Only rarely do those whose policies lead to war find themselves bearing the brunt of the inconveniences, not to say the dangers of war. All of this is easily rationalized, but lurking behind much of this kind of rationalization is a violation of the pole of individual value. When it comes to treatment of the enemy in war it is all the easier to regard whole populations as being beneath any human consideration. The polarity of individual/social requires, however, that we not simply disregard the value of the individual.

(ii) *Freedom/Responsibility*

This is a similar presumption since freedom is personal or individual in its roots and responsibility is social in its context. In a theological perspective we speak of God's gift of freedom and of man's responsibility to God for the exercise of that freedom. Somehow these two must be kept in tension. To be real, God's gift of freedom to every person must be radically individual and uncontrolled. Even the idea of submitting one's will to God's will, if it is authentic, must continue in the most radically personal sense to be an expression of our freedom and not an abdication of that freedom to some power which is altogether external to ourselves. And yet, freedom itself cannot be exercised in a vacuum. Apart from a context of responsibility – something outside ourselves which is worth responding to – freedom is meaningless. This point is of great importance in the ethics of H. Richard Niebuhr, who emphasizes the responsive character of all ethical action. In our moral life, we exercise our freedom by responding to our relationships with God and fellow beings. 'All action, we now say, including what we rather indeterminately call moral action, is response to action upon us.' The important question to bear in mind is, 'To whom or what am I responsible and in what community of interaction am I myself?'.[8] But, on the other hand, that self which responds does not do so only reflexively. It is not a self unless it responds freely, and that freedom cannot be abrogated in the name of responsibility without undermining the meaning of responsibility itself.

Many of the ideological debates of the turbulent decade of the 1960s illustrate the results of emphasizing one of these poles, freedom and responsibility, at the expense of the other. For instance, a number of political jurisdictions in the United States considered laws prohibiting racial discrimination in the sale and rental of housing. Opponents of the laws contended that they would destroy the sacred freedom of the individual to determine the disposal of his or her own property in any way he or she should see fit. Proponents argued against this that minority group persons in the housing market needed protection for *their* freedom to obtain housing. Many on both sides failed to keep freedom in tension with responsibility to the community, although in my opinion this failure was particularly evident among the opponents of such legislation. Freedom by itself cannot be an absolute; but neither can it be absolutely denied.

During the social disorders of 1967 and 1968 (with persisting echoes thereafter), many Americans called for a kind of 'law-and-order' which seemed to suggest that public responsibility could be had by trampling upon freedom. It was urged by some that society had become 'permissive' and that recent judgments by the courts were encouraging this permissiveness. The attitude was often unaccompanied by much concern for traditional freedom of expression or of freedom from the arbitrary exercise of the state's police powers. Curiously, some of those most anxious to support a repressive exercise of the state's police powers also seemed anxious to avoid any regulation of personal freedom to acquire guns, etc. – so this debate also had its ambiguities. At the same time, some advocates of civil liberties pushed the cause of individual freedom so hard as to betray an evident lack of concern for the concrete results of anti-social exercises of freedom.

Some of the hardest moral dilemmas in jurisprudence concern the rights of the accused to freedom prior to conviction versus the need to protect the public. Further dilemmas occur in such areas of social policy as the regulation of pornography and the distribution and use of harmful drugs. We cannot enter into careful consideration of the best resolution of such dilemmas here; but most such dilemmas illustrate in a typical way the operation of a polar presumption, for it is morally wrong to treat the issues as though *only* freedom or *only* social responsibility were at stake. Both are engaged together. A resolution which disregards freedom altogether will tend to be wrong from the standpoint of social responsibility, and a solution which neglects social responsibility will in the long run work to the detriment of freedom. I happen to believe that law should, where possible, be rather permissive about pornography. For the sake of freedom, the burden of proof should be against coercive restriction of movies, literature, etc. At the same time, it seems clear that pornography can debase community values and human sensitivities in ways which ultimately undermine respect for freedom itself. Thus, while placing the burden of proof against legal coercion in this field we may, at the same time, place a burden of proof against irresponsible exercise of that same freedom from coercion. The distinction must in this way be made between legal freedom and moral freedom, between legal restraint and moral restraint. Certainly even legal freedom cannot be absolute in such areas, but the burden of proof can be in its favour.[9]

The polar character of the relationship between freedom and

responsibility can be demonstrated rather sharply by pursuing literally the implications of the standard Jeffersonian quotation that that government is best which governs least. The *reductio ad absurdum* of this was supplied by Thoreau who added that 'that government is best which governs not at all'.[10] Few people really believe that freedom can extend to the point of absolute legal anarchism. We may be willing to place a burden of proof against all coercion, but implicitly most of us would also place a contrary burden of proof against complete anarchism as a method of guaranteeing freedom. We understand that there must be some context of responsibility before the community or we shall lose our freedom. The polar presumption will not, by itself, define for us the correct relationship between these two poles, but it will help us to avoid neglecting either side altogether.

(iii) *Subsidiarity/Universality*

This presumption refers to the level of social organization at which problems should be addressed. The term subsidiarity, as we noted in Chapter 2, is an outgrowth of Roman Catholic consideration of this question. According to the doctrine of subsidiarity, as developed in various papal encyclicals, social problems should be dealt with at the most immediate (or local) level consistent with their solution. Any problem that can be solved by the family ought not to be referred to the state; any problem that can be solved by a local community ought not to be taken over by regional or national government. In the name of subsidiarity, twentieth-century Popes have resisted state dominance in the field of education and affirmed the moral rights of private ownership. The principle itself suggests a tension, for the higher collectivity must certainly be invoked when necessary.[11] But it also needs to be seen in relationship to the reverse principle that problems can be dealt with most responsibly on the widest possible scale. Since solutions to problems, however immediate they may be, tend to have ramifications far beyond the immediate situation, a case can be made in the name of responsibility for the involvement of the wider community in arriving at solutions. Can education in

America best be dealt with locally? Perhaps so; but then how is the wider community to protect itself from the results of poor educational systems in many localities? How can resources then be redistributed from wealthier to poorer communities and states? This dilemma has been posed at the ideological as well as practical level by the movement for neighbourhood government and neighbourhood control of schools and community development corporations in contemporary America. Maximum claims by some advocates of this movement amount to total control within the neighbourhood, with only the loosest thinking about how the various neighbourhoods should relate to one another.[12] In part this movement has been a reaction against the inexorable development of immense, impersonal institutions of government, industry, education, and even religion. Local people have lost a sense of participation in the vast, impersonal institutional forces which seem to control their destinies and, withal, problems are not being solved effectively because those who control the solutions are remote from local realities. Perhaps in the interaction between the vast corporate institutions and the local movements we can see an irreducible polar tension at work. Most important problems have both universal and local dimensions. All of us exist both locally and universally. We do not want to trade our local identity and powers of self-determination off for a fragmentary and often illusory slice of participation in the politics of society as a whole. But at the same time we do not want to cede the opportunity to affect the destiny of history on the larger scale.

Much of the rhetoric of nationalism and self-determination in the revolutionary movements of the Third World points toward this same tension. Taken literally, self-determination or self-development or independence have the incompleteness of polar terms, for total independence and self-determination are never possible, either practically or morally. Practically the world has become far too interdependent. Morally, the whole world is in at least one sense the unity of interaction and co-operation. Taken in the sense of its ultimate claims, nationalism has become a dangerous anachronism in a world where the behaviour of each nation affects all others. Nevertheless, criticism of a one-sided quest for self-determination can itself become one-sided. The slogans 'self-determination' and 'self-development' may not be so much in opposition to true universalism (as represented by world federalism, for instance, or the concept of world law) as they are in opposition to imperialistic controls by more powerful nations and multi-national business corporations. Imperialism is not genuine universalism; rather, it is a perverted form of localism. It is the domination of one local group by another. Still, even ideal universal forms of social organization, such as those encouraged by world federalism and 'world peace through world law' need the corrections of subsidiarity, for world-scale institutions cannot hope to manage most local problems. We cannot hope to define a proper relationship between universality and subsidiarity here. We can only say that something is missing when either is neglected. The burden of proof must be borne by the total disregard of either.

(iv) *Conservation/Innovation*

It is a part of the timeless folklore of humanity, that some people are more prone to change while others seek to maintain the *status quo*. It is not unusual for older people to be more conservative, more resistant to change, more protective of established values; nor is it unusual for younger people to be more inclined to seek change and to be impatient with things as they are. This may be true in part because, up to a point, the older people become, the more apt they are to acquire personal stakes in existing social reward systems. Nevertheless, neither change nor conservatism could become by itself a defensible presumption for all people. It is probably a good thing that some people tend to place the burden of proof against change and that others tend to place it in favour of change. The truth is that in any social situation there are likely to be *some* values worth preserving in the ongoing continuity of human experience, and it is equally true that in most social situations some change is morally imperative. We can safely make this kind of flat generalization about almost any society, even before we know anything about it in detail. If God is at work in a society's history, which he surely is, then there are values present to be preserved. If sinful human beings are also there, motivated by selfish interests, as they surely are, then there are bound to be unjust relationships and institutions which need to be reformed or uprooted.

We should place the burden of proof, therefore, against the notion that *everything* about any situation needs to be changed. But we should also reject the presumption that *nothing* should be changed. In the light of human finitude and sin and in view of the static and dynamic elements of ongoing history, basic values will be neglected if either change or changelessness is made into an absolute. Thus, Walter Rauschenbusch's forthright statement that 'if a man wants to be a Christian, he must stand over against things as they are and condemn them in the name of that higher conception of life which Jesus revealed'[13] needs to be corrected by Rauschenbusch's own appreciation for *some* present embodiments of the good – such as some features of family life, some achievements of political democracy.[14] Total commitment to change promises nothing for future achievements, and thus change itself, when absolutized, becomes meaningless. But on the other hand, William James' conservatism, as expressed in his 1891 essay on 'The Moral Philosopher and the Moral Life', needs correction in the opposite direction. James wrote that

> The presumption in cases of conflict must always be in favor of the conventionally recognized good. The philosopher must be a conservative, and in the construction of his casuistic scale must put the things most in accordance with the custom of the community on top.[15]

This passage can be corrected by some of the themes of James' own pragmatic method, which suggests a perpetually developing appreciation of the meaning of the good and hence some real openness to change. But both these quotations, one from a theologian and the other from a philosopher of the Progressive Era, should remind us how easily we can be trapped into rhetorical abandonment of either existing values or of needed changes.

This rhetorical problem is probably inevitable in every dynamic period of history, for in such periods self-conscious forces for change or in resistance to change are most intense. The rhetoric of revolution, which was loosely employed in the latter 1960s (even by theologians), often seemed to suggest that *any* revolution was to be supported by properly radical Christians. During the same period, reactionary elements dug in to resist *all* change or revolution and thus to identify Christianity with the whole of an existing social way of life. But the burden of proof must be placed against both change for the sake of change alone and sameness for the sake of sameness alone.

It is worth remembering at this point that the term 'radical' is not properly placed in polar opposition to 'conservatism'. To be a radical, to have a radical point of view, is to approach problems at the root. The true radical will therefore understand (at the root) that some proposed changes are a threat to basic values which need to be preserved. But he or she will also be first to support needed revolutionary changes in deeply-entrenched injustices. To illustrate the point in relation to the women's liberation movement: a true radical may well perceive gross injustices in many of the roles to which women have been relegated under the guise of protection of the family and of honouring motherhood. He or she may find language itself a subtle reinforcement of oppression, as male metaphors are utilized to convey images of strength, creativity and independence, while female metaphors suggest passiveness and dependency. Thus the radical may be led to demand sweeping social and cultural changes. At the same time, the radical may be concerned over the loss of primal institutions of marriage and family which historically have offered protection and nurturing for the most intimate relationships and commitments of love between persons of opposite sex and between parents and children. Through the inclination to defend such institutions the radical may properly be called conservative. Radicalism, in this way, is deeper than either conservatism or change in themselves. We are always called to be radical in our perceptions.

(v) *Optimism/Pessimism*

Optimism and pessimism are not forms of moral principle or judgment, but they do represent opposing types of attitude toward situations which need to be kept in balance. They represent answers to the following question: Should the Christian make judgments and act on them in the expectation that what he believes to be good is also a real possibility? If the answer has to be negative, then the positive presumptions of Chapter 3 are essentially meaningless. But the answer cannot be fully affirmative so long as human sinfulness and finitude exist. Christian realism must be both hopeful and sceptical. It should be neither deluded and naively optimistic nor cynically pessimistic. Cynicism flourishes in the belief that the good is always powerless in the actual world. Without some hope, moral endeavour itself becomes pointless, for 'work without hope draws nectar in a sieve, and hope without an object cannot live' (Coleridge). On the other hand, unreal expectations breed disillusionment and ultimately cynicism when they are dashed to pieces on the rocks of reality.

Some people are more likely to relate to life pessimistically and others optimistically. Each can make a positive contribution to the community of moral judgment provided that the opposite pole is also an element in his or her respective thinking. The theologians of hope have stressed the grounds in Christian faith for a long-run attitude of optimism, despite all present frustrations of the good. They remind us, as does the mainstream of Christian tradition, that the Christian eschatological perspective is always ultimately optimistic. In the *long* run, at least beyond human history, God's loving will can in faith be expected to prevail. But the tension between optimism and pessimism cannot be left simply as a tension between total pessimism about the present world darkness and optimism about God's ultimate redemption of life beyond history. Pessimism and cynicism will continue to distort our moral perspectives unless something of that long-run eschatological hope can also infect the short-run concrete present reality. In terms of Christian hope, it is probably impossible to sustain much hope for life beyond history in the absence of some evidence of God's redeeming power within the events of history. Our rhetoric sometimes belies our deeper attitudes at this point. Throughout Christian history there have been those who seem to have abandoned all prospect for the experiencing of goodness in this world. But even among the sectarians who advocated and practised withdrawal from the hopelessly evil world there has usually been some effort to organize the social life of the faithful in such a way as to embody God's intended goodness – a little beachhead of God's kingdom in the fallen world. Most Christians have gone beyond that little shred of optimism in the expectation that it may be possible to organize the good with some effectiveness.

Sometimes they have gone too far in the other direction. One recalls with some embarrassment the goal of the early twentieth-century Student Volunteer Movement and its goal (and presumed expectation) of making the whole world Christian 'in our generation'. Some of the less cautious representatives of the social gospel movement of the same period spoke of 'building the kingdom of God on earth' as if that were a manageable human possibility within a foreseeable period of time. The 'Constantinian Christianity' against which Eastern European Christian theologians have reacted with such force – the Christianity of triumphal Christendom – represented many centuries of Christian determination to organize a thoroughly Christian civilization without sufficient self-criticism or awareness of how subtly demonic selfishness can infect lofty ambitions for the success of the gospel.

Use of optimism/pessimism as a polar presumption requires us always to hope, but not too much. The burden of proof stands against either total optimism or total pessimism concerning future events. We must always act on the presumption that there are some possibilities – but not unlimited possibilities – in every human situation. After the political victories of the Civil Rights Movement in the 1960s, American society witnessed a period of conservative reaction in the so-called 'white backlash' and a corresponding sense of frustration and impotence developed among many black people. Resistance to racial desegragation which had previously been most evident in the South tended now to centre in northern urban areas. Black people in the northern ghettos were finding it difficult to escape poverty. Many felt themselves to be locked into vicious circles of low income, inadequate education, poor housing, and political vulnerability. The urban riots of 1967–68 reflected this pent-up frustration. In a different way, the more individualized forms of urban crime and violence and drug addiction were also based upon hopeless frustration. Not infrequently during this period black intellectuals found themselves seriously questioning whether there had been any accomplishments at all during the Civil Rights Movement. Its major gains seemed to have been on paper. In the real world, blackness seemed still to represent second-class citizenship and dehumanization. Martin Luther King, Jr remained a symbol of goodness and nobility, but after his assassination he also became for many a symbol of naiveté and tragedy. In retrospect, it is apparent that neither the most euphoric claims concerning the accomplishments of the Civil Rights Movement nor the reactive pessimism were altogether reasonable. Clearly the movement had not fully ushered in the new day of freedom from racism; but equally clearly the legal gains had been quite real. My purpose in citing this historical illustration, however, is not to assess the Civil Rights Movement but rather to say something about the climate of Christian moral judgment regarding race relations during the aftermath. The polar optimism/pessimism should in periods of that kind lead one to keep faith with the hopes nourished by previous accomplishments while also maintaining realism about the incompleteness of those accomplishments. If *everything* during the civil rights period had been failure, the logical conclusion (actually drawn by some) was that further expenditures of energy would be equally useless.

In the 'Catechism of a Revolutionist', attributed to the Russian anarchist Nechaev (1847–82) and widely influential in the anarchist movement, we are treated to a display of rhetoric which simultaneously exhibits both extremes of optimism and pessimism about historical possibilities:

149

The Association has no aim other than the complete liberation and happiness of the masses, i.e. of the people who live by manual labor. But, convinced that this liberation and the achievement of this happiness is possible only through an all-destroying popular revolution, the Association will by all its means and all its power further the development and extension of those evils and those calamities which must at last exhaust the patience of the people and drive them to a general uprising.

By Revolution the Association does not understand a regulated movement after the classical Western model – a movement which, always bowing to the property rights and the traditions of the social systems of so-called civilization and morality, has until now limited itself everywhere to the overthrow of one political form in order to replace it by another and striven to create a so-called revolutionary state. Only that revolution will be beneficial to the people which will destroy at the very root every vestige of statehood and will annihilate all of Russia's state traditions, institutions and classes.

The Association therefore does not intend to foist on the people any organization from above. The future organization will no doubt evolve out of the popular movement and out of life itself. But this is the business of future generations. Our business is destruction, terrible, complete, universal, and merciless. . . .[16]

Here we have utter pessimism about any redeeming possibilities within the present forms of social organization combined with stupendous optimism about the goodness that will simply blossom forth, unaided, after the present social organization has been smashed. This extreme illustration is worth pausing over because it is not so far removed from the tendencies of other revolutionary movements which paint too stark a contrast between present evils and future goodness, thus neglecting altogether the mutual correctives of optimism and pessimism as they pertain to both present and future social life. The burden of proof should be against both extremes.

But this requires us to face again the question raised at the beginning of this chapter: does the use of polar presumptions tend to lead us into social complacency? Does it cut the nerve by relativizing both present situations of evil and future possibilities of good? One answer to this is that to the contrary it takes both evil and good seriously wherever it finds them – either in the present or in the future. Those who despise or disregard the goodness at work in every present situation are not likely to contribute much to its future possibilities. Those who do not see the evil possibilities in their future visions have probably diagnosed present evils incorrectly. The attitude of complacency, on the other hand, is likely evidence that one has broken down the polarity of optimism/pessimism: either things are so bad that nothing I do will make any difference or things are so good that they will continue to be good and to improve regardless of what I do. Maintenance of this polarity is absolutely crucial to the avoidance of complacency.

But this also means that we cannot, in our moral judgments, be judicial bystanders, observing the ongoing flow of life in Olympian detachment. Christian moral judgment is action-oriented. In the final analysis it is a strategic perspective – a planning of action to contribute to God's intended good. A concluding chapter in the present volume will attempt to relate moral judgment to effective social strategy.

We must, however, turn next to the problem of moral influence and human authority, because in all of our uses of moral presumptions we are inevitably influenced by the judgments of others. The question we must face is under what circumstances should we yield our moral judgments to the influence or determination by others?

6

Presumptions of Human Authority

Thus far we have considered the problem of judgment and decision-making as if it were simply a matter of each person's solitary responsibility. In a sense it is an individual matter. Moral responsibility, if it has any distinctive meaning at all, is preeminently a personal thing. We cannot entirely delegate either our minds or our wills to others without undermining our integrity. We permit ourselves to become mere things or instruments when we allow our moral decisions to be made completely for us by others.

In the first chapter we noted the breakdown of various traditional sources of external authority on the basis of which Christians of the past have often relied for feelings of moral certainty. In part, this breakdown reflects a growing awareness that we no longer have adequate reasons for accepting such external authorities without question. We can no longer believe with our minds that such authorities as scripture, church, and tradition are *necessarily* right and applicable to the decisions we face. Since our minds are no longer wholly convinced, it would be an abdication of moral responsibility for us to turn our moral will over to such external authorities without further question. We have to have *reasons* which convince us that the direction of our judgments and decisions is in harmony with our faith. We cannot simply delegate this to an external authority unless, in some sense which is credible to us, we have sufficient reason for doing so.

But having stated the problem of moral judgment in such an individualistic way we are forced to remember that we are not

152

simply individuals. We are also social by nature. A purely individualistic approach to moral decision-making is in conflict with the individual/social polar presumption and with the insight that even within our individuality there is a profoundly social dimension. That 'self' of which we are aware in our self-understanding is itself substantially a product of our interaction with others. Moral judgment is personal in its essence, but it is also social in character. Our most private-seeming perceptions and judgments are all infected by the perceptions and judgments of others. In the beginning, each of our earliest childhood moral judgments overwhelmingly reflect the values and perceptions of parents or other nurturing adults. The residual power of these earliest influences often persists throughout life, unconsciously shaping our moral perspectives. As we grow up, however, other influences also come into play, including the effects of peer groups and all forms of leadership which affect us.

Contemporary social psychology has demonstrated in a powerful way just how significant these influences can be. The evidence is particularly compelling in the insights of reference group theory.[1] Basic to this body of knowledge is the factual observation that people tend to derive values and perceptions from the groups with which they identify themselves: 'a commonplace subscribed to by the man-in-the-street as well as by the social scientist is the proposition that many of the attitudes of an individual are greatly influenced by the norms of groups to which he belongs.'[2] The reason for this is in large measure that the relationships we have with others in our group experiences are important to us. We conform to the values and share the perceptions of the group largely so that we will be accepted by it. The sharing of perceptions and values is intimately linked to one of the most fundamental needs of our humanness: to be responded to positively by others in shared experience – to be accepted and valued. Through this acceptance of our self-hood by others (what Charles Hampden-Turner and others have termed 'self-confirmation'[3]) we gain identity and meaning. We may, of course, belong simultaneously to more than one reference group; we may identify with groups by which we are not recognized; the 'group' may be historical (it is possible to identify with persons and groups long dead, adopting through imagination values and perceptions having their conjectured approval); the form of reference identification may even be negative, in the sense of a rejection of values and perceptions associated with groups we reject or that we are rejected by. The social realities summarized by the theory of reference groups is obviously very complex.

The pioneering experiments with small groups by Solomon E. Asch provided compelling evidence of the degree to which we can be led to conform to judgments and behaviour patterns emanating from a group consensus. The subjects of his experiments were placed in small groups with the task of determining the length of certain lines. All but one of the members of each of the experimental groups were instructed to give a single, obviously false answer when questioned about the length of the line – thus testing whether the unsuspecting subject would be able to trust his own (more nearly correct) judgment or whether he would yield to the unanimous pressure exerted by the erroneous judgment made by the other group members. Many of the individuals thus tested went along with the group rather than trust their own judgment. Sometimes they yielded to the group with apparent uneasiness, and some exhibited considerable emotional agitation. It is interesting, however, that when even one of the pre-instructed members of the group was told to dissent from the majority opinion, the subject of the experiment was found to be much freer to make up his own mind.[4] We may conclude that the fact that the other dissenter obviously was accepted by the group despite his disagreement showed that the issue would not affect being accepted by the group. 'Normal' people could disagree on such a point. Other, later experiments have shown somewhat disturbingly that many subjects will go so far as to inflict serious suffering on others in order to conform to what they believe the group or an authority figure (such as a social scientist conducting the research) expects them to do.[5]

Must we conclude from such experiments (and the resulting

body of social scientific theory) that we are controlled by groups and other forms of authority despite everything we have said about personal moral judgment? To concede this altogether is to abandon the morality in moral judgment. The degree of group influence, while great, is still variable. In none of these experiments have all subjects exhibited the same measure of control. A few, while manifesting some psychic pain at their own deviation, nevertheless have had inner resources to dissent from the absurd or the immoral. Their behaviour can also be subsumed under reference group theory, but it may suggest the influence in their cases of an absent or a transcendent reference. If the polarity of individual/social is based on reality, we may suppose that even in the cases of those most easily swayed toward immediate social conformity some shred of a subjective 'I' is interacting with the overpowering 'they' of the group. Few people, if any, can stand aloof from all social conformity, but for most of us there is at least the possibility of choosing the reference groups and individuals by whom we care to be influenced in our moral judgments. And there is reason to suppose that as a part of the social fabric our own moral perceptions will influence those of other people.

It is important to speak thus of our judgments being 'influenced' by other people, but not being *determined* by them. Absolute conformity to the judgments of others is not consistent with Christian faith, for it necessarily absolutizes other people whom we know to be both finite and sinners. But there may well be reason consciously to accept, even to seek out the judgments of others in order to be influenced by them. When we approach the judgments of others in this spirit, we are involved in a different kind of presumption from those dealt with in previous chapters: now we treat the judgment of particular individuals or groups as *probably* moral or true and we then require other judgments to bear the burden of proof. This is what happens when we give 'great weight' to the opinions of particular people. It is not that those opinions will necessarily be followed, but only that for various reasons those opinions will be followed unless it can be proved to us that they should be set aside. As indicated in Chapter 2, this is what usually happens in some form in executive decision-making where a generalist must consult those with specialized expertise. The judgment of the specialist may not be followed, but it probably will be unless a convincing case is mounted to oppose it. When we choose to follow a particular human 'authority' we give him or her the benefit of the doubt. The earliest of life's moral authorities, the parents or parent-substitutes, often exert this kind of continuing influence for many years whenever we come upon problems which have been anticipated by the values they have passed on to us. Sometimes this influence persists throughout a whole lifetime. We may well be open to new insight (we certainly *should* be), but we are still likely to measure each new viewpoint against those early moral influences and to require the new viewpoints to bear the burden of proof. Frequently, of course, this happens quite unconsciously. That is one reason why we can often anticipate the fundamental stance on social issues of people when we know how and when their formative years were spent. For instance, it has often been noted that children raised during the Depression years of the 1930s tend to take a different attitude toward material things than those who have only lived with affluence. Similarly, Margaret Mead points out how important it is to know whether one was born and received early nurture before or after the great watershed of World War II and the beginning of the nuclear age. [6] Those born after this watershed have always lived in the environment created by television, nuclear danger, instant communications, jet travel, etc., while those with earlier roots have mental habits developed before the emergence of these immense changes. The older group is not really able to function in the traditional role of the elders of society since members were not themselves steeped in the emerging new cultural situation.

There are no elders who know what those who have been reared within the last twenty years know about the world into which they were born. The elders are separated from them by the fact that they, too, are a strangely isolated generation. No generation has ever known, experienced, and incorporated such rapid changes, watched the sources of power, the means of communication, the definition of humanity, the limits of their explorable universe, the certainties of a known and limited world, the fundamental imperatives of life and death – all change before their eyes.[7]

The unconscious influence of the authority of elders may be weaker in our time than in any recent generation. But there is no way to avoid the influence of human authorities of various kinds, which means that the choice of authorities and the manner in which we permit ourselves to be influenced by them are serious moral questions.

A. *The Selection of Moral Authorities*

We must therefore now address the interesting question of how we should go about choosing those individual and group 'authorities' by which we wish to be influenced in our moral judgments? Which authorities are most likely to reflect Christian insight into moral questions? Under what circumstances should different kinds of authorities be permitted to influence our judgments?

For these to be meaningful ethical questions, we must be able to give reasons for choosing to be influenced by some rather than others. But a somewhat intricate distinction needs to be made. Our reasons for choosing one authority over another are not the same thing as the reasons the authorities themselves offer in support of the judgments they have made. When we allow ourselves to be influenced by another person or group as an *authority* this means that to some extent we choose to follow their lead even when we do not fully understand their own reasons. When we treat specific human authorities as probably or presumptively right this means that we choose to listen to them more than to others and, in cases of lingering doubt, to continue to follow these human authorities rather than others. We will follow even apart from the intrinsic persuasiveness of their presentation of a case in favour of their judgment.[8] We follow their lead partly because we have reason to believe they will be right even when we do not fully understand them.

Every rationalistic or individualistic age naturally shrinks from accepting such leadership on the grounds that we should not commit ourselves to any judgment we cannot personally comprehend. But how can we possibly comprehend for ourselves the relevant facts of all the situations in which we must make judgments? Even when our understanding is very great do we not need to compensate in some measure for the needed corrective which others can give? Pure rationalism is not humble enough concerning the limitations of our capacity to know, and pure individualism overlooks the depth of our dependency upon the influence of others in all areas of life. It is certainly true that all of us, even the most rational and independent, will in fact be influenced by the judgments of others whose judgments we have, for whatever reason, come to trust. Still, as we have said, such influence is morally responsible only when we can give solid reasons for our trusting and only when our trusting functions as a presumption – open to modification if it becomes evident that the trusted human authority is probably wrong.

I wish to consider now four forms of human authority which can be treated as sources of dependable presumptions for judgment.

B. *Presumptions*

(i) *The Community of Faith*

On matters of moral judgment an obvious case can be made for relying upon that reference group which most clearly expresses our deepest personal values. Christians can scarcely ignore the church as a source of presumptive authority, and strong and sometimes persuasive claims have often been made for the church as *the* authority for Christians on moral issues. In a previous chapter we have been critical of certain key aspects of Paul Lehmann's 'contextual ethic', but here we may note with some admiration his insight into the way in which the Christian '*koinonia*' shapes and influences, but does not violate, the moral judgment of the Christian. It is in the *koinonia* that Christians arrive singly and together at those moral judgments which best express the meaning of what God is doing in human history 'to make and keep human life human'.[9] While Lehmann's method of moral judgment is basically intuitive (and therefore subject to the criticism that it offers little actual guidance) it does at least implicitly subject intuition to the test of consensus within the company of the faithful. This is certainly better than purely individual intuition. Moral judgments arising as a group consensus among those sharing the same basic faith are likely (1) to be purified of individual idiosyncrasy and self-interest and (2) to represent a cumulative reflection of the best insights of the entire group. To be sure, even the church can sometimes also function to debase the lofty purity of the individual, but if it is really the church it is a community of faith based upon and accountable to authentic Christian values.

The consensus of the community on moral questions is registered in some form in virtually every kind of Christian church. Sometimes the process is highly authoritarian, sometimes very democratic. The old-style and purist Society of Friends waited for the 'sense of the meeting' to develop – a visibly democratic process, possibly qualified to some extent by the inner dynamics of group life in which some participants tend to be more equal than others. The end result of this consensual-formation has been highly influential in the judgments of individual Quakers, particularly since a consensus could not be registered in most cases until all were truly agreed. Other Protestant bodies also have means of developing moral consensus, often through formal declarations at national, regional, and local levels, both denominationally and ecumenically. The student of ecumenical and denominational pronouncements on moral questions is struck by the capacity of those who participate in formulating them to put aside local biases and self-interest when challenged to work together in formulating a distinctively Christian judgment on an issue. Assuming, as we must, that Christians often experience internal conflict between their faith perspectives and their self-interests and idolatries, we might expect this to happen with some frequency. The collective judgment, formally determined, is certainly a better index to the deeper Christian consensus than a casual public opinion poll of the same Christians is likely to be. This is why the statement that church pronouncements do not represent the thinking of grass-roots Christians is usually superficial. Round up the dissident Christians and give them the solemn responsibility of formulating a truly Christian response to a controversial social issue, and the effect of this new responsibility upon their judgment is likely to be noticeable.[10] For such reasons, the authority of church bodies may, with good reason, be given a presumptive status by Christians.

In most Protestant churches a somewhat less democratic form of moral authority is frequently expressed through the pastor's sermon. This is typically an individualistic and one-way form of influence. Dialogue is generally not encouraged by the way in which this is institutionalized within the life of the church, and when it is the pastor's position in the dialogue is clearly weighted more heavily than that of laymen. I believe there ought to be more dialogue and more opportunity for laymen to register their own convictions on moral issues in an effort to influence the community. Nevertheless, when it is not corrupted too much by the pastor's self-interest, there are sound moral reasons why Christians should allow themselves to be influenced to a considerable extent by this form of communication. The pastor has, in effect, been designated by the community to reflect deeply on the meaning of Christian faith and to speak clearly and honestly to them about its implication for their lives as well as for the pastor's. They are likely to know the pastor's personal limitations, intellectually and otherwise, and to take these into account. But the process by which the pastor was originally designated and trained for this form of leadership and the freedom and responsibility which have been institutionalized into the role are all likely to be conducive to more insightful moral leadership than might be expected from a random sampling of individual Christians. It is not irrational, therefore, to suppose that Christians will receive from the pulpit a form of moral leadership which is worthy of respect. It will be all the more worthy of respect if it is known that the pastor has gathered into his own judgment the best insights available from the moral perceptions of others in the congregation, so that the base of moral experience from which he draws is not limited to his own personal life and study. This is all a relative moral authority, of course – a presumptive influence, not a source of infallible directives to be followed at all cost. Relatively, the weight of a serious consensus by groups of Christians will usually be greater than that of the leadership of individual pastors.

Within Christianity as a whole, the maximum claims for the moral authority of the church have been advanced by Roman Catholicism. These claims have gone far beyond the presumptive authority of which we speak, to the point of insisting that the church, through its properly designated channels of authority, is worthy of the unqualified obedience of believing Christians. Few Protestants or communicants of Eastern Orthodoxy accept the maximum claims of Tridentine Catholicism, and increasing numbers of Catholics either reinterpret the substance of these claims away or reject them altogether. Nevertheless, it is important for Ecumenical Christianity to continue to explore the insights of Catholicism on the question of the magisterial authority of the church and to struggle toward a new ecumenical consensus which retains the valid insights concerning the authority of the church.

Honest dialogue may require both a yes and a no to this Roman Catholic tradition of authority. Few Christians who are not otherwise committed to Roman Catholicism can say yes to the maximum claims advanced by the first Vatican Council, which defined the dogma of papal infallibility. It is worthy of mention that even that Council did not accept the most sweeping claims for papal authority on the part of some leaders of the church. The English Catholic W. G. Ward, for instance, wrote that 'all direct doctrinal instructions of all encyclicals, of all letters to individual bishops and allocutions, published by the Popes, are *ex cathedra* pronouncements and *ipso facto* infallible'.[11] Others spoke of the Pope as 'the Man with whom God is for ever, the Man who carries the thought of God' whose inspired directions 'we must unswervingly follow' or as a man who, when he thinks, 'it is God who is thinking in him'.[12]

Such excessive rhetoric, which comes close to deifying the Pope, is patently arbitrary. But even the more restrained dogma, which limits the Pope's infallibility to carefully circumscribed dogmas of faith and morals, and which has, as such, only been exercised once since the first Vatican Council,[13] could not readily be accepted by any Christian who considers the Pope to be a human being alongside other mortals. The second Vatican Council, in the Dogmatic Constitution on the Church (*Lumen Gentium*) greatly broadened – and some might say weakened – the exclusively papal locus of infallibility. This authority was more clearly marked off as a gift to the whole church. Still, it treats infallibility as an exercise of the whole college of bishops, acting with the Pope:

> The infallibility promised to the Church resides also in the body of bishops when that body exercises supreme teaching authority with the successor of Peter. To the resultant definitions the assent of the Chuch can never be wanting, on account of the activity of that same Holy Spirit, whereby the whole flock of Christ is preserved and progresses in unity of faith.[14]

The basis thus remains for the claim that the human authority of bishops and Pope (or Pope alone, acting properly for the whole church) is necessarily an expression of the Holy Spirit and therefore to be obeyed without question by the faithful. This is a claim that few Protestant or Orthodox Christians would wish to make, even for the church taken as a whole.

In recent years, the dogma of infallibility has been subjected to continuing scrutiny by Catholic thinkers. Some have sought new interpretations, seeking to preserve the serious intent of the dogma while avoiding superhuman claims for a human authority. Others have so sought to circumscribe the definition of an exercise of infallibility that it could remain only a theoretical problem.[15] Possibly the issue ought not to concern us any further here, since 'infallibility' has been exercised, so far as the church is concerned, only once incontestably and that in relation to a comparatively minor (and morally inconsequential) matter. But the problem must be pursued for both negative and positive reasons by all Christians. Negatively, even a rarely exercised infallible authority continues to distort all Christian perceptions of the real authority of the church and can potentially be used in the future much more than it has in the past. Positively, however, the claims of authority which have been registered here by the Roman Catholic Church may convey a dimension of the truth which all Christian ethics needs to hear.

From an ecumenical standpoint, the most promising interpretations which are developing within Roman Catholicism are those which are frankly critical of the term 'infallible' as being too ambiguous and misleading to be useful. Edward Schillebeeckx, for instance, speaks of 'ideological and sociological difficulties that seem almost insoluble' surrounding the term 'infallibility',[16] and Hans Küng gained wide support (and opposition) for his proposal that the term be abandoned in favour of the more accurate designation of the 'indefectibility' or constancy of the church's being in the truth.[17] According to Küng, the word is ambiguous on two counts: first, its connotation in some translations as implying moral impeccability and second, its linkage to supposed infallible propositions. 'Would it not be better,' he asks, 'to sacrifice the word in order to save the reality, instead of saving the word and sacrificing the reality?' Of course the reality referred to by the term 'infallibility' can mean different things to different people. But this is Küng's point: many Catholics have been led by the term away from a theologically defensible understanding of how it is that the Holy Spirit keeps the church in the truth despite the sum total of individual errors. His own conception of 'indefectibility' is summarized as follows:

> If the Church is no longer in the truth, she is no longer the Church at all. But the Church's being true is not absolutely dependent on quite definite infallible propositions, but on her remaining in the truth throughout all – even erroneous – propositions. However, in order to bring out the fact that the Church's being means being true, for clarity's sake we shall speak, not simply of the indefectibility or perpetuity of the Church, but of her indefectibility or perpetuity *in the truth*. What is meant here then is that the Church remains in the truth and this is not annulled by the sum total of individual errors. . . .

In this way the word 'infallibility' would remain ultimately reserved to the one to whom it was originally reserved: to God, who can neither deceive nor be deceived and who alone is infallible in the strict sense.[18]

There is a certain sense in which Küng's conception reverses the order of things and affirms that the church is, through its indefectibility, protected from the errors of popes and bishops – as from other errors – in order to remain in a fundamental state of truth. In a somewhat similar reformulation, Schillebeeckx speaks of 'the infallible guidance of the Holy Spirit manifested in an imperfect historical objectivization in the Church'. Rather than using the term 'infallibility', he would prefer to speak of 'a correct, legitimate judgment concerning faith which is faithful to the Gospel and ultimately binding on all believers'. Dogma must be 'subjected to the criticism of the totality of faith within the whole of history'.[19] Thus Schillebeeckx also distinguishes between the faith of the church that it will, if it remains faithful, be led by the Spirit in harmony with the truth of the gospel and the more dubious proposition that specified pronouncements by particular church leaders (acting individually or collectively) should be followed unquestioningly.

Charles E. Curran discusses the teaching authority of the church with a recognition both of the centrality of this responsibility and of the risks of error which the church must run in accepting it. The church, he writes, 'must raise its voice on particular issues facing the world and society today with the understanding that it does not speak with an absolute certitude but proposes what it thinks to be the best possible Christian approach with the realization that it might be wrong'. It 'should avoid the dangers of theological and philosophical actualism by showing the various criteria and principles which enter into its judgment in this particular case'. It must recognize that the more concrete and particular its judgments are, the greater will be the risks of error. It therefore fulfils its responsibility as a moral teacher on two levels: 'to express constantly and continually develop the various criteria, principles, goals, and ideals which the Christian incorporates into his decision-making process and at the same time, but in a more hesitant manner, propose some concrete solutions for the manifold problems facing contemporary man.'[20] A good deal of the teaching responsibility of the church lies in helping people to think more clearly for themselves – rather than handing over answers to be accepted passively.

Curran accurately anticipates that 'such an understanding of the teaching mission of the Church in these specific moral questions should not be an obstacle to the union of Christians, for it closely resembles many of the theoretical approaches adopted in Protestant circles'.[21] Many Roman Catholic scholars would doubtless prefer to address the question whether it adequately reflects the *Catholic* position. It may be that a consensus simply does not yet exist to support a position like Curran's. Yet, combined with the insights of Schillebeeckx and Küng, this may well be a position which Roman Catholicism can increasingly accept as the most authentic interpretation of what really can and should be meant by the unfortunate term 'infallibility'. I do not believe this undermines at all the role of designated leaders (Pope, bishops, priests) in articulating that consensus which develops around moral issues under the guidance of the Holy Spirit within the church. But it does require a more modest expression of the consensus by those whose office it is to do so, and it suggests that the consensus on moral questions should be accepted somewhat more tentatively (than the word infallibility implies) by other Christians.[22]

Such tentativeness can be most clearly acknowledged by regarding the pronouncements of the church as having presumptive standing among the faithful. As members of the community they are obliged to take the church's efforts at moral guidance seriously. This means that they will in some sense place the burden of proof against contrary viewpoints. The more profoundly democratic a community of faith is, the more successful it is likely to be in securing this kind of presumptive support for its formal moral leadership. But whether the church is explicitly democratic or not, continued membership within it implies a commonality of moral perception which ought to find expression in this kind of presumption.

Even among those Roman Catholics holding the more traditional interpretation of papal infallibility, that power is usually believed to have been exercised very rarely. The more common, and not infallible form of papal teaching, is the encyclical. While the traditionalists hold encyclicals in high esteem (and the popes themselves have endeavoured to write them so as not to appear to be contradicting the encyclicals of their predecessors), their status is not that of dogma. Among faithful Catholics they have enjoyed great prestige but not always slavish obedience. For Catholics, the great encyclicals ought to carry the force of presumption. Even the encyclical *Humanae Vitae*, reaffirming the usual prohibition of artificial contraception, should perhaps be presumed right by faithful Catholics until a burden of proof has been met by serious opponents. The fact that that burden has long since been met to the satisfaction of large numbers of thoughtful Catholics should not diminish their similar initial presumption in favour of future encyclicals. At the same time, the prestige of the papal teaching authority can only be enhanced by humble acknowledgment of human limitations when some such teachings have been tested and found wanting within the Christian community.

As we have already noted, Protestant and Eastern Orthodox Christian communities have not sought to develop such highly centralized forms of teaching authority, but the faithful of those communions do well to treat their own church pronouncements and statements by properly designated leadership with a similar presumptive attitude. This should include statements by the World Council of Churches and other ecumenical bodies.

(ii) *Tradition*

A presumption in favour of the moral teachings of inherited tradition is in fact but an extension of regard given to the teachings of the community of faith. Tradition is the cumulative deposit of the moral experience of that community through time. One must be cautious in treating this form of authority with too much respect, lest the result simply be conservative or even reactionary. Nevertheless, if we can assume basic identity with the faith and values of previous generations in our religious community, we should give considerable weight to the collective judgment of these generations of forbears on the problems we face today. A presumption in favour of such a judgment will be all the greater, of course, if it reflects a consensus of moral teaching in more than one previous era and if previous generations have been known to face problems and alternative solutions comparable to our own. The relationship between past and present in the moral experience of a community of faith was stated particularly well by Alexander Miller:

> We may have to live life without general principles, but we do have the resources of a cumulative inheritance. The community to whose *ethos* or *mores* we are concerned to conform, which has its life from Christ and its charter from the Scriptures, is a living community of faith, in whose corporate experience most of the problems we confront have been up for decision either in the precise form in which we meet them, or in forms not unrelated to our contemporary dilemma. Communities not only generate mores, they form habits. And just as any wholesome family inculcates habits of restraint and consideration which condition conduct, so the ongoing life of the Christian *koinonia* fosters a life of such a style and shape that it predetermines conduct in many a representative situation.[23]

Miller acknowledges that these habits may be bad as well as good, but when this is the case 'the best resource for their correction is within the tradition of the Church itself, in the recollection of its primal origin and its original charter'.

The burden of proof against a presumption of tradition can more easily be met if it can be shown that the tradition was peculiar to a particular historical context with its own socio-cultural uniqueness. If, for instance, we are to regard St Paul's condemnation of long hair styles among men as a kind of tradition, it can be shown quite easily that this was nothing more than a reflection of the peculiar taste of a particular period – having no claim upon Christian conscience in any way. Regrettably, some traditions have been able to gain considerable prestige over long periods of time which nevertheless have been exposed as thoroughly inconsistent with the basic Christian presumptions after much experience. One must remember here the long and tragic Christian experience with slavery and with the persecution of heretics. If time alone were the determinant, we would still be forced to hold presumptions in favour of the institution of slavery and the coercive measure against heretics because in both cases more generations of Christians accepted these barbarisms than have been in revolt against them. Nevertheless, in both cases liberating historical experiences and more careful theological analysis have shown us that many previous generations of Christians were flatly wrong.[24]

Christian traditions concerning marriage and family may provide us with a more positive illustration. Granted, practices among Christians have varied widely through the centuries, including promiscuity, ascetic chastity, homosexuality, polygamy, and various forms of monogamous marriage, and that these and other variants of marriage and family organization have all been endorsed seriously at certain times by particular groups of Christians. It remains true that the mainstream of Christian experience and teaching has continued through the centuries to affirm the moral wisdom of covenant faithfulness in monogamous marriage. This fact is particularly impressive in the light of the wide variations of historical context respecting other aspects of social, economic, and political life. Christians of many eras, on the basis of their values of love and their concern for sexual fulfilment and the nurturing of the young have concluded from their collective experience and experimentation that the inviolate covenant of monogamous marriage is the best institutionalization of sexual and familial life. Our own era, with widespread breakdown of monogamous marriage and with much experimentation with other 'life-styles', is clearly putting this kind of tradition to the test. The Christian ought surely to be open to the *possibility* that new institutionalizations of sexual and familial relationship will be equal to or even better than the old in protecting and enhancing human fulfilments. But this long tradition should at the same time operate as a kind of presumption in his or her own decision-making. A burden of proof should still have to be met before Christians abandon the institutions of marriage covenant and family in light of the vast amount of Christian moral experience which previously has confirmed them.

Most of the truly difficult decisions facing Christians in our era are troublesome precisely because they are so new. The 'church of the ages' – the historical extension of the community of faith – has had but little opportunity to acquire experience in dealing with these new problems. This is not so much the case with problems of familial and political relationship, for such problems are perennial, but with the management of new technologies and the new environmental problems posed by mankind's increasing dominance of the earth. What kinds of urban planning provide the most humanizing possibilities? How much wilderness needs to be preserved? What are the moral consequences of cloning? Of heart transplants? Should we pursue the technological capability to determine the sex of our offspring? What is the optimum population size for planet earth, and by what means can we best attain it? How much of the economy should be private sector and how much public? In an increasingly world-wide economy, how can inflation and recession and injustice be prevented?

What is at stake in answering such questions may remain fairly clear to the Christian who understands his own basic moral presumptions. But tradition does not provide us with very many clues as to *how* the basic moral presumptions of Christians are involved in these problems, and it may be a mistake to try to stretch tradition beyond its base in the actual experience of previous generations of people.

This cautionary note needs especially to be heeded by the scholars and teachers within the community of faith who are too ready to impose a largely irrelevant past on to a largely uncertain present. Otherwise, however, the biblical and historical scholars of the church provide, in a sense, the main linkages we have between Christians of other generations and those of the present. Their weight in the dialogue on moral questions within the community of faith ought therefore to be very great.

(iii) *Technical and Factual Expertise*

Sincere Christians are most apt to be wrong in their moral judgments, not because of wrong basic values but because of inadequate grasp of the factual situation and difficulties in relating facts to values. God himself must shudder at some of the moral pronouncements which church bodies have sometimes solemnly offered forth in his name to guide the thinking of the faithful, totally innocent in their technical and factual errors. Such erroneous judgment did not begin with the Galileo case, nor is it likely to end soon. Clearly the human authority presumption for the community of faith and tradition needs to be supplemented by a presumption in favour of factual and technical expertise. Some would argue, in fact, that many problems ought simply to be turned over to the experts.

Putting aside for the moment the question of how we know who the experts *are*, this is a possibility which needs to be examined. In his critique of the World Council of Churches Conference on 'Church and Society' at Geneva, in 1966, Paul Ramsey was particularly critical of the tendency by church bodies to make judgments which are too specific on political and social questions.[25] (The most important case in point involved statements of that Conference on America's role in Vietnam.) Such questions may not even present moral and theological issues:

> It is high time for it to be acknowledged on all sides that not every decision is a moral decision, and not every moral decision is a Christian decision. The bearing of God's will and governance in relation to every aspect of human life cannot possibly be construed in such fashion that supposes that there is a Christian shape or style to every decision. Concerning a great many choices it has to be said that only a deliberately or inflexibly imprudent decision would be wrong, or an uncharitable exercise of prudence. The principle of prudence (among a Christian's teachings) definitely refers the matter in question to the magistrate or to the political process for decision; and Christians as such can say no more than that this is the case.[26]

In Ramsey's judgment, therefore, we are best advised to refer such decisions in their entirety to those having greatest factual contact with the problems. Should we at least acknowledge a presumption of human authority here, placing the burden of proof against those who challenge the competence and wisdom of those whose office it is to engage the facts directly?

To some extent we must certainly do so; but an important caution must be raised. *Much* depends upon the values as well as the competence of those to whom we propose thus to delegate our moral judgment-making. I shall have more to say concerning the specific problem of presumptions in the political realm, but note here in Ramsey's words the importance of the principle of prudence. I know of no principle of prudence which can be invoked by Christians to delegate their judgments on moral questions to those whose basic values are different from their own. Prudent judgments are those which wisely relate means to ends. They necessarily involve technical grasp concerning the means to be employed. But just as necessarily they involve value-impregnated choices of ends to be sought. How can we presume the moral rightness of those experts or authorities whose 'prudence' is in the service of ends which are not commensurate with Christian faith? 'Prudence' is not some ethic all of its own upon which all 'prudent' people can agree and to which all persons, Christians and non-Christians alike, owe moral allegiance, although Christians may, for their own reasons, unite with non-Christians in regarding a particular course of action as prudent.

In retrospect, some of the moral debates among Christians concerning the morality of American participation in the Vietnam War bear renewed scrutiny. Those who opposed the war on Christian moral grounds were often told that 'we should trust the President; he alone has access to all the facts'. Aside from the necessary presumption that even the President of the United States is a fallible sinner, rigorous moral judgment-forming needed to question more seriously whether the ends being sought by the President and, indeed, the President's whole value frame of reference, could be approved. The known access of a President of the United States to vast information-gathering sources is not enough to validate the goals served by his policies. In the case of the Vietnam

War it is worthy of more than passing notice that even the President's sources of information were deeply flawed. In his perceptive analysis of this period, David Halberstam demonstrates how captive the whole administration was to assumptions about Vietnam and Communism which were not accurate. Moreover, as doubts began to grow among top advisers and decision-makers, many were inhibited by their own career aspirations from admitting previous errors and challenging any present policy commitments. In some respects, ironically, the President was the 'very last to know'.[27]

Still, there is a methodological respect which must be paid to expertise. Having established what are the most dependable sources of factual and technical knowledge, we do well to give them the benefit of the doubt on factual and technical questions. In doing so, we must be rigorously careful not to permit such expertise to determine the broader questions of judgment and policy unless we have *other* reasons to suppose that the factual experts are *also* persons who share our basic moral presumptions and who have the ability to connect their factual and normative perspectives. Most of Paul Ramsey's prudent magistrates would have a difficult time meeting such a test. How many recent Presidents of the United States or other high officials have been fully committed to the value and equality of all human beings and to the fundamental unity of the whole human family in God? Does not 'prudence' among such political leaders more generally mean the capacity to serve the concrete and sometimes grossly selfish interests of powerful constituencies? In treating the judgments of such statesmen must we not always take carefully into account the interests which sustain them in power?

Great ecumenical conferences, such as those of the World Council of Churches, and the highest moral teaching authorities of the Roman Catholic Church, such as the Pope and Council, generally have sought to make use of experts whose technical competence is beyond question but who also manifest personal commitment to the church's basic values. This is not an easy selection to make, but I could not agree with Ramsey in treating this as virtually impossible when he writes that

> The notion that laymen who are experts, for example, in the political
> and economic sciences can enable the church to speak a relevant
> Christian word to today's world and at the same time to point out the
> particular policy to be followed is simply an illusion. It takes an expert
> to pick an expert. Or rather the experts disagree; and if there is any
> reason at all and not just an accident why one set of experts and not
> another comes to council, the decisions concerning which ones are to
> be picked to inform church councils will inevitably be made by some
> *curia* or persons in control of setting up such councils in terms of the
> particular interests, positions, or trends of thought the experts are
> already reputed for.[28]

Ramsey feels that 'we must resist the temptation to believe that
what needs to be done is to improve the church's use of "experts".
It is the aim of specificity in the church's resolutions and
proclamations that should be radically called in question.'[29]

Here, in other words, we are invited to leave expertise to the
experts (rendering, we might say, unto Caesar what is Caesar's)
and to eschew all efforts to give specific point and illustration to
the moral teaching of the church. But when the church abandons
the field of specificity in moral teaching it really abandons the
field of moral teaching altogether. Even the teaching of generalities
and principles and attempting to affect the ethos will be pointless
unless the meaning of the generalities and principles can gain
concrete footage. In his many writings on moral questions, Ramsey
has not himself avoided the responsibility to combine ethical
principle with what he considered to be the best available empirical
expertise in such wide-ranging fields as international affairs,
medicine, civil rights, and genetics. Why restrict the church, the
community of faith, to the generalities? I do not think it is because
he wants to save the principalities and powers of this world from
the church's criticism. It is more likely because he fears that the
church's mistakes on concrete matters will obscure the force of
its witness to the fundamentals of its faith. Surely that risk is
present. But how, in this life, can we avoid the risk of being
mistaken? Does not the church run a greater risk in conveying the
impression that moral life should be left to pious generalities,
detached from the real world of tough-minded magistrates

and expert elites, and that the latter should be permitted to run things to suit their own self-interested conceptions of prudence?

All the same, picking our experts to provide factual authority can be difficult. Surely it is not simply a matter of expecting only the experts to pick experts – for then even the executive or legislator would never be able to determine which experts could be trusted presumptively. The lay world always knows its experts best by the visible results of their work. Has the plumber in the past, generally speaking, been able to stop the leaks? Have impressive numbers of cancer patients been cured by acupuncture? by cobalt treatments? by surgery? by Christian Science practitioners? Have engineers and architects with particular kinds of credentials managed to build bridges and skyscrapers which did not collapse with the spring rains and high winds? Have social scientists, international relations experts, economists, and other authorities in the policy-relevant academic fields good predictive records which are translatable into effective policies? Accreditation standards which have been developed in the various guilds and professional societies represent, more or less, the forms of mutual recognition by persons whose specialized results can also be perceived by those who are not specialists. If I have had successful results from two or three plumbers I am more likely to trust a completely unknown person who is in some fashion, personal or impersonal, recommended by these plumbers as a fellow plumber of like competence. This may seem fairly obvious, but must be recalled lest we treat expert elites as some twentieth-century equivalent of the mystery cults – knowable only through initiation.

The critical use of expert presumption requires that more be said, however, about how to minimize the risks. In a useful analysis of this problem, Daniel D. McCracken proposes a series of questions to be taken into account by decision-makers who are not specialized experts when evaluating the advice of those who are:

1. Is the proposed expert actually well-informed in the precise subject area?
2. Does the expert have a hidden agenda, i.e., motivations for giving

the technical testimony that might make his technical testimony unreliable?
3. Is the expert seeing the issue in a too-narrow technical light?
4. Has the expert gone out of his field completely?
5. Is the decision-maker looking for information or ammunition?[30]

These critical questions ought not to lead us away from the use of technical experts as sources of human authority, but they do tell us something of the difference between real expertise and merely apparent expertise. In relation to the first of these questions, for instance, McCracken warns us that many experts continue to give advice long after they have lost touch with the details of their own field. Number two suggests that the expert may have a conflict of interest in offering testimony if one kind of advice will be more profitable to him personally than another. Number four reminds us that the policy question being faced by the decision-maker is likely to be broader than the expertise of the technician. We should not assume that technical competence confers wisdom on these broader aspects of a question. The military expert may well know all about logistics and fire-power without knowing anything about the nuances of international diplomacy and the psychological and cultural factors at work in a conflict situation.

Thus, within the comparatively narrow bounds of relevant technical information the benefit of the doubt can be granted to the experts and a corresponding burden of proof must be borne by those whose credentials cannot be recognized as clearly. McCracken's questions point to areas in which such a burden of proof can sometimes be met. And even the best technical expertise must not be presumed right in determining, overall, what is the best *Christian* judgment.

We may note briefly that the first three presumptions imply division of labour among like-minded people in moral decision-making. No individual can possibly keep up with all the important issues, particularly in a democracy where the responsibility of citizens is more far-ranging. Inevitably we shall have to find ourselves leaning upon others in areas which lie outside our own competence and interest. Most of us probably have informal and possibly unconscious ways of doing this. For decisions on how to vote in the school board election we may particularly trust one person's judgment, even though that person's views on international relations may seem to us to be totally unreliable. Within the community of faith such divisions of responsibility often go unrecognized, but they remain very important to the healthy decision-making process. Where we lean heavily upon the overall judgment of any other persons we ought, of course, to be clear in our own minds that their value presuppositions are as dependable as their facts.

In this connection the questions should be raised whether the known *unreliability* of the facts and values of certain persons should create a negative presumption: if 'they' are for it, we must presume it to be wrong. Translated out, what this means is that if other persons or groups are known to be against our own fundamental values, we should presume that any social policies they favour will likely be opposed to what we stand for. Pacifists may rather automatically oppose suggestions coming from the Pentagon. Liberals will vote against Congressmen earning too high an approval rating by the Americans for Constitutional Action, just as conservatives will react to those approved by Americans for Democratic Action. And so on. I suppose this kind of prejudice is inevitable and, to some extent, a prudent part of decision-making. But we ought never to forget that just as every person must be presumed to be part sinner, so everyone must be expected to be on the side of the angels at least some of the time. Mussolini's alleged improvement of Italian rail service and Napoleon's sale of Louisiana to the United States need not have faced a burden of proof from Christians, although the net effect of the careers of both those leaders may have been decidedly on the negative side. Doubtless even the Communist Party and the John Birch Society would be in agreement on the need for an adequate sewerage system.

(iv) *Civil Society*
To a striking degree, people permit their actual judgments to be formed for them by law and civil authorities. As noted above,

during the height of controversy over the Vietnam War, millions of Americans continued to support national policy on the grounds that 'the President alone has all the facts'. One suspects, however, that something more than that rather questionable assumption is needed to account for such widespread support for policies which created so many difficulties. It is also interesting to observe the turnaround in popular attitudes toward the government of mainland China during the years before and after President Nixon's famous trip to that country and the subsequent admission of that government to the United Nations. For twenty years public opinion polls had showed unremitting hostility to 'Red China', and statements favouring US recognition of the People's Republic of China were widely regarded as being tantamount to treason. (A study conference sponsored by the National Council of Churches during the 1950s brought some disrepute upon that body by treating this possibility even as a discussible prospect.) Most explanations of this turnaround in public opinion emphasized either that the time was at last ripe or that this was a political action which only a conservative President, such as Richard Nixon, could possibly have taken. Such explanations, whatever their validity, missed the real point: a large enough body of citizens was unconsciously prepared to support presidential leadership on this kind of question – either to continue the isolation of mainland China or to deal with that country in the same way as with others. Similarly, during the early years of the Vietnam War when large majorities of citizens supported President Johnson's war policies (and those of President Kennedy before him) equally large majorities might well have supported virtually any other course of action, including abandonment of all involvements, provided the policy were interpreted as important to vital national interests or to world peace. I know no other way to account for the great body of evidence from the entire Cold War period of the popular readiness to alternate between anti-Communist paranoia and euphoria over summit conferences and evidences of detente. On such matters, it has not been so much a question of public readiness for new moves as it has been presidential leadership that has determined the course of action. Plainly, on matters of utmost substance, large numbers of people are prepared to have their judgments dominated by the political leadership. A passage from the wisdom of Confucius illustrates the universality of the attitude:

> Tzu-chang asked about government. The Master said, 'The requisites of government are that there be a sufficiency of food, sufficiency of military equipment, and the confidence of the people in their ruler.' Tzu-chang said, 'If it cannot be helped, and one of these must be dispensed with, which of the three should be foregone first?' 'The military equipment,' said the Master. Tzu-chang again asked, 'If it cannot be helped, and one of the remaining two must be dispensed with, which of them should be foregone?' The Master answered, 'Part with the food. From of old, death has been the lot of all men; but a people that has no faith in their rulers is lost indeed.'[31]

While not as explicit, Romans 13 and I Peter 2.13 express similarly high esteem for governmental authority.

To be sure, not all Christians have gone along with this. Michael Novak would, for instance, be numbered among those who wish to reverse this presumption in favour of the rightness of governmental authority:

> In the United States, it is assumed that government officials are speaking the truth until the opposite can be proven, and they are seldom if ever vigorously challenged or cross-examined in public. Merely 'objective' or 'neutral' reporting, therefore, immeasurably strengthens the hand of government. The public hears the government's point of view, which is treated respectfully, even with a certain awe and restraint, and then commented on as if it were an example of reasonable discourse. . . . It would be much more healthy if Americans assumed, now that television has made government propaganda so powerful, that their government is always lying or, at the very least, coloring the truth.[32]

In one of his letters, Lord Acton made the same point:

> I cannot accept your canon that we are to judge Pope and King unlike other men, with a favourable presumption that they did no wrong. If there is any presumption it is the other way against holders of power, increasing as the power increases. Historic responsibility has to make up for want of legal responsibility. Power tends to corrupt and absolute power corrupts absolutely. Great men are almost always bad, even when they exercise influence and not authority; still more when you

to civil disobedience in such dehumanized situations. All the same, a *presumption* should exist, against civil disobedience itself first, and then against seeking to avoid the consequences of the action if civil disobedience should prove necessary. Acceptance of the consequences, in the manner of Gandhi and Martin Luther King, Jr, confirms respect for the state even when one must disobey it.

Civil disobedience can even be understood as a possible Christian responsibility on behalf of the state. As Christian political thought has well understood from the time of Augustine, the state's injustices are themselves the most likely cause of its own disintegration. By recalling the state to equal respect for all its citizens and devotion to the unity in love of the whole community – first by active criticism as a citizen and then, if necessary in the extreme cases, by civil disobedience – the Christian can be seen as acting for, not against the best interests of the civil society.

The discussion of presumptions of human authority could continue here with endless specificity, for the fabric of human influence in society is almost infinitely complex. In a summary comment, we must return to the point that no human authority should be treated as absolute and that those human authorities which are to be regarded as presumptively right must always be tested in relation to the basic moral presumptions derived from our faith. We must not avoid being influenced by others, for we are finite beings and we are social by nature. But we are also creatures of faith with personal freedom, critical judgment, and the capacity to transcend social influences. Methodological presumption, applied to the choice of human sources of authority, can help us bridge the distance between our personal decision-making and social influences.

7

Ideological Presumptions

A variety of circumstances have combined over the past half
century to make ideological thinking unfashionable in Christian
intellectual circles. The tendency of ideological consciousness is
to treat particular forms of social organization as ideal, whether
these are past, present, or only potential.[1] Much Christian thinking
(particularly beginning with Karl Barth) has been critical of this
kind of thinking for reasons which have already been outlined in
the first chapter above. God is understood to transcend such man-
centred thinking. God reveals himself in the event of Jesus Christ,
not through human ideological thinking. The idealisms of
nineteenth-century theology and even of the Social Gospel
Movement came to be regarded as idolatrous or as a form of
salvation by works. Man, in Christ, came to be seen as liberated
from a 'sacralized' culture (Gogarten, Bonhoeffer).

This theological tendency has been reinforced greatly by
revulsion against the use of Christianity to justify the political
and economic interests of privileged classes in Western society.
In the United States, Reinhold Niebuhr led the way in merciless
exposure of the economic, racial, and national interests masked by
Christian ideological thinking. Some of the most penetrating judgments upon this Christian 'ideological taint' have come from
Eastern European theologians, working in Marxist countries. This
is not altogether surprising because a fundamental stock-in-trade
of Marxist analysis has been the exposure of all religion as justification of class oppression and as a psychological consolation for
those who have been dehumanized by that oppression. Theo-

logians, operating under the pressure of that not altogether
unfounded criticism, have had to find ways of interpreting
Christian faith which are clearly outside the framework of ideological commitments. Such thinkers as Josef Hromadka and Jan
Milic Lochman have sought to extricate Christian faith and practice from the old 'Constantinian' era of Christendom – the period
of special power and privileges for the church and Christian
believers. While criticizing Marxism at various important points,
these theologians have hailed the birth of the 'post-Constantinian
era'. For example, Lochman writes that

> as far as men can judge, this era, covering nearly the whole of church
> history until now, is at an end for us. . . . The individual Christian as
> such is no longer protected and privileged by his society; his public
> prestige is not increased on account of his being a Christian; he no
> longer conforms to a desirable rule but is, rather, an exception, not
> the householder but a stranger and sojourner within his culture.[2]

The post-Constantinian situation is clearest in the Marxist
countries, but to discerning people it is also true of the West. The
church's capacity to organize society on its own terms clearly has
come to an end. How should the church react? Eastern European
theologians, and others influenced by Karl Barth, emphasize that
the church's reaction must not be either simple adaptation to any
new emerging situation (such as Marxist socialism) nor should it
be in defensive reaction against it. Most of all, it must be free to
proclaim the gospel to each new age and, in the name of the
gospel, to resist bondage to absolutisms of all kinds. In its freedom, it must also respond humanly to the emerging new possibilities in socialist countries. Only recently have such thinkers as
Lochman begun to explore how this freedom in the gospel can
mean co-operation with others in the clarification of ideological
thinking:

> If theology and the church do not respond to a sharp ideological
> situation in their society with anti-ideological negatives, but prove
> their evangelical freedom by critically constructive participation in the
> questions arising from this situation; and if, in doing this, they commit
> themselves with concentration to the truth of the gospel, then the way
> opens, even in the face of a pronounced ideology, for a meaningful
> mission and service in the church and in society.[3]

We must recognize that 'ideology is an enterprise full of risks' but it 'is a part of human reality, an element of human life'.[4] Lochman's own ideological leanings are suggested by his vigorous approval of the 'socialism with a human face' of the Dubcek reform period in Czechoslovakia (1968), a movement from which 'democratic socialism was not alien'.[5] In recent years a number of theologians have emerged in Africa, Asia, and Latin America to challenge the ideological biases of the West and to call for various versions of socialist society.[6] It is not yet clear, however, whether some new consensus will develop around the question of how, exactly, Christian faith should be related to ideology. 'Christendom' is everywhere on the defensive. Yet it is unclear to what extent Christian faith can become a sanction and inspiration for new forms of social order.

The question is important for our analysis because ideology poses the problem of how moral judgments can be related to the overall organization or conceptualization of society. To be sure, in a certain sense the positive, negative, and polar presumptions discussed above can be described in ideological terms. They are an attempt to draw out of the Christian faith certain rationally manageable, value-relevant terms of reference with which to address the concrete choices of society. They are the foundation stones, in a sense, for an ideological style of thinking about society (and thus, we have been able to illustrate them, in part, by reference to ideological tendencies). But the further step of asserting that Christian faith and these presumptions require some kind of methodological commitment to overall social visions must still be raised. How can we relate ourselves to the broader issues of social order without subordinating Christian faith to an ideological perspective and without prostituting Christian faith to selfish interests? How can we avoid the risks of being wrong when we are, after all, thinking about what is 'best' for four billion people in the global family?

If we seek to avoid these risks by responding only to the judgments which are thrust upon us we can only do this by reverting to an intuitive style of thinking. Making use of our positive, negative, and polar presumptions we may well take each decision as it comes and do the best we can within the immediate environment of our decision-making. It would doubtless seem less pretentious to avoid relating our judgments to an overall scheme of what we want society to become; but since our judgments could scarcely miss *affecting* what society is to become, we will to a large extent have reverted to intuitions about what will be best. Such intuitive judgments can be as pretentious unconsciously as they might have been when rendered with conscious intention. Whether consciously or unconsciously, Christians *are* responsible for the full context of their moral decision-making. As we make our decisions, whether consciously or unconsciously, we shall always be engaged in ideological thinking. There is, as Lochman wisely observed, no way to avoid this in the real world. Man is, indubitably, 'an ideological being – a *homo ideologicus*'.

A. *The Christian and Civilization*

What this must mean is that in faithfulness to God, the Christian accepts responsibility for the whole of civilization – not to preserve selfish interests masked as religion nor to create a new human-centred idolatry, but in faithfulness to the God whose loving concern embraces the whole world. We cannot concede that this is a 'post-Constantinian age' or a 'post-Christian era' if we mean by these terms that the church should now relinquish attempts to organize the world on the basis of Christian presumptions. The many centuries of 'Christendom' have overlaid such a statement with so many distortions of the faith that the statement itself risks serious misunderstanding. Nevertheless, abandonment of a sense of responsibility for the shape of the world's future is tantamount to abandoning the gospel itself.[7]

A dominant view today, which strangely shapes the perceptions of many Christian sectarians, Barthians, pacifists, and revolutionaries alike, is that the attempt to give a Christian shape to Roman civilization was precisely the time when the early church bit the apple and fell from grace. The church, thinking it had converted Constantine and through him the rest of Roman civilization, woke up centuries later to discover that the church had itself been converted – away from the gospel – to an official civil religion based upon power interests and idolatries. I do not want to overdraw the portrait, but something like this is really intended when the terms 'Constantinian' and 'Christendom' are used pejoratively to characterize the period when Christianity became the dominant, organizing faith of Western culture. It is important for us to decide whether it was the culture-transforming, civilization-building vocation of Christians that was wrong in principle, or whether that vocation was to some extent carried out in a faulty way. Until this question is answered, all efforts directed toward acceptance of Christian responsibility for civilization may be dismissed as a new, unacceptable triumphalism.

Doubtless some thinkers have made overstated claims for past Christian civilization. The writings of Christopher Dawson, T. S. Eliot, and Emil Brunner sometimes leave this impression. Dawson, for example, writes that

> a Christian civilization is certainly not a perfect civilization, but it is a civilization that accepts the Christian way of life as normal and frames its institutions as the organs of a Christian order. Such a civilization actually existed for a thousand years, more or less. It was a living and growing organism – a great *tree of culture* which bore rich fruit in its season.[8]

Dawson concedes that 'in its origins, it was a civilization of converted barbarians and it retained certain barbaric elements which reasserted themselves again and again in the course of its history'. Nevertheless, he believes that the Christian culture which developed during 'the great centuries of the Middle Ages' can now, in retrospect, be regarded as 'the classical age of our culture'.[9] In defence of such statements, Dawson argues that only when a civilization or culture as a whole is grounded in a living faith will it have vital creativity and unity. Better a civilization of barbarians who have this unifying centre than a decadent society without it. But even though the centre of living faith is not itself a manipulatable thing (it must, he remarks, be renewed in each generation), faith cannot serve as a creative basis of civilization if the vocation of civilization is itself regarded as irrelevant. The 'great centuries' were periods of living faith and cultural vocation. Emil Brunner, who also regarded faith in this way ('if culture is to become and to remain truly human, it must have a culture-transcending centre'[10]), joins Dawson in citing the loss of a Christian centre as reason for the decline of civilization: '. . . the history of civilization during the past hundred years has made clear beyond any doubt that the progressive decline of Christian influence has caused a progressive decay of civilization.'[11]

The principal objection to such stated and implied admiration for Christian civilization is that it underestimates the corruption occurring to the living centre of faith when it became the basis for conscious efforts to manage civilization. It is, at bottom, a question of power. The problem is instantly placed in a more pessimistic perspective when we see what happened to people who refused to organize their lives on the basis of Christian symbols and goals in such a 'Christian' civilization. The reverse side of their suffering was the external prosperity enjoyed by those who accepted Christianity because it was more comfortable to do so. To the non-Christian and the Christian dissenter, Christian civilization is idolatry and arrogance – a world of alienating power.

John Howard Yoder, as we have already seen, is well aware of this in his criticism of much contemporary Christian ethics. Yoder vigorously condemns what he considers to be the typical Troeltschian way of limiting the alternatives to either the acceptance of the full responsibility for governing political life (which means sharing in the moral compromises associated with governing) or the withdrawal from relevance in order to maintain our moral perfection. Yoder reminds us that had Jesus' own perfectionist ethic not been politically relevant he would hardly have posed a problem to those who had him crucified. But the relevance of Jesus was not in any attempt to control the political order. It was in his witness to the good, in the light of which the evil of human political authorities was revealed. Jesus' relevance was not in trying to make history move in the right direction, but in providing powerful impetus among men for resistance to its moving in the wrong direction. This is different from both poles of the Troeltschian church-sect typology. It is not an acceptance of responsibility for the future course of society (the church-type), but neither is it a withdrawal from the social arena (the sect-type). Rather, it is a witnessing within the social arena in such manner as to challenge the dominant assumptions of those who rule. It is an acceptance of servanthood to the whole community of mankind. This is politically relevant, but not in the sense of the church-type. It is perfectionist, but not in the sense of the sect-type.

Yoder does not finally concern himself about the actual shape of the future: 'the calculating link between our obedience and ultimate efficacy has been broken, since the triumph of God comes through resurrection and not through effective sovereignty or assured survival.'[12] We should be faithful to the good as we are given to see it, but we should not use evil means to gain any end. The end we can leave in God's hands. This eschatology becomes explicitly relevant to the theme of the present chapter in Yoder's emphatic rejection of Christian responsibility for the establishment of any particular, Christian vision of what society ought to become:

> There is a widespread recognition that Western society is moving toward the collapse of the mentality that has been identified with Christendom. Christians must recognize that they are a minority not only on the globe but also at home in the midst of the followers of non-Christian and post-Christian faiths. Perhaps this will prepare us to see how inappropriate and preposterous was the prevailing assumption, from the time of Constantine until yesterday, that the fundamental responsibility of the church for society is to manage it.[13]

'And might it be,' he asks, 'if we could be freed from the compulsiveness of the vision of ourselves as the guardians of history, that we could receive again the gift of being able to see ourselves as participants in the loving nature of God as revealed in Christ?'

Yoder's writing is at least a good reminder of one truth which less rigorous minds often forget: that there is no way to organize and govern society without also doing some evil in the process.

From an opposite, yet strangely compatible viewpoint, Luther said as much: 'take heed and first fill the world with real Christians before you attempt to rule it in a Christian and evangelical manner. This you will never accomplish; for the world and the masses are and always will be un-Christian, even if they are baptized and Christian in name.'[14]

Thus the problem is again before us which was addressed in different form in Chapter 4: Should a Christian use evil means to a good end? The problem in the present context is that one cannot govern without making use of an external system of incentives, a system whereby people will be motivated to do what we want them to do. In classical Christian literature the nature of the incentives is usually expressed with harsh, coercive symbolism. The state is the 'sword', protecting the innocent and punishing the wrong-doer. The sword (or the gun, or prison, or nuclear bomb) is a powerful, but negative incentive. We will do what we are asked to do at least because of the undesirable consequences of not doing so. But the structure of incentives is actually much more complex and subtle in actual society. We cannot fail to note the importance of a reward system in every society It is one thing to bear witness to the intrinsic good of God's intended kingdom and hope that, by one's words and example, others will be encouraged to live by these same positive incentives. Yoder will happily go this far in the direction of a new Christendom. But it is quite another thing when we begin to discover that in the actual shape of society there are a thousand points at which the structure of things depends upon more selfish rewards and punishments.

Interestingly this formed the essence of Kierkegaard's 'attack upon Christendom'. Christendom had made the affirmation of Christianity the most profitable form of behaviour and therefore the clarity of the gospel had become hopelessly compromised by the numbers of Christians who weren't really Christians at all. Christendom certainly rewarded being a Christian – and the reward was not confined to the intrinsic values promised in the gospel. Those who have thought seriously about the implications of Christian civilization have always had to recognize this. Walter

Rauschenbusch certainly implied something about use of selfish incentives for good ends in his famous definition of a 'Christianized' social order. Whereas the present social order tends to 'make good men do bad things', the Christianized social order will be one which 'makes bad men do good things'.[15] External incentives are implied by the word 'make', and it is as interesting to note that good people can be 'made' to do bad things as it is to observe that a better social order will 'make' bad people do what they otherwise, all things considered, would prefer *not* to do – namely, do good. T. S. Eliot doubtless had similar thoughts in mind when he remarked that in a Christian civilization 'it is not primarily the Christianity of the statesmen that matters, but their being confined, by the temper and traditions of the people they rule, to a Christian framework within which to realize their ambitions and advance the prosperity and prestige of their country'.[16] The reverse would be equally true, where the 'general ethos of the people' is not Christian and a politician, whether Christian or not, would have to live within the limits set by the different ethos. But my point (and Eliot's) is that the politician or anybody else who is in the market for personal rewards (such as being able to realize one's ambitions) will have to do it on the basis of the general shape of the society. To set up a 'Christian' society or civilization is not to avoid external forms of motivation, it is simply to redirect them in the service of what are considered to be 'Christian' ends. But by tempting people through use of external rewards we may undermine what must, for the Christian, be the only real incentives.

Accordingly, as we project our ideologies and utopias, we confront what could be called the dilemma of Christian civilization: Any supposedly Christian civilization will create social, economic, and cultural rewards for being 'Christian' – and thus, paradoxically, where Christianity prospers most and thus brings greatest prosperity to its adherents and leaders, one can least know whether people are Christian out of pure faith and devotion or for the sake of those personal advantages. In an earlier generation this was popularly referred to as the dilemma of 'rice Christianity'.

But can we really avoid this dilemma through the kind of moral perfectionism proposed by Yoder? Has he successfully outlined a way of avoiding both sectarian withdrawal from God's world and, at the same time, the evils which always seem to be involved when we rely upon external rewards and punishments to influence the course of human history? As a preliminary response, it must be said that in so far as moral perfectionism really is his position, the result is bound to entail withdrawal from responsibility from those problems which can apparently only be dealt with through use of those less-than-perfect means. Referring the problem of results or outcomes to God is only verbally a solution to the dilemma. That has always been the sectarian position: God will make things work out for the best so long as we do not dilute our commitment and seek to attract people solely on the basis of faithfulness. In other words, to assert that God *will* do what needs ultimately to be done about human history does not make this some third option over-against Troeltsch's 'church-type' and 'sect-type'. Yoder's concern that Christian witness and servanthood be politically relevant is a modification of the sect-type response, but his unwillingness to compromise in order to supply some human direction to history is distinctly a sectarian position.[17] Of course we have already examined the implications of this position from the standpoint of its apparent neglect of a doctrine of creation.[18]

But the question then emerges whether the sectarian approach, as modified by Yoder, may not even so be the morally preferable one. Yoder mounts a highly convincing argument in support of the pure expression of Christian love and service as the only way Christians can hope to be faithful to God's kingdom of love and righteousness. He further suggests that we begin by seeking to put the church's own house in order: 'A social style characterized by the creation of a new community and the rejection of violence of any kind is the theme of New Testament proclamation from beginning to end, from right to left.'[19]

But now we must remind ourselves that the essential problem is broader than the use of raw, coercive violence: it is the attack upon the integrity of others through use of external incentives of all kinds, including fear (of violence) and vanity and venality and ambition. The dilemma of civilization is not limited to those who seek objectives for the whole of society nor to those who belong to social establishments of various kinds. It is well to remind ourselves that even the most radical, revolutionary, or sectarian movement – including those most disdainful of the creature comforts and vanities of the establishment – rewards the faithful with psychic compensations and ego enhancements not intrinsic to the movement's objectives as such. How can one *know* that the revolutionary leader is motivated more by the cause than he is by the gratifications involved in leadership? How can we be sure that the leader of the sectarian movement, or the pacifist, is not activated by the prestige he gains within the movement? In the case of the writers of radical or sectarian or pacifist literature, it is even possible in some cases that the gratifications and vanities of publication may be more important than the cause. These are hard words, and this is of course a sword by which we can all be slain. But that is exactly the point. All of society, including the 'new community' to be created by Christians, is subject to the dilemma of civilization because every community, new or old, has quite worldly rewards and punishments to distribute. The New Testament church is in no sense an exception, as the book of Acts and most of the epistles make clear.

These words are not written in cynicism, because God's power of grace – the power of resurrection – is also at work. But it is pure sectarian nonsense to hold that this power of grace is at work in some altogether novel, categorically different way in the management of the new community and in the movement of Christians than it is in the life of society at large. The church, as we have asserted on other pages, is surely called to be a fellowship of those whose devotion to God is clearer and more radiant. When it is true to its calling, it understands, as no other fellowship can understand, that God's gift of grace transforms all of life. But that does not mean that the church will be able to do something with its own life that is utterly different from what Christians can do in society – both because there are recurrent possibilities of evil in the management of the church and because there are recurrent possibilities of good in the management of society.

I have not, however, gone into Yoder's position again in order to dismiss it, but rather to say that the problem he raises – the maintenance of the relevance of the gospel to society without losing the gospel – can better be treated through methodological presumption, applied now on the level of our broader visions, dreams, and ideologies. The problem really is *not* whether or not Christian faith can tolerate attempts to direct the course of social history. Such attempts are inevitable. Nor is it whether or not Christian faith should countenance the use of extrinsic forms of motivation. This, too, is inevitable, even when we seek to avoid it within the life of the church itself. Rather, it is in the faithfulness with which we do this planning. The question must always be, *which* ideological conceptions *really do* manifest faithfulness to God, and how can we serve those conceptions more effectively. In part, that question must be reserved to the next chapter on social strategy. But we must also concern ourselves here with what ideologies are most Christian in presupposition and how we can best learn from the experience of Christians who have supported the wrong kinds of models of civilization, perhaps also for the wrong reasons. Those models which, to the best of our faithful, co-operative thinking, do exemplify obedience to God's kingdom, must then receive presumptive force in guiding our concrete judgments and decisions.

B. *Two Tests of 'Christian' Civilization*

The four positive and two negative presumptions dealt with in Chapters 3 and 4 can be taken to represent the decisive elements in Christian thinking about civilization. The positive presumptions reflect the purposes while the negative (and polar) presumptions define limits in our ideological thinking. In a moment I wish to illustrate how these presumptions can enter into our thinking about these matters and how ideologies and utopian constructs can themselves establish the more inclusive presumptions to guide our judgments.

But it may be observed now that in our consideration of the Christian and civilization we have seen two basic flaws in the allegedly 'Christian' civilization (or Christendom) which have most concerned its modern critics. The first of these was the pretension, bordering on idolatry, with which Christian symbols and institutions were thrust upon non-Christians. This has always been a sin against pluralism, but it is all the more evident during the present highly pluralistic age. The second was the use of sub-Christian incentives, including violence, to control people and to shape their future. In any discussion of the possibility of a more Christian civilization, therefore, we might as well begin by saying that the avoidance of such things is an important test of such a civilization.

Christians play interesting games with the term 'pluralism'. Increasingly we are all for it. But we also assume that to make a more 'Christian' society somehow must entail further sinning against pluralism. Why should this be so? If a Christian really believes that society *ought* to be pluralistic, then he either regards pluralism as a necessary social implication from Christian faith (or at least compatible with it), or he holds his pluralism in spite of his Christianity. If the latter is the case, then he has a problem. But if the former is true there should be no reason why pluralism must be offensive to the Christian. Why can we not stipulate that a truly Christian society is one which is fully hospitable to the freedom of non-Christian points of view? Christians ought not to seek to create a civilization in any sense that would prematurely vitiate the claims made by non-Christian, un-Christian, and anti-Christian views of reality. We ought not to seek a new triumphalism, enforcing Christian ascendancy over all other perspectives. Indeed, the capacity to accommodate the social interests and creativities of every non-Christian person or group must stand as a criterion of a truly Christian civilization. The old Christendom was based upon exclusive (and sometimes idolatrous) claims for Christian symbols and practices. But it is quite another thing to seek to ground culture in a Christian perspective which *in principle* welcomes the contributions of all the pluralisms of the modern world while retaining *in principle* theological grounds for criticizing them.

The positive principle of Christian theology is at once affirmative of the goodness of being, the ultimate value in God of existence, and the potentiality of an authentic witness to God being found in any or all other faiths. In one sense it may appear narrow by seeking to lead persons into basing their lives and social structures in Christian faith. Nevertheless, it recognizes that any such grounding which prematurely violates the witness of any other faith is contrary to Christian faith itself. The reason for this is partly in the Christian recognition of God's capacity to speak a creative new word (or a needed word of judgment) through those who seem most alienated from the community of faith. A Christian approach to social pluralism has its theological roots in the belief that there is no human being whose life exists outside the boundaries of God's sovereign activity. Any 'Christian civilization' which disregards this is more likely to be offensive to the gospel than supportive of it. That point has been made in countless ways by the critics of Christendom. The burden of proof ought to be *against*, not for, the restriction of non-Christian viewpoints and activities in a Christian society. The old 'thesis-anti-thesis' view of religious liberty, happily in decline these days, should be reversed. Rather than accepting religious liberty only when it can be shown conclusively that the true faith and practice cannot be enforced upon everybody, we ought to insist upon religious liberty unless it has to be limited for absolutely overriding social considerations.

Similar response should be made to the question whether the civilization-building and maintaining vocation necessarily entails an unacceptable component of use of sub-Christian incentives, including violence. We have already sought to establish that it is an illusion to suppose that one can avoid the problem by avoiding the responsibility. Nevertheless, it would stand as an important test of a Christian approach to civilization whether such forms of non-Christian incentive are always made to bear the burden of proof. The internal governance of sectarian communities may provide us with some helpful models for the wider society, although even in such communities there may sometimes be too much use of coercive practices (such as shunning) in social control. The burden of proof, in a seriously Christian society, should always be against violence and coercion and the organization of economic and social incentives in such a way that social effectiveness depends upon people doing what needs to be done for the wrong reasons. Human sinfulness doubtless means that some use of wrong incentives will prove necessary within every group, but as we make judgments affecting the shape of civilization it should be with a presumption against it. We should also go further in reminding ourselves that the fact that wrong incentives can exert such power often means that large numbers of people are given insufficient opportunity to experience human fulfilment. Use of external incentives should be limited, where possible, to those things which lead people toward, not away from, real human fulfilment.

The question whether a civilization substantially meeting such tests should be called 'Christian' is then probably a semantic issue of no great importance. Certainly no civilization will be a perfect manifestation of the implications of the gospel; but any can be much more so or much less so. Certainly Christians and their churches have a vocation to shape their judgments in accord with the more so and away from the less so.

C. *Ideological Formulations*

It is beyond the scope of the present book to take up the wide variety of possibly Christian ideological formulations definitively. Throughout, we have had to use such materials only suggestively and illustratively. The meaning of our discussion of Christian ideological formulation should now be tested, however, with reference to more concrete examples of possible ideological thinking. I wish here to consider, only briefly and suggestively, the ideological problems posed by political and economic life. In both of these broad areas, we confront immense difficulties if we are forced (or feel forced) to make judgments as Christians without the benefit of an overall normative conception – an 'ideal model' – of what politics or economics involves and how it should be structured if God's will were truly to be done on earth.

D. *Political Ideal Models*

In the most general sense, political ideology is concerned with the organization of social decision-making at the level of the state. In principle, it entails the activity of everybody within the limits of the state, and in this sense the state can itself best be described as society acting as a whole. Most political theorists would add to this that the state functions through law and that it is invested with the ultimate powers of coercion.[20] The political order potentially affects all of the conditions of human existence. Not surprisingly, the power to determine the policies of the political order is vigorously contested.[21] Political ideologies are mainly concerned with the determination of how that power should be allocated and exercised.

It may be noted quickly that some political ideologies are on the face of it contrary to aspects of Christian faith. The difficulties with traditional monarchy were noted as early as the Old Testament in the dire predictions by Samuel, the last of the pre-monarchical Hebrew judges, who warned of tyrannies and injustices and pointed out that the people would be treated like slaves if they should create a monarchy for themselves.[22] Even under the most benevolent of monarchies, there is a sense in which that is still true. Society is organized paternalistically, which always means, I take it, that 'father knows best'. Such paternalistic authority may seem justified by the ignorance of the people or by the wisdom of some kings and aristocracies. But proper respect cannot, in that kind of system, be shown to the God-given possibilities in human nature. Moreover, proper recognition cannot be given to the human limits and sinfulness of every monarch. Traditional monarchy is, furthermore, an offence to Christian understandings of mutuality, since it creates nearly insuperable class and caste barriers to normal human interaction. Relationships are dominated by the superiority of some and the inferiority of others. Hereditary monarchy and aristocracy tends to heighten this problem, of course.

Political fascism is even more alien to Christian understanding, even though it often appears disguised in the clothing of populist egalitarianism.[23] Monarchy can at least be respectful of individual rights; but fascism swallows up the personhood of its subjects into the absoluteness of the state. As Mussolini stated it, 'fascism conceives of the State as an absolute, in comparison with which all individuals or groups are relative, only to be conceived of in their relation to the State'.[24] The glorification of power in fascism frequently reflects deep social anxieties and the fear of disorder; but it is profoundly idolatrous in its theological implications. The value of the individual as a child of God is transformed into his utility to the state. His freedom is real only in so far as its expression coincides with the will of the state or in so far as it is irrelevant to the state. His life becomes *public* in the most awful sense. In the polarity individual/social, the individual is lost and therefore, also, the social character is perverted. Fascism also tends to be a chauvinistic creed, to disdain peace, to glorify aggressive warfare against 'weak' and 'inferior' peoples. In its particularly virulent Nazi form, fascism was racist. In a word, fascist ideologies run counter to virtually all of the positive, negative, and polar presumptions discussed in this book.

Political anarchism has attracted numerous followers in various forms over the past two centuries. Essentially, it is the view that political power is itself the root expression of evil and should be abolished altogether. Typically, anarchism presupposes a highly optimist theory of human nature. As we have seen in Chapter 4, Tolstoyan anarchism regards coercive governmental institutions as the source of evil; once the coercive structures have been abolished, man's goodness and creativity will be free to blossom forth spontaneously. By far the most important form of political anarchism is Marxist Communism, which views the 'withering away of the state' as a scientifically predictable outcome of a successful socialist revolution. In the Marxist form, political power is an expression of class exploitation and class conflict. In the classless society which will follow the revolution, there will be no need for the coercive state – only for politically neutral institutions of economic administration. Although the point is not often enough understood, Marxist anarchism also rests upon the assumption of the nearly flawless goodness of human nature when the latter is not alienated by exploitation. Communism, in its political ideology, is often mistaken for a fascist-type totalitarianism primarily because its conception of the state during the period of revolutionary struggle and consolidation makes similar demands upon people and involves similar disregard for individual human rights. Ultimately, however, it is anarchist. The problem with anarchism in its various forms, again, lies in its understanding of human nature. Its conception is contrary to Christian insight into the sinful character of man, but it also appears to deny even human freedom to sin in the ultimate society. As many commentators have noted, these ultimate expectations lead to a blind spot concerning methods to be employed by the party and state during the interval leading up to the classless society.[25]

These major ideological tendencies come in countless forms and variations. Our purpose is not to catalogue them but to illustrate how ideological tendencies can in themselves be contrary to Christian faith. Logically, what this means is that a Christian cannot organize his or her political thinking on the basis of these ideologies and that the Christian will tend to place the burden of proof against particular policies which have as their principal rationale their being an outgrowth of one of these ways of thinking. Christians often have to live and work in situations dominated by such ideological tendencies. But their own point of view must be in serious tension with them.

But Christian political thinking can relate much more positively to some forms of democratic ideology. Let it be noted with care that when speaking of democratic ideology as being a fit framework for Christian thinking, I have in mind the political tradition and not *laissez faire* economics. Moreover, we are discussing ideal models and not the current institutional practices of any particular country, such as the United States. With these caveats, we can cite four interlocking principles of democratic ideology: the concept of popular sovereignty, equality before the law, majority rule, and secure civil rights and liberties. Each of these is worth a brief commentary in relation to Christian thought.

The idea of popular sovereignty has ancient, non-Christian roots, principally in Stoicism and in Greek experience with the city-state. The Stoic political philosophers held that the ultimate location of political power is in the people of the civil community – not in their rulers. While much Stoic political philosophy was subsequent to the development of Roman Imperium, these philosophers held that even the emperor is not finally sovereign. His powers are delegated to him by the people, if not explicitly then by implication. The civil community is a political and legal covenant. This idea had significance in medieval political thinking and emerged in the modern world through such philosophers as Hobbes, Locke, and Rousseau, each of whom expressed it quite uniquely.

Some Christian social philosophers, such as Jacques Maritain, have been reluctant to speak of popular sovereignty – not because of anti-democratic attitudes but because they consider any human claim of sovereignty to be pretentious. Only God is ultimately sovereign.[26] From a theological standpoint this is a point well taken. But it only raises in different form the question of the human channels through which God's political sovereignty can best be exercised. Christians, in other words, clearly do hold political power to be responsible to a transcendent frame of reference. But the question is, what human beings have this responsibility? Very strong theological reasons exist for considering the old classical idea of popular sovereignty to be more compatible with Christian faith than any alternative. Only popular sovereignty recognizes in political terms the ultimate responsibility which every person has before God. Every other conception of political sovereignty implies that some self-designating persons stand between all others and God. The term 'self-designating' must be used here since those who participate in designating the ruler have a share in sovereignty. The maximum case for 'divine right of kings', such as that of James I of England ('The state of monarchy is the supremest thing upon earth: for kings are not only God's lieutenants upon earth, and sit upon God's throne, but even by God himself they are called Gods'),[27] emphasizes that the king has his powers directly from God and is responsible only to God for their exercise. Similar claims have been made for various forms of theocracy involving rule by priestly castes.[28] All such political ideologies presuppose theologically unacceptable distinctions between those persons who have this *a priori* political relationship to God and those who do not. Popular sovereignty, on the other hand, means that all are called to be citizens as well as subjects, though some will be singled out for the offices of government in some way. The concept of popular sovereignty was well-expressed in the formula of the responsible society by the First Assembly of the World Council of Churches (Amsterdam, 1948): 'A responsible society is one where freedom is the freedom of men who acknowledge responsibility to justice and public order, and where those who hold political authority or economic power are responsible for its exercise to God and the people whose welfare is affected by it. Man must never be made a mere means for political or economic ends. . . .'[29] Here responsibility to God is joined with responsibility to the people, and it is implicitly recognized that no ruling elite can consider itself solely responsible to God or its own conception of justice or truth or human well-being. In our time this obviously calls into question the claims and pretensions of strong-arm dictators who have set aside constitutional electoral systems. But it also raises questions which need to be taken seriously by revolutionary elites who presume to determine the future destiny of an entire society. In evaluating the latter, much depends upon whether or not the revolutionary intent is to establish institutions which genuinely reflect popular sovereignty.

The other three principles of democratic ideology can be described as corollaries of popular sovereignty. Equality before the law is clearly implied by the conception of each person as 'king'. Since political authority is ultimately derived, on the human level, from the whole body politic, all stand equally in relationship to the law of the body politic. Equality before the law must also be seen as a necessary political application of the presumption of equality, which was discussed in theological terms in Chapter 3. Majority rule also follows from this: if all are equal but unanimity of judgment on policy questions is not possible, then the larger number of equal people should carry the presumption over the smaller number. This does not mean that the larger number is necessarily right (G. K. Chesterton once remarked, somewhat cynically, that 'the majority is always wrong'), but only that there is a greater probability of rightness attached to the views of the majority than to those of any given minority.

Some have concluded that democratic ideology stops here. If it does, then nothing is to prevent a majority from running rough-shod over a minority. But the guarantee of civil rights and liberties for all, whether in a majority or minority, is also presumed by democratic ideology. There are some things that a majority can never do as an expression of democratic rule. It can never violate the right of minority persons to exist, to be free to dissent from policies established by the majority, and to be free to express themselves in the market place of ideas. One could add other basic human rights which have come to be accepted in the context of democratic ideology. It is only a metaphorical way of expressing the rationale for this, but I rather like the observation that we enjoy the rights of kings. The king must be free to express his will, to have unlimited access to information needed for governing, to worship as he pleases – and he must be free from arbitrary arrest and harassments of officers of the law who are, after all, *his* officers.

These points concerning democratic ideology do not mean that we have become gods, but only that no human beings should be allowed to be simply the political subjects of the will of others.

All should be free to participate in social decision-making, although only some will serve as officers and legislative decision-makers. When democratic ideology was engaged in the death-struggle with fascism and in the immediate post-war world, these ideas would scarcely have needed vindication among thinking people. Democratic slogans and ideas were dominant everywhere and were evidently the wave of a new humanist future. They had, indeed, considerable importance in the struggle for liberation which swept across Asia and Africa during the course of which a billion people changed their political status. But today the case has to be made again, and from a more defensive posture, among those who regard democratic ideology as a mask for Western socio-economic privilege. I shall turn in a moment to the problem of economic ideology. But before doing so the question must again be put rather sharply: What *political* alternative to democracy is more in harmony with Christian faith and humanistic values? Shall we accept an alternative which does *not* treat all persons as sovereign? which does not function by majority rule (and if not, by what minority are we to be ruled, and how, aside from the barrel of a gun, is this minority to be chosen)? which does not consider equality before the law? which does not respect the civil rights and liberties of the people? Credible arguments can be mustered that democracy is not workable apart from favourable economic relationships. The Watergate scandals established beyond doubt that vast economic power can be translated into gross political inequalities. Experience in smaller countries of the Third World, such as Chile and Guatemala, clearly indicate that foreign economic interests can utterly subvert the democratic political process and deliver the institutions of power into the hands of predatory elites. But these are not arguments against democratic ideology; they are arguments against the subversion of democracy. The use of democratic ideological slogans to mask selfish privilege must be seen first of all as an inauthentic application of democratic ideology – not as its logical consequence.

The overall case for political democracy is impressive enough to make this ideological model a presumptive point of reference.

Other things equal, or when in doubt, political decisions ought to be supportive of this ideological perspective. The burden of proof should be against solutions to the problem of political organization which are not consistent with it. If, under particular and extreme circumstances, it should be necessary for a minority to seize control of a society and rule it in disregard for the sovereign rights of all of the people, they must bear the burden of proving that the consequences of their not doing so would be even worse. In some of the African countries following independence the claim was made that small educated elites had to rule their lands through tightly-controlled, one-party governments until more people could be prepared for leadership and tribal rivalries could be brought under control. We cannot here go into the merits of any of these cases; but it seems to me that a Christian should be willing to entertain the possibility of this being a true statement of the political problem. If so, a case could be made that the present elite represents the possibility of future democratic society. But in a doubtful case the presumption should be in favour of efforts to involve all persons within the society in the blessings and responsibilities of self-government. At this writing, the minority white governments of southern Africa show utter disregard for popular sovereignty and equality and basic civil rights in the name of protecting 'civilization'. In such cases it seems quite evident that sufficient proof could not be brought forth to justify such a deviation from democratic ideology.

Similarly, revolutionary movements, which are not in themselves democratically organized, must bear the burden of proof that their present methods are necessary for the sake of a future democratic possibility. It can never be assumed that the possibility will automatically be fulfilled unless there is already a deep commitment to it.

In the United States much judicial attention has been given to the meaning and limitations to be placed upon items in the Bill of Rights. Are freedom of speech and press and religion to be considered absolutes, and if so how far do they extend? If they are not absolutes, then what can justify limitations placed upon them?

In the main, the courts have given the rights great presumptive weight without treating them quite as absolutes. Civil liberties are, for example, to be respected fully unless their exercise is inadvisable because of a 'clear and present danger'. Freedom of speech is to be respected unless it inordinately violates the desired peace and quiet and other rights of others. Freedom of the press is to be protected zealously unless by its exercise innocent persons are libelled, etc. In such instances, the presumption is properly placed in favour of the implications of democratic ideology, whether or not one regards the burden of proof as having been met sufficiently to justify exceptions.

E. *Economic Ideal Models*

Economic ideologies are concerned with the systems of production and distribution of scarce values. In the main, economic life involves material needs and wants, although some scarce values (such as theatrical entertainment and copyrights) are not exactly material. On the other hand, some material things, such as air and sunlight are plentiful enough not to be described as 'scarce' values in the economic sense under most circumstances.

Much social controversy over the past two hundred years has involved the mutually exclusive claims of competing economic ideologies – of which there have been a bewildering number. One recalls the traditionalist defences of slavery and feudalism, mercantilism, the emergence of private enterprise and free market capitalism, and the various reformist and revolutionary kinds of socialism, including nineteenth-century utopias, syndicalism, the single tax movement, Fabianism, and Marxism. Such economic ideologies embody an organizing conception of the facts of economic life and a more or less clear attitude toward the moral values which the ideologies purport to protect or advance. Strong vestiges of traditionalist economic organization remain in the modern world, with feudalism and even slavery still existing here and there. When put in ideological form, such traditionalist economic systems tend to be paternalistic and to place great emphasis upon fixed and inherited social stations. Invariably they are offensive to conceptions of equality. Their models of mutuality are paternalistic, involving the mutual 'loyalties' of authority and subject. Often they are highly restrictive of the freedom and opportunity of the subject classes. While some of the language of the New Testament tends to support such ideological conceptions ('slaves obey your masters', etc.), these are the points in New Testament teaching which seem most bound to the technological and cultural situation of an age now past. It is difficult to reconcile the paternalistic ideological assumptions of a St Paul in his concrete teaching on specific socio-economic and political questions with St Paul's own deeper insights on grace and freedom (as contained, for instance, in Galatians and Romans). Some of the older natural law conceptions in the Thomistic tradition tended to support this kind of ideological paternalism in economics. But traditionalist economic ideology, the defence of the *ancien regime*, is now everywhere very much on the defensive.

The great watershed in twentieth-century economic ideology still lies between *laissez faire* capitalism and socialism. Few people are either all for one or the other. But these two ideological frameworks represent the assumptions which people tend to accept and on the basis of which actual decisions are made.

According to *laissez faire* ideology, the economic role of government should be restricted to the protection of property and the adoption of regulations guaranteeing fair competition. Economic enterprise is fundamentally a private thing and should be kept so. Individuals should be free to invent, to produce, to invest, to buy and sell in a free market without interference. Competition among those who produce and sell will assure maximum efficiency in both production and distribution because buyers will select the best products at the lowest prices. People will be motivated to work hard and to produce creatively because they will themselves benefit from this productivity. In a free-enterprise economic system, as Adam Smith remarked, each person's vigorous pursuit of his own selfish interests will, 'by an invisible hand', redound to the greater good for all – because only by producing and selling goods and services needed and wanted by others under favourable terms will each person be able to serve his own selfish interests. Under free-enterprise capitalism everybody who is willing to work will find it possible to earn a livelihood and mankind will be assured of continuing material progress and prosperity. Or so the ideology holds.

In its Western ideological form, *laissez faire* capitalism has been supported by what is loosely termed the 'Protestant ethic', an individualistic work ethic emphasizing work (in relation to one's calling) and thrift (in relation to 'stewardship'). It was summarized by John Wesley's 'Gain all you can. Save all you can. Give all you can.' But in its economic ideological form, the 'give all you can' is to be replaced by an 'accumulate all you can' – it being understood that accumulation is not idle wealth but the development of capital enterprise for the production of still further wealth. Not that ideology is altogether opposed to giving. Persons of substantial wealth should be benefactors of mankind through their endowment of libraries, and universities, and museums, and art galleries. Indeed, by their acquisition of wealth, such persons will have demonstrated their greater capacity to determine which institutions of culture are most deserving of such philanthropy. But the hallmark of the 'Protestant ethic' is its emphasis upon work and its judgment that, economically speaking, we tend to get what we deserve, whether wealth or poverty.[30]

In assessing the influence of this *laissez faire* ideology we should be reminded again that the influence persists despite the fact that no present-day economy is a pure example of its logic. To be consequential, an ideology need only shape the consciousness and with it the judgments of people who believe in it. American business and labour interests may both compromise away the purity of *laissez faire* capitalism when their concrete interests are at stake, but both have often enough demonstrated their mental captivity to the ideology itself. It is something like sinning against our ideals when practicality and self-interest seem to require it, but continuing to espouse the ideals and to put them into practice whenever we consider it feasible. We should also remember that the ideological emphasis upon work in *laissez faire* capitalism is by no means unique to that ideology. Where, for instance, could one find a greater emphasis upon an ascetic work ethic than in contemporary China?

John C. Bennett, who is himself critical of capitalism, points to three of its advantages which should not be lost to our thinking:

> The first is that it has always taken seriously the problem of incentive. . . . Second, capitalism as a method of economic organization has the advantage of encouraging many independent centers of economic initiative. . . . A third advantage is that capitalism stands for the value of having at least segments of the economy let to impersonal and automatic forms of regulation instead of attempting to include all economic processes in one vast plan at the center. Christian realism about the sin and finiteness of man provides warning against the attempt to plan everything. Such pretentious planning involves too great concentration of power.[31]

While agreeing with Bennett as to the importance of these values, it seems more than questionable whether *laissez faire* capitalism, as an ideological frame of reference, can serve as vehicle for Christian moral judgment. Bennett refers to major points of conflict between capitalism and Christian faith, as enumerated by the Oxford Conference on Life and Work in 1937:

> (1) the tendency of economic institutions to enhance the acquisitiveness of men, (2) the shocking inequalities in economic opportunities and in access to the conditions on which the welfare of all depends, (3) the irresponsible possession of economic power, (4) the difficulty of finding ways of making a living that do not conflict with one's sense of Christian vocation.[32]

While these criticisms seem pointed more at actual practice in the countries most influenced by capitalism than they are at *laissez faire* ideology as such, a strong case can be made that these flaws are almost bound to result wherever the ideology is taken seriously. The enhancement of acquisitiveness is the full intention of the ideology. That is what is supposed to lead to the cornucopia of benefits for society as a whole. Inequality likewise is absolutely implicit in the capitalist scheme of incentives. Indeed, the ideology proclaims the great value of 'getting ahead', presumably of others.

Thus, we are led to value ourselves in proportion to our material superiority over others. It takes little analysis of the real world to discern that the reverse is more likely to be the case: wealth is more likely to correlate with sin than with righteousness. Even the desire to be superior to others is in itself a sin against God's intended human community of love and brotherhood. Even were this not so, the materialism of this acquisitiveness should be a serious flaw from a Christian standpoint. And even were *this* not so, *laissez faire* leaves to chance and the 'invisible hand' what should be the first objective of every economic system: serving the economic needs of persons in community. The theory is that all will be best if cared for in this way and that those who are not well cared for (the poor) will in fact have deserved their poverty through their own moral inadequacies. But it is not so in the real world. Only as Western capitalistic countries have moved away from the pure ideology through adoption of more liberal social welfare programmes have the needs of helpless and innocent poor people been met. In the United States these programmes have been strung together illogically and often wastefully precisely because they have been hampered by the confines of *laissez faire* ideology. Welfare programmes have had to be constructed half-apologetically, the meeting of needs being supplanted to irrelevant formulas for self-reliance (irrelevant because the vast majority of poor people could not under any circumstances become fully self-sufficient economically). The problems of *laissez faire* are compounded by international exploitation of the raw materials and labour of poorer countries by the wealthier ones. In sum, *laissez faire* capitalism is principled selfishness and irresponsibility when it is implemented seriously.

The other main contemporary economic ideology is socialism in its now numerous variations. Joseph A. Schumpeter's definition of socialism is satisfactory up to a point. He speaks of it as 'that organization of society in which the means of production are controlled, and the decisions on how and what to produce and on who is to get what, are made by public authority instead of by privately-owned and privately managed firms'.[33] As an ideology, socialism also contains both practical and ethical rationales. The main point is that economic power is formally responsible to the whole of society, through the state, and not simply to those who hold it as private wealth. Accordingly, economic decisions are much more likely to be made in such a way as directly to benefit everybody and not simply those who own the instruments of production. Marx's theory of industrial crisis makes this point in moral terms if not in the scientific sense he imagined. According to Marx, industrial crisis and economic depression occurs when there is no longer enough purchasing power in the market to absorb the products of industrial production. In such a situation, industry no longer has any incentive or economic capability to continue to produce since it is owned privately and must make a profit. *Laissez faire* ideology might assert that this loss of market demand reflects consumer disinterest in the products of industry. But to Marxist analysis, the same phenomenon is better accounted for by the fact that workers always receive less in wages than the market value of what is produced – the balance being kept by the capitalist as surplus value. In the long run (usually every ten years or so) production catches up with and passes the available purchasing power of wage workers. One after another, industries are forced to cut back on production. More and more workers are thrown out of work, thus losing the wages needed for purchasing power. A vicious circle thus develops in which unemployment constricts the market of industry's products, leading to further unemployment and economic depression. Whether or not this account of economic crisis has been rendered obsolete by subsequent economic theories (especially those of John Maynard Keynes), the ethical point has a certain validity. Under capitalism, economic decisions will always be made for the benefit of investors, even if the decisions that have to be made lead straight into public economic disaster. Under socialism decisions can at least be based on social, not private, objectives. There is no need for the scandal of unused plant capacity and stockpiles of products and food rotting because of the lack of private purchasing power. There is no obstacle to full production and full employment since nobody has to make a private profit for production to occur. Inequalities may exist in fact, but unlike capitalism there are no inequalities in principle. The incentive for planned obsolescence is removed.

In the abstract, the case for socialism seems indisputable. In actuality there are also problems with socialism which the Christian should note. The most important is the problem of power: who is to control economic power when it is a state monopoly? Private economic power centres are irresponsible in very large measure, but at least there is some accountability to the market (diluted as that accountability may be by private monopoly conditions and saturation advertising). Where political and economic power are united, however, the latter will be no more responsible than the former. Socialism combined with any political system other than democracy will be no more responsible than the political system – a point which most of the Marxist socialist countries have demonstrated too well. Even combined with democracy, socialism could tend toward the corruption of the political institutions by placing too much power in the hands of officer holders – power which could be used to perpetuate officials in office and generally contribute to corruption. Socialism, while meeting rather well the test of the positive moral presumptions, needs to be checked rather carefully in relation to the negative ones. Does it offer enough hedge against man's sinful tendency to seize and use power selfishly?

The other main problem with socialism is that it may weaken individual initiative and diminish the responsiveness of the open market. While these points are sometimes offered as definitive objections to socialism, they are merely points where socialism is sometimes undeveloped. In principle (that is, in the ideology) there is no reason why the market mechanism cannot be used nor why individual initiative cannot be stimulated in a socialist economy. Even within the American civil service there are instances of great initiative and creativity (such as in programmes of the National Institutes of Health, the Public Health Service, and the US Forest Service). Meanwhile, most of the socialist countries, including the Marxist ones, employ a market system of sorts without doing violence to their ideological purity. Some, such as Yugoslavia, even encourage development of new economic initiatives in the form of co-operatives.

From this brief discussion there may emerge the rudiments of an economic ideology which is more or less compatible with Christian faith. It would, I believe, be a form of democratic socialism. Its economic institutions would be responsible to government, and government would be responsible to the people. In the development of both governmental and economic institutions care would be taken to keep too much power from becoming concentrated in a few hands. Economic initiative would be encouraged and rewarded, although a truly 'humanized' society would be one in which the grateful recognition of service rendered would be sufficient reward. The presumption in the distribution of economic benefits would be for equality. Use of incentives creating inequalities would be kept to the minimum required by the general condition of human sinfulness. Small-scale business activities, including what Robert Theobald calls 'consentives',[34] would be consistent with this. Major industries and, in the long run, intermediate industries should, however, be publicly capitalized and owned.

An important component in Christian ideological thinking about economics must be the question of social welfare. I refer to the provision of certain services to the public at minimal or no charge – including health care, education, public transportation, and a basic income guarantee.[35] Such welfare provisions can be provided under welfare capitalism, of course. In a system of welfare capitalism, business and industry are permitted to function more or less without restraint, but they are then taxed heavily enough by government to finance generous welfare provisions for the whole society. This continues to place too much emphasis upon selfishness an economic motive and to concentrate too much power in private hands, although it is a great improvement over pure *laissez faire*. Welfare capitalism acknowledges the responsibility of all economic endeavour to the whole community, but it continues to permit great inequality and large concentrations of potentially irresponsible economic power. An equally important reservation concerning welfare capitalism is that it often continues to lodge the burden of proof against further needed extensions of the welfare principle. The presumption continues to favour private wealth-building.

One of the worst things about *laissez faire* ideology is that it puts a quite irrational burden of proof against public expenditures of all kinds, including those for the arts and other culturally-enriching and community-building activities. Historically, only those public expenditures which clearly expedite private economic activity – such as the building of railways, highways, and airports – have not had to confront an initial negative prejudice of great magnitude. Education serves economic activity in this way, but even so it is probably fortuitous that the emergence of common schools and the concept of universal free state school education preceded the full ascendancy of *laissez faire* in America. Otherwise state school education would almost certainly have faced the resistance with which universal health care proposals have been greeted in recent years. Military expenditures have not usually had to face much resistance in recent years in this country, but this is readily interpreted in terms of the defence of existing institutions of private economic activity.

In recent years, both capitalism and socialism have been challenged by the wastefulness and ecological irresponsibility of modern technology. Polluted rivers and smoggy air can exist under either form of ideological sponsorship, and government presumably requires higher standards under either system. *Laissez faire* probably has the greater blind spot at this point, however. It is a good deal easier for a private corporation to dump its refuse on to the public and to regard this as a good bargain than it is for a publicly controlled enterprise to do so. In the former case, the business is likely to increase its profits by lowering its costs. In the latter, the public disposal of pollutants must be entered into the ledger as a cost and dealt with responsibly. The steady, predictable resistance to environmental control measures by private industries in the United States illustrates the point. But concern for ecology belongs in a Christian economic ideology as one of the givens, and it cannot be said that socialism has always made this a prominent concern.

Some Christians would go even further and argue that Christian economic thought should establish a presumption against modern, large-scale technology as such. That is clearly the tendency of some of the work of Jacques Ellul on this subject[36] and many Christians who are responsive to the ecology movement concur. I believe it is too late to advance the outright dismantling of modern technology as a serious proposition. In balance, the benefits of technology in liberating human beings from heavy physical toil and the uncertainties of climate and season and food supply probably outweigh the problems of technological civilization. Even were this not so, it is doubtful whether any substantially lesser technological base could adequately feed, clothe, and shelter the present world population. The most promising solutions to the problems posed by modern technology may turn out to be those which involve further technological development. For example, the harnessing of the power of the sun and the development of safer forms of nuclear energy might be ways of solving some of the problems of contemporary technology.

In a widely quoted and in many ways very sensible book, the British economist E. F. Schumacher proposes a sweeping change of current attitudes toward large-scale technology. His interest is partly one of reversing the present ruinous rate of exploitation of the earth's finite resources and partly one of restoring a human sense of proportion to economic activity. His proposals for small-scale technology and his economic analysis are worthy of deeper study and stand as a reminder that many of the further technological developments of which I have spoken need to be in the direction of smaller-scale activities. It is difficult to relate Schumacher's work to any of the traditional options in economic ideology, and he may have significant things to say to all of them.[37]

Conclusion

These ideological illustrations cannot be treated here in greater detail. That is an important continuing task for Christian ethics and, indeed, for every responsible Christian. I have intended by their use to suggest how the basic presumptions of Christians can be translated into broader conceptions of what society ought to be. Such ideal models of social organization cannot usually be judged by their immediate practicality, although we should question the adequacy of any model which is on the face of it impractical. Ideological thinking helps us to organize our moral judgments even when confronted by the illusiveness of our noblest conceptions of the good. By accepting the presumptive validity of our ideal models of society, we at least know what a compromise is when it is forced upon us. We can at least require deviations or exceptions to bear the burden of proof.

We must remind ourselves yet once again that no ideology is to be regarded as an ultimate in itself. All ideal models gain their value from their adequacy in reflecting God's loving purposes for human existence. Since none of us is God, we cannot expect to have perfect models even in our heads, much less in the actual world.

8

Moral Judgment and Social Strategy

There is a certain danger implicit in the preceding discussion of moral judgment. It is that we shall unconsciously assume an olympian detachment from *acting* on the basis of our judgments. Analysis of our ideals and consideration of what ought to be done can easily become a spectator sport. We can easily assume that intellectual comprehension of issues properly discharges the office of Christian moral judgment. We can become like the 'ivory tower intellectuals' of whom the Marxist philosopher Laszek Kolakowski speaks: 'Thus, the intellectual wants to reserve for himself the right of moral judgment of social reality without any responsibility for the course of social events.'[1] Even among Christian ethicists and theologians the word 'practical' sometimes carries a tone of condescension, despite the fact that if Christian faith is not permitted to organize our practical experience it is nothing at all. We can drift into the style of life attributed (perhaps unfairly) to the American socialist leader Norman Thomas:

> Norman Thomas was not regarded as dangerous. He preached Christian ethics in government in a perfectly respectable way. At no time did he appear to offer the possibility of putting these ideals into practice. Therefore, he was never hated the way Roosevelt was hated. He was never identified with an organization that seemed about to do anything practical. Here was the kind of Socialist that a decent Socialist was supposed to be – for whom romantic college professors could vote. He symbolized a conflicting ideal without creating a practical working institution which interfered with any of the ideals that Socialism contradicted.[2]

Christians have a responsibility to be not only wise judges but committed activists; and not only committed activists, but strategically effective activists. Moral judgment must therefore be related to social strategy. Christian social strategy is the attempt by Christians to organize most effectively their capacity to achieve theologically appropriate social objectives. It is the attempt to seek such objectives *intelligently*. It can be contrasted both with visceral, unco-ordinated, unplanned activism and with abandonment of the effort to achieve social objectives at all.

At certain points, which will be discussed later in the chapter, methodological presumption may have significant contributions to make in resolving important dilemmas of strategic method. For instance, it may help us to speak to the question whether Christians should employ violence in revolution and to what extent they should appeal to unworthy motives in order to achieve important goals. Before proceeding to that point, however, it may prove helpful to explore the systemic context of social action and the theological and practical problems of relating means to ends in social strategy.

A. *The Dilemma of Christian Social Strategy*

We shall have to focus in a particular way in this chapter upon the moral dilemmas involved in strategic use of 'the system'. In a way, this dilemma corresponds to the dilemma of Christian civilization discussed in the preceding chapter. But here we shall be concerned with the purposive activity of Christians, not with their detached judgments. The question we must face now is to what extent those desiring to achieve social objectives should work in and through 'the system' and to what extent they should work outside it to achieve their goals.

The question has both ethical and practical ramifications. Ethically it involves the legitimacy of the system. Practically, it is a question of what, in fact, can be accomplished through the system. The dilemma occurs as the Christian strategist faces the possibility that the apparently effective forms of strategy may not be moral and that the apparently moral forms of strategy may not be effective. The dilemma appears in its sharpest forms as we relate to social systems. The social system itself may appear to be moral. But it may also appear that important moral goals can only be gained by pursuing methods *outside* the system. For example, political democracy (a morally approvable procedural system) may in given circumstances have to be bypassed for the sake of such important moral goals as peace or economic justice. On the other hand, an important goal sometimes can be gained only by seeking it *through* the normal channels of an immoral system. Then the question is whether one should engage in actions which, while promising success vis-a-vis a particular goal, will at the same time strengthen an immoral system. The dilemma is particularly frustrating because, for the Christian, effectiveness itself must be defined in moral terms.

The whole problem is much more complex than many social activists and publicists suppose since social systems are themselves almost infinitely complex phenomena. They exist on many different levels, organizing different aspects of life which are sometimes parallel, sometimes hierarchical in relation to each other. Despite the great diversity of social systems, there is a sense in which all known social systems are interrelated – illustrating Walter Muelder's dictum that 'mankind is the unit of co-operation'.[3]

Our understanding of the word *system* must therefore be broader than that implied by most rhetoric in defence of or in opposition to 'the system'. We may understand the term to mean all regular patterns of social interaction in which the expectancy is widely shared that certain forms of action will evoke predictable results. Social systems, according to Wilbert E. Moore, minimally consist of 'role-players or actors in interaction governed by rules of conduct that entail rewards for compliance and penalties for non-compliance'. He notes that

> such systems may vary in size from a pair of friends to the large national state, in duration from the barely more than transitory encounter to a nominally eternal administrative organization, in range of common interests from the collector's club to the family or community, and in a multitude of other ways. No simple and universal

explanation, such as sociability, will account for this variety, and dealing with variety has been one of the main preoccupations of social science. Descriptive generalizations about particular types of systems and explaining the types in their settings constitute the bulk of our very incomplete knowledge of 'social systems'.[4]

We can speak meaningfully of political systems, economic systems, familial systems, etc., on the basis of the principal objectives of the system and the nature of distributed rewards. We all participate simultaneously in a complex web of social systems.

Defined in this broad way, it is evident that social strategy has to operate in and from social systems of some sort. A totally revolutionary strategy – one with absolute discontinuity as its objective – is inconceivable. The practicalities of strategy cannot simply be determined, therefore, by a decision for or against social systems, and to some extent our presumption must be against efforts to do so. It is rather a question of determining which kind of goals can and ought to be sought as the objects of a Christian social strategy and what kinds of strategic methods, either from within or outside a defined social system, are relevant to the desired changes.

B. *The Objectives of Christian Social Strategy*

The first requisite of Christian social strategy is a clear understanding of its objectives: What social changes or stabilities are to be sought, and why, precisely, should Christians work for such goals? The broad outline of an answer to these questions is anticipated by the positive presumptions of Chapter 3, but more needs to be said here concerning the identification of the working objectives of social strategy. Social strategy may be particularly complex for Christians because the identification of the good in concrete social form involves both tangible and intangible realities. It is much easier to organize strategy around clearly tangible goals. But in a Christian perspective, tangible ends are subordinated to intangible ones. The intangible goals are the ultimate, intrinsic objectives; the tangible objectives are mainly instrumental. For instance, the immediate goal of much Christian social action in the United States during the 1960s was racial desegregation. That goal could be spelled out in terms of the destruction of certain quite tangible barriers to authentic human interaction among persons of different racial backgrounds. But the more ultimate goal was integration – a transformed spiritual and relational reality. In effect, tangible goals such as desegregation were means rather than ends. To speak of the ultimate goals of the Christian as intangible is not to say that they are unreal, but rather that they are not measurable. In the last analysis they are dependent upon factors over which strategy and action can gain no final control. Fulfilment of the community of love and justice which Christians understand by faith to be the kingdom of God necessarily involves the attitudes of free human beings. And both the freedom of persons and the theological point of reference transcend the manipulable objects of experience. In the light of the problems of human finitude and sin, we can only speak of relative approximations of the kingdom of God – not of its perfect realization within human history.

But of what might an approximation to the kingdom of God consist? To speak of approximations or of 'proximate ends' may seem to suggest that, while the transcendent reality of God's kingdom cannot be realized fully by human agency, some proportion of it can. It suggests that we can come more or less close to the goal while never expecting finally to achieve it. But the problem with this way of viewing our proximate goals is that no matter how close we come to devising the best external arrangements and institutions, the gap between such objective factors and the intrinsic realities of loving community remains yawning before us in the absence of an affirmative response from other free human beings. Man may continue to be estranged from fellow man in spite of favourable external arrangements. Notwithstanding improvements in the objective situation, we find ourselves, as Christian strategists, further away from God's intended community of love because of a deepening human selfishness. Thus, progress toward the ultimate, intrinsic goals cannot be measured only in terms of objective improvements in the human situation.

A more promising approach to this problem treats proximate ends quite frankly as instrumental goals. Certain tangible goals are sought because they *serve* the more ultimate, transcendent realities. This approach to the development of actual goals for Christian strategy is consonant with the conclusions we have already drawn from Bonhoeffer's distinction between the ultimate and the penultimate and from Barth's formulation of the doctrine of creation. When we identify human needs on the historical plane, it is not to suggest that such needs are identical with man's transcendent nature and destiny. But meeting the mundane needs serves the transcendent all the same. While instrumental goals (the proximate ends) cannot be regarded as intrinsic or ultimate, they are invested with a moral seriousness derived from the intrinsic or ultimate. Food for the hungry man is not ultimate. But since in the world of existence human beings need food in order to survive, and since human survival without dehumanizing degrees of suffering is a precondition of human participation in God's intended family of love on earth, it follows that food for the hungry man belongs to God's intention and is therefore properly to be regarded as a 'Christian' goal. We may speak similarly of other economic, social, political, and legal conditions and relationships. Programmes to erase famine or illiteracy or racial discrimination gain ethical status from the fact that such conditions make it more difficult for people to live a human life in community – as that life is most profoundly disclosed to Christian understanding. The creation of better governmental institutions, housing, educational institutions, social security, guaranteed income, economic justice, etc., can represent efforts to improve the conditions necessary to human life in community.

Is Christian social strategy thus restricted to the pursuit of objective conditions on the instrumental level alone? While the ultimate, intrinsic realities which are the final goals of Christian action cannot be reduced to objective conditions, there is, nevertheless, a sense in which the Christian strategist can act more directly in pursuit of the ultimate itself. That is by his attempt to communicate to others (the alienated and unjust, the oppressor and oppressed alike) his own full acceptance of them as children of God, brothers and sisters and fellow heirs of the promise. Social strategy has a certain symbolic character which is distinct from though related to actions to change objective conditions. A given line of social strategy may be useful on either or both levels, or its utility on one level can be negated by its disutility on the other. Both levels of strategy have their risks. Communication or symbolic action may lead to neglect of objective conditions and serve as a mask (or, in the bad sense, an ideology) for the maintenance of evil conditions. Action dealing with objective conditions alone may, on the other hand, neglect the deeper human realities those conditions are intended to serve.[5] People who are serious about either of these levels will be serious about the other as well. A good illustration of both is afforded by the 1963 march on Washington, which was sponsored by American civil rights organizations. On the more obvious level, the march was designed to get Congress to enact legislation to establish objective conditions considered necessary for the restoration of black people to full participation in the life of American society. But a very important aspect of the churches' participation in the march was the desire to communicate a reconciling acceptance of and identification with these disinherited people.[6]

Both types of social strategy are important and both gain their ethical legitimation from the quality of the goodness which they serve. They suggest that the key strategic questions, which locate the goals for Christian strategy, are these: (1) What are the objective conditions necessary or desirable to the life of persons and communities in the kingdom of God at this time in history? and (2) How can we best communicate the reconciling reality of that kingdom to persons estranged from it?

The church itself is a characteristic embodiment of these twin aspects of Christian social strategy. It cannot be viewed simply as an agent of change, for it also has its own corporate embodiment, its own objective structure and dynamics. It can be studied empirically as a social phenomenon, and often it must itself be the target of the social strategy of Christians. But neither is the church purely temporal for, as the church, it also is a fellowship of faith. As such it can bear witness to the transcendent realities of its faith, while seeking in its own institutional life to embody those realities and while acting to secure conditions appropriate to those realities in the world.[7]

With this understanding of the objectives in mind, we must return to the problem of Christian social strategy in relation to given social systems.

C. *'The System' as a Problem in Strategic Practicality*

It has already been observed that social strategy must operate in and from social systems of some sort and that the practicalities of strategy cannot simply be determined by a decision for or against working within the system. But now we must remember that any social system involving leadership (as all clearly do) has a hierarchical power structure which can either be confirmed or challenged by the strategy employed by the social change agent. Thus the key question: Should the attempt be made to work *through* this existing power structure, or should the change agent try to organize a new power base from which to gain control of the entire system?

The problem can be illustrated in the social science literature on racial desegregation in which the role of the 'gatekeeper' has been emphasized.[8] The gatekeeper in any social institution is understood to be the person who, more than others, ultimately determines whether minority group persons are to be admitted. An industrialist might be the gatekeeper so far as job opportunity is concerned, a real estate agent or apartment house manager could be the gatekeeper in housing, a minister the gatekeeper in respect to church membership. To effect desegregation one tries to persuade the gatekeeper, either through rational or moral appeal or through pressure tactics. The legitimacy of the gatekeeper's position in the social system is not generally questioned in the social science literature on this subject published in the 1950s.

The basic concept is readily applicable to other problems of social strategy. The gatekeeper can be understood as the point where the power of any social system, as a system, is focused. Thus, in legislative politics, a committee chairman may exercise a gatekeeper role in the operative system; or, in a local school system, the superintendent or key board members may play the role. In many cities of medium size, a rather small elite often exercises the gatekeeper power for most key local decisions in business and politics.

A fundamental decision confronts the social change agent as he contemplates the system. Will he attempt to work through the gatekeeper, thus in effect supporting existing power relationships, or will he attempt to challenge the gatekeeper by constructing a new series of power relationships? Attempts during the late 1960s and early 1970s by the US Senate Foreign Relations Committee to share powers in foreign relations exercised predominantly by the President could be understood as a modified attempt to construct new power relationships. On the other hand, efforts to influence the President's policies (via telegrams, visiting delegations, etc.) can be understood as working through the gatekeeper and thus confirming existing power relationships. If the change agent does decide to work through the existing power structure an inevitable consequence of his decision is to confirm and probably strengthen that structure – even if he is successful thereby in gaining his own immediate objectives. From a purely practical standpoint he ought therefore to weigh any negative effects in strengthening an existing power system against the positive effects in gaining his original objectives.

One social scientist, James B. McKee, raised precisely this question in relation to what he considered to be the over-reliance of social scientists upon existing gatekeepers in their race relations strategies in the 1950s. Working primarily with existing power elites, he argued, gives them 'effective control over the scope and direction of the program, keeps the issue out of the hands of more militant leadership, offsets the chance of the rise of new leadership, and thus lessens the threat to the status quo in power, and offers a fresh and important situation to be exploited for validation of its moral and civil leadership'.[9] Considerations of this kind led the Office of Economic Opportunity, in devising its local community action programmes, to prescribe the 'maximum feasible participation' of poor people themselves. Community Action Councils were purposely structured so as to keep as much power as possible over the designation and funding of local projects in the hands of poor people. Existing community leadership, including public officials, was not given a dominant role. The effect (eventually perceived and often countered by most local political leadership) was to begin to create a new power base.

The inability to arrive at clear choices between working with existing elites or attempting to replace them can seriously weaken social strategy, although some combination of the two is not unthinkable. One of the weaknesses of the McCarthy Presidential campaign of 1968 was the confused interaction of two major goals: peace in Vietnam (and a reordering of national priorities) on the one hand, and reform of the procedures of the Democratic Party on the other. The second objective, while it was consonant with the drive for nominating convention delegates in a few states, precluded effective bargaining with the important kingmakers, such as Mayor Richard Daley of Chicago and the top leadership of the Labour Movement. Similar problems plagued the McGovern Presidential campaign of 1972, although Senator McGovern did succeed in gaining the Democratic nomination which had eluded Senator McCarthy in 1968. The genius of Senator Robert F. Kennedy's 1968 Presidential campaign, on the other hand, was its apparent ability to attract reformers (whose most important substantive issue was peace in Vietnam) without necessarily alienating the existing political gatekeepers. But the key to this strategy was its emphasis upon peace in Vietnam and its relative lack of emphasis upon reform of the party's procedures.[10]

The basic strategic decision we are considering involves a choice between a *reformist* or a *revolutionary* orientation, as these terms have been understood in classical socialist circles. But we must remember that even these terms are relative. This relativity can be illustrated in relation to that same McCarthy campaign during the explosive year 1968. In comparison with the approach of militants who viewed all electoral politics with contempt, the McCarthy campaign was reformist. But from the standpoint of the White House and Democratic Party loyalists, the campaign might properly have been called revolutionary because it sought structural changes in the *de facto* power system. The campaign was reformist in the sense that it sought reforms without challenging the underlying system of Constitution and law. But it was revolutionary in the sense that it challenged the nominating system in the Democratic Party in a fundamental way.

We need to be clear that the choice between violent and nonviolent tactics does not correspond to this decision whether to work through or against a power elite. Violence can be directed toward the overthrow of a power system, either by removing it directly or by making it impossible for the system to govern. But violence can also be employed to wring concessions out of a power system; that is, it can be used to influence a particular decision without challenging the power system fundamentally. Likewise, nonviolent tactics are not necessarily reformist. Gandhi's campaigns for Indian independence show how non-violent tactics can be used for revolutionary purposes in destroying a whole system of power and replacing it with another.

Moreover, the choice between strategies of education and strategies of direct action does not correspond to this decision whether to influence or work against elites. Education can be directed toward the enlightenment of an elite, or it can be directed toward the masses in order to begin the formation of a new, revolutionary base. Similarly, direct action can merely refer to the actions of a power elite in the social process (such as President Truman's executive order desegregating the US armed forces), or it can mean direct action to replace a power elite. Somewhere in between, direct action can be used as a means of persuading or influencing a power elite. Education and direct action are both significant aspects of all social strategy. Education is properly understood as preparation for action, whether in the context of a predominantly revolutionary strategic perspective or a reformist one. In either case, the choice between reliance upon education rather than action must hinge upon one's assessment of the degree of readiness to take action. The two, education and action, belong together in social strategy.

D. *Strategic Analysis of Social Systems*

Ethical questions involved in the decision whether to work with or against a power elite will be considered below. Before dealing with those issues we should, in a preliminary way, consider certain practical problems. The social strategist must balance the undesirable consequences against the desirable. What are the resources available for this, and what are the foreseeable obstacles if one should desire to circumvent or replace a power elite?

We return to the observation that social systems are complex webs of interdependency. Systems are more or less functional with respect to ends and needs. Robert Merton has pointed out that social phenomena may serve both 'manifest' and 'latent' functions. The former represent the publicly recognized purposes. The latter refer to less obvious forms of need-gratification.[11] We must expect great resistance in attempting to dislodge the leadership of a social system if that leadership is viewed as highly functional by a large proportion of the participants in the system. Attempts to replace the seniority system of congressional committee leadership survived most attacks upon it because it served political and personal functions viewed as necessary by a large enough majority of members of Congress. Even the House of Representatives Rules Committee, which was notoriously obstructive for a period of years under the leadership of Congressman Howard Smith, performed latent functions which were apparently appreciated even by many congressmen who publicly called for reform. It buried bills which congressmen had introduced only as a result of political pressure, and in other ways it saved them the embarrassment of having to vote on politically divisive measures.

Similarly, big city political machines, in spite of their notorious corruption, often performed needed services that were valued highly by newly-arrived immigrants.

Revolutionary change in leadership generally presupposes existing widespread discontent or the capacity to create such discontent within the system. Accurate analysis of the manifest and latent functions performed by a social system, including analysis of the participants' perceptions of those functions, should therefore precede any judgment as to the practicality of challenging the system's power elite. In some cases, it may be evident that the elite is imposed or exploitative or simply inadequate and that discontent either exists or can be aroused. In other cases, where there is no prospect of developing a new power base, it may be more practical to work through an existing elite.

A new power base can sometimes be established by involving outside forces or forces derived from a more inclusive system. For example, the revolution in voting rights for black people in the South could hardly have been accomplished through persuasion of existing southern power elites; nor could the white majority, particularly for the sake of that objective, have been used as a power base to replace those elites. But it did prove possible to involve the wider federal system of the United States to accomplish that objective and thereby also to begin to reconstitute the power structure of the South itself. The 1968 Soviet invasion of Czechoslovakia is a comparable illustration (practically, if not morally). Those in Czechoslovakia wishing to re-establish an authoritarian Stalinist regime during the Dubcek reform period (1967–68) found themselves quite powerless within Czechoslovakia itself. The overwhelming majority of the Czech people and most Czech institutions eagerly supported the reforms and were determined to resist a return to authoritarianism. The actual destruction of the reform movement could be effected only by power imposed from the wider Warsaw Pact system, in particular by the power of the Soviet Union. This outside power was able to return the tiny authoritarian circle (probably only a small fragment of the Communist Party itself) to rule.

The problem is thrown into sharp relief by the strategy and tactics of many New Left activists in the late 1960s. While, on the face of it, the tactics of disruption and confrontation (and, in extreme cases, of bombings) seemed to restrict more than to enlarge the revolutionary power base, those employing such tactics regarded them as contributing to ultimate control of the American political system. In a perceptive study of protest movements of this period, a task force of the National Commission on the Causes and Prevention of Violence summarized the case for confrontation tactics as argued in New Left documents and as stated by New Left leaders in interviews with Commission staff.

1. *Confrontation and militancy are methods of arousing moderates to action.* The creation of turmoil and disorder can stimulate otherwise quiescent groups to take more forceful action in their own ways. Liberals may come to support radical demands while opposing their tactics; extreme tactics may shock moderates into self-re-examination.

2. *Confrontation and militancy can educate the public.* Direct action is not intended to win particular reforms or to influence decision-makers, but rather to bring out a repressive response from authorities – a response rarely seen by most white Americans. When confrontation brings violent official response, uncommitted elements of the public can see for themselves the true nature of the 'system'. . . .

3. *Confrontation, militancy and resistance are ways to prepare young radicals for the possibility of greater repression.* . . .

4. *Combative behaviour with respect to the police and other authorities, although possibly alienating 'respectable' adults, has the opposite effect on the movement's relationships with non-student youth.* Educated, middle-class, non-violent styles of protest are poorly understood by working-class youth, black youth, and other 'dropouts'. Contact with these sectors of the youth population is essential and depends upon the adoption of a tough and aggressive stance to win respect from such youth. . . .

5. *The experience of resistance and combat may have a liberating effect on young middle-class radicals.* Most middle-class students are shocked by aggressive or violent behaviour. Thus cultural fear of violence is psychologically damaging and may be politically inhibiting. To be a serious revolutionary, one must reject middle-class values, particularly deference toward authority. Militant confrontation gives resisters the experience of physically opposing institutional power, and it may force students to choose between 'respectable' intellectual radicalism and serious commitment to revolution, violent or otherwise.

6. *The political potency of 'backlash' is usually exaggerated.* Those who point to the possibility of repression as a reaction to confrontation tactics wish to compromise demands and principles and dilute radicalism. Repression will come in any case, and to diminish one's efforts in anticipation is to give up the game before it starts.[12]

In this overall strategic perspective, even an increase in overt repression may be desired because it helps to heighten the contradictions within the system, creates wider public awareness, and increases the discontent from which a revolutionary power base can be formed. The defeat of liberal reformism may, in this light, be welcomed. Sometimes things 'have to get worse before they can get better'. Acting out of this kind of perspective, the Provisional Irish Republican Army (Provisional IRA) has sought to create disruption and confrontation wherever possible. Use of bombing and other terroristic tactics has not led to popularity. But popularity is not the organization's objective. It is more interested in disrupting the normal flow of community life and frustrating all normal or liberal means of dealing with the challenge. It would not welcome moderate solutions to the political problems of Northern Ireland, and its terrorism can in part be understood as being designed to prevent such solutions from occurring. Its assumption is that when Irish and British patience finally breaks down in the anarchy of violence and counterviolence, the Provisional IRA will be able to play a leading role in the radical reconstruction of Irish politics. Similar strategic objectives have been at work wherever radical revolutionaries have made major use of terrorism and disruption.

Such a perspective is not on its face unthinkable. But its strategic practicality would seem to depend upon the accuracy of key assumptions concerning the degree to which society, as a systemic whole, is already functional. We should remember that in very few instances have genuinely revolutionary movements succeeded in industrial countries. Those few instances of success have almost invariably represented right-wing movements or coups – sometimes as reactions to ill-conceived left-wing revolutionary efforts. The reason for this may be that in industrialized countries too many people believe they have too great a present stake in the existing system – thus leading them to react negatively to what they perceive as threats to the existing order. Revolutionary strategies can thus create more power base, not for revolutionaries but for reactionary demagogues.[13] But, on the other hand, there are numerous illustrations of success by reform strategies which do not threaten the underlying system of order itself. Such strategies can be perceived as improving the functional character of the society. In recent history, revolutionary movements have had much greater success in non-industrial societies where very substantial discontent already exists.

Strategic analysis must therefore encompass realistic study of the balancing of forces potentially aligned for or against change. Equilibrium theory, of the kind developed by Robert M. MacIver, seeks to develop a typology of possible balances of this kind.[14] In his typology, a 'tense equilibrium' is a highly polarized situation accompanied by emotional stress. Overt conflict is likely to result in general deterioration of the situation rather than in either side gaining its objectives. An 'indifferent equilibrium' is one in which there is little strong sentiment either for or against change – a situation in which vigorous leadership can be very effective. A 'precarious equilibrium' is one in which change is very likely, but in one direction only – as in the case of a rock precariously perched on the side of a cliff. Here the question is whether or not the *status quo* can be maintained; if it is not, the direction of change is clearly predictable. A 'moving equilibrium' is a dynamic situation in which there is no stable *status quo* to be defended or attacked but rather a flux of events presenting greater or lesser opportunities to all parties.

While few social situations are likely to illustrate any of these types perfectly, such a conceptualization provides useful tools for analysis. For example, careful analysis may show that a situation is actually an indifferent equilibrium and that overwhelming support could be found for change – in spite of the initial fears of leaders that strong action could precipitate polarization. In some such situations people are likely to follow the established leadership in almost any direction. As we noted earlier, this was almost certainly the case with respect to American Presidential leadership on the China and Vietnam questions. During the periods of major escalation of the Vietnam War, from 1965–68, when public opinion generally seemed to support all of President Johnson's moves, it is not unlikely that the people would just as readily have supported total disengagement or other alternatives. It is quite possible that the public was interested in supporting the presidency as a basic national institution, but comparatively it was indifferent to particular policies regarding Vietnam.

Or, to use another illustration, during the fragile career of the Weimar Republic, the democratic centre was precariously balanced between a militant left and a militant right – both regarding the centrist regime with contempt. In retrospect, it is evident that this was a 'precarious equilibrium'. The situation was highly unstable; but change, if any, would be toward the right and, ultimately, fascism. Major movement toward the left, as envisaged by Communists and other radical socialists, was never a real option. Social change agents on the left therefore had only the real options of helping to preserve a *status quo* (which might in the long run have proved most useful to them) or permitting power to move sharply to the right – which in fact happened.[15] In the Russian revolutionary situation of 1917 precisely the opposite kind of precarious equilibrium existed. There the military forces, workers, peasants, etc., would hardly have tolerated a swing rightward, back to the Czarist regime. But a fragile centre proved vulnerable to pressure from the Bolsheviks on the left. Those interested in preventing a Communist victory could have acted relevantly in that situation only by strengthening the constitutional democratic regime. There was no possibility of a Czarist restoration.

Such assessments must be made with great care. Timid conservatism may too readily believe that any change will be for the worse. Immature radicalism may too quickly assume that any change will be for the better. Specific analysis of the situation is required.

E.   *Strategic Reliance upon Government*

A very basic strategic question involves the choice of primary reliance upon government as over-against non-governmental power systems for social change. Should churches, for example, deal with poverty or housing problems for the elderly or medical care problems directly (using their own resources) or should they seek to involve the government in such areas? Should the attempt be made to impose more serious governmental regulation or even to nationalize the corporations?

In an analysis of this problem, George D. Beam has argued that in fact little is to be gained through the political arena: 'With the expansion of the civil service to include more and more government employees, with the increasing wealth and consequent power of conglomerates, pension trusts, and insurance companies, and with the continuous demand for technically sophisticated and expensive defence equipment by the military, the *initiative and direction* of American policy has shifted out of the political arena to the areas of administration, economics and the military.' He therefore contends for a strategy of 'action geared toward taking over and making one's own the real factors of contemporary society – the administration, the economy, and the military'.[16] Presumably this should be done directly in some way, not through regular political channels.

It is fairly arguable that non-governmental power centres and the major civil service bureaucracies can be infiltrated or otherwise influenced. Creative efforts have been made to do just that in recent years.[17] The Project for Corporate Responsibility was at least partially successful. Church and educational groups have begun to make some small difference in the policies of corporations and banks through the manipulation of invested funds. Social change movements have in recent years become much more effective in such manoeuvres because of a growing understanding of actual power relationships. In particular, the potential economic power of such hitherto passive institutions as pension funds has been exposed to view. And, of course, highly respectable but otherwise powerless groups can sometimes create bothersome public relations problems for powerful vested interests.

Without overlooking the value of such non-governmental strategic approaches, it needs to be remembered that only government brings to focus the power of the whole conglomerate of social systems making up a national society. As we have already noted, political power is in principle superior to other forms of power, including even private economic wealth. Political power is therefore the maximum point of strategic leverage upon everything else. Private measures can gain control over small segments of decision-making, but only government possesses ultimate power over the whole. For all the difficulties in using the political system, it is still probable that government is the most strategic point of access to the decisions that will affect most social issues. Redistribution of income, control of the environment, international policies, the definition and enforcement of civil rights, control of police policies, reform of prisons, transportation, housing, medical policies, population stabilization – these all can be affected more profoundly by government than by any other form of power.

This should be particularly obvious in relation to economic matters. The funds available from private groups for welfare projects are nothing compared with the sums available through the taxing powers of government. Even with very sacrificial giving, all the churches in America would be hard-pressed to mount a welfare programme equal even to present inadequate public welfare programmes.[18]

This is not to suggest that all social strategy must be oriented toward governmental action. Some objectives doubtless cannot be reached in this way, and sometimes the political climate is so utterly unfavourable as to present the strategist with the choice between actions through private channels or no action at all. Moreover, non-governmental groups can sometimes stimulate social change through small-scale demonstrations of new possibilities or through action to create conditions to which government must then respond. Action in non-governmental groups can also establish power bases relevant to governmental action. Significant power in any non-governmental system is likely in various ways to translate into power in the governmental system itself if approached intelligently.

F. *'The System' and Dilemmas of Strategic Moral Judgment*

Christian social strategy must be committed to ethical criteria of 'effectiveness'. Nothing 'works' unless it succeeds morally. We have already defined the objectives of Christian social strategy as (1) the objective conditions necessary or desirable to the life of persons and communities in the kingdom of God, and (2) the communication of the reconciling reality of that kingdom to persons estranged from it. These proximate goals are understood as serving the fullest possible realization of God's intended loving community of humankind on earth. How does such an understanding of strategic objectives affect our approach to social systems? In a very immediate sense, it precludes our ever treating persons simply as functions of systems or as enemies to be disposed of or disregarded. But it also confronts us with the deeper moral dilemmas anticipated in the preceding chapter.

The basic dilemma remains that posed by Walter Rauschenbusch's statement concerning the difference between Christian and un-Christian social orders: 'An unchristian social order can be known by the fact that it makes good men do bad things . . . a Christian social order makes bad men do good things.' It is plain in this that Christian social strategy must declare war upon all systematizations of violence or racism or economic injustice in which even good people are, in effect, compelled to perpetuate social evil by participating in ordinary institutional life. But, if effective strategy requires use of systems of power, it will involve the change agent in whatever evils there are that are ancillary to the system – whether intended by him or not. Making use of the power systems and structures of society, whether or not these are governmental, almost inevitably involves the Christian in sanctioning coercion or in appealing to sub-Christian motivations or in confirming stratification systems in which 'inferiors' are alienated from 'superiors'.

One necessary answer to this dilemma is that the Christian social strategist, in his choice of methods, places every means under the transcendent criterion of God's ultimate intentions and not merely under the criterion of effectiveness in reaching a proximate goal. Every measurable objective is still only a proximate or penultimate end. Thus, the Christian cannot chart his social strategy on the basis of simple pragmatic calculations. In the more ultimate perspective, some apparently effective approaches are not understood to be effective at all.

But to leave the problem at this point is probably to become irrelevant to most human experience. To be human is to be involved in systems which perpetuate evil; it is even to contribute sometimes to their effectiveness in perpetuating evil. Many even of those who protest most vehemently against the involvement of Christians and churches in immoral social systems urge co-operation with revolutionary movements whose violent methods present prima facie contradictions to the community of love envisaged by Christian ethics. Similarly, Christians who have recoiled at the participation by some of their radical brethren in revolutionary movements have often been blind to their own personal and corporate involvements in vast systems of institutionalized racism and violence. The ultimate criterion of the kindgom of God remains above all Christian strategy and action. But the tension between that criterion and human systems cannot be represented as simple negation.

We return, therefore, again to the concept of moral presumption. Our initial presumption must be in favour of methods and movements believed to be directly consonant with God's intended kingdom of love and justice. Our initial presumption must be against all that seems to alienate or repress or coerce fellow human beings. Such a presumption needs to be open, however, to the possibility that that which is presumed to be the better or worse may, in specific circumstances, not prove to be so. A strategic method which is initially presumed to be wrong will not be employed unless it can be shown to be necessary for the sake, not of a purely proximate end, but of the ultimate end. Would worse evil ultimately befall man if the problematic means were not used than would if it were? As we have already seen, just-war doctrine illustrates the method. According to that doctrine, social violence is presumed to be off limits for Christian participation or approval unless in a given case war is able to meet several criteria. In cases of continuing doubt, one should *not* engage in social violence.

Lest this approach be dismissed too quickly as temporizing with evil, let us remind ourselves that the alternative is some form of anarchism. Anything other than social anarchism is at least open to the use of some social coercion, some reliance upon other than purely voluntary observance of social norms; and thus to limit the moral freedom of others. If we are to sanction and make use of social systems which 'make' bad people do good things, then we are already involved in the use of methods which are problematical under the transcendent criterion of God's kingdom of love. The worst of it is, we may also have to make use of systems which at least tempt good people to do bad things. We may have to rely upon economic or other incentives which foster selfishness, since the functioning of any social system is likely to depend upon motivations which are extraneous to the purposes to which we intend to put it. We may have to make use of stratification systems which deepen human alienation. We may feel that we have to appeal to the unadulterated sense of self-interest of exploited people in order to organize them into an effective new power base for change.[19] In situations where new power bases are manifestly impossible to organize, we may have to co-operate with selfish power elites and thus provide them with further legitimation. But genuinely Christian social strategy does not merely try to weight the negative against the positive in some kind of cost-benefit or preponderance-of-the-evidence analysis. It seeks to maintain the tension by placing an initial burden of proof against the negative. When in doubt, the benefit of the doubt is accorded to the positive.

That the burden of proof can so often be borne results from the universality of human sin. We are required, as Luther saw, to erect dykes against sinfulness. But, as Luther also saw, the human strategy of the gospel must operate in two realms simultaneously: the level of dealing in and through human institutions and the level of proclamation of the gospel. Luther's method of correlating the two tracks was inadequate. But his approach is a useful reminder that it is never enough merely to deal with tangible goals. There must be a parallel strategy of witness.

The social strategies of Martin Luther King, Jr, illustrate a more creative way of relating the two. King was ready when necessary to bargain with corrupt power structures for the sake of tangible improvements in the situation of black people. But the concrete actions of his movement were interpreted as, directed toward, and consistent with human reconciliation. His campaigns were based upon the wise ethical assumption that, if anything, repression more seriously damages the spirit of the oppressor than that of the oppressed. The strategic formula thus included (1) maximum arousal of a sense of injustice and discontent among the oppressed (thus heightening and making more visible the conflict between oppressor and oppressed) combined with (2) strong motivation within the new base of power thus formed for reconciliation with the oppressor – but on the basis of justice rather than subservience. The combination represented by this formula relieves the first part from self-centredness by emphasizing that both the oppressed and the oppressor have a common (though often unrecognized) interest in overcoming injustice. Love for the oppressor requires us to insist that he abandon oppression. The strategy was effective politically in that its commitment to non-violence tended to shift the onus for violent counter-reactions on to the opponent – thus extending its own base of political power to include many of those who abhor violence and disorder. The strategy had revolutionary impact upon American society. But it was not revolutionary with respect to the basic constitutional system. Its victories, by and large, needed to be registered *within* the political system in the form of new definitions of rights and responsibilities.

Subsequent spokesmen for the New Left have questioned not only whether strategic objectives can be gained effectively through democratic political processes, but even whether it is moral to try. George D. Beam, for instance, cites the tendency in 'usual politics' to confuse 'the values of democracy with the means used to attain them'. He argues that the procedures of majority rule and compromise can result in gross evils. Compromise is to be rejected 'when the procedure does not result in the implementation of democratic values'.[20]

This viewpoint, which cannot be considered in detail here, raises the broader question of what stake a Christian social strategy may have in the maintenance of procedural systems. To be committed to a procedural system, as Beam rightly notes, is to be willing to accept a distasteful outcome. But the whole history of civilized human life suggests the preferability of procedural systems other than raw power struggles. Compromises resulting from commitment to what is regarded on the whole as being a good procedural system have to be evaluated not simply in terms of the immediate issue at stake but also in terms of the wider social results of breaking down the procedural system itself. The *nature* of the procedural system is thus itself of concern to Christian social strategy. A procedural system based solely upon majority rule, without provision for the guarantee of certain basic rights, could not be accepted as ideal by Christians. This point has already been discussed in relation to democratic political ideology. A truly democratic procedural system can be given presumptive status by Christian social strategy.

G.   *The Systematic Consolidation of Strategy*

Much social strategy fails, ultimately, not because it is defeated but because its victories are not consolidated and preserved. Even revolutionary strategies may not be prepared for consolidation on a *moral* plane. It may simply be assumed that the new power elite will of course govern *for* the people whereas the old governed *against* them. But Christian social strategy is concerned, not simply with the attainment of conditions more conducive to God's intended community of love and justice, but also with the permanence and future improvement of those conditions and with the way in which people respond to each other in the new situation. In part, the institutionalization of new conditions into social systems may require some new reliance upon social coercion or even violence – as when laws establish penalties for the violation of the civil rights of others or when new cultural attitudes make it less profitable for businessmen to pollute the water and air. But effective consolidation in a Christian perspective seeks to incorporate opponents into the acceptance of new definitions of justice and human decency. Moral consolidation is incomplete without reconciliation. The prospect of reconciliation should, as we have emphasized in other words, be an ultimate criterion of Christian strategy.

Notes

1 Moral Commitment and Ethical Uncertainty

1. This way of stating the problem of the volume is, of course, quite Kantian. The distinction between moral will and moral intelligence and judgment lies at the heart of all of Kant's writings on ethics. The following passage is characteristic: 'The supreme principle of all moral judgment lies in the understanding: that of the moral incentive to action lies in the heart. This motive is moral feeling. We must guard against confusing the principle of the judgment with the principle of the motive. The first is the norm; the second the incentive. The motive cannot take the place of the rule. Where the motive is wanting, the error is practical; but when the judgment fails the error is theoretical.' Immanuel Kant, *Lectures on Ethics*, Harper and Row, New York and Evanston 1963 [ca. 1780], tr. Louis Infield, pp. 36–37. This distinction is, however, also assumed by most thinkers in the history of ethics, even though some have attempted to reduce morality entirely to the will, as though we could be sure that a good person would always do good things, and some others have attempted to reduce it entirely to the mind, as though we could be sure that an intelligent person would always be a person of good will. The basic approach to Christian moral judgment to be outlined in the present volume will differ from Kant's in important respects.

2. See particularly H. Richard Niebuhr, *Radical Monotheism and Western Culture*, Harper and Brothers, New York 1960.

3. These three approaches are distinguished from one another and elaborated in H. Richard Niebuhr, *The Responsible Self: An Essay in Christian Moral Philosophy*, Harper and Row, New York 1963, and Edward LeRoy Long, Jr, *A Survey of Christian Ethics*, Oxford University Press, New York 1967.

4. This point is made particularly forcefully in Paul A. Carter, *The Decline and Revival of the Social Gospel: Social and Political Liberalism in American Protestant Churches, 1920-1940*, Cornell University Press, Ithaca, New York 1956, pp. 44, 92–95.

5. Encyclical *Casti Connubii*, paragraph 54.

6. Frederick Elder, *Crisis in Eden: A Religious Study of Man and*

Environment, Abingdon Press, Nashville 1970, contrasts 'inclusionist' and 'exclusionist' views of the relationship of man to nature. The latter emphasizes man's separation from and mastery over nature. The former sees man as a part of nature and dependent upon it. Obviously this 'inclusionist' perspective would tend to be closer to the older natural law theories by stressing the normativeness of nature. By whatever name, the 'inclusionist' view has clearly (and properly) made a significant impact on thinking in recent years. This has been a useful corrective to the practical and theoretical arrogance of a generation of secular pragmatism priding itself upon having come of age in the mastery of all things. Nevertheless, is there not a permanent, irreducible sense in which humanity has been given a kind of dominion (for good or ill) over nature? Do not man's intellectual and technological capabilities give him a uniqueness which could be claimed by no other aspect of nature?

7. Leo Pfeffer has commented that 'it is substantially true that the problem of compulsion in religion is a heritage of the monotheistic worship which Moses commanded must, under penalty of death, be accorded to a jealous God. The history of religious persecution flows directly from Moses' command to slay the three thousand men who worshipped the golden calf to the Spanish Inquisition and the exiling of Roger Williams and Anne Hutchinson by the Puritan fathers.' *Church, State, and Freedom*, Beacon Press, Boston 1953, p. 6. See also Francesco Ruffini, *Religious Liberty*, tr. J. Parker Heyes, Putnam, New York 1912, p. 19, for a similar analysis.

8. Tillich, *The Protestant Era*, tr. James Luther Adams, University of Chicago Press 1948, p. xii.

9. Ibid.

10. Ibid., p. xiv.

11. Ibid., p. xv.

12. See Reinhold Niebuhr, *The Nature and Destiny of Man*, Scribner, New York 1943, II, pp. 213 ff.

13. Richard Niebuhr, *Radical Monotheism and Western Culture*, loc. cit.

14. Dietrich Bonhoeffer, *Letters and Papers from Prison*, tr. Reginald H. Fuller, Macmillan, New York 1962 [1953], Letter to Bethge, 8 July 1944, p. 214, and Enlarged Edition, SCM Press 1971, p. 346.

15. Ibid., 18 July 1944, p. 222 and p. 361.

16. Gabriel Vahanian, *No Other God*, George Braziller, New York 1966, p. 32.

17. Joseph Fletcher, *Situation Ethics: The New Morality*, Westminster Press and SCM Press 1966, p. 59.

18. Ibid., p. 68. The point is obscured, however, by his earlier assertion concerning love that it 'is for the sake of people and it is not a good-in-itself', p. 61.

19. Ibid., pp. 95, 71, 26, 31.

20. Ibid., p. 67.

21. Ibid., p. 61.

22. See especially his books *Justice and the Social Order*, tr. Mary Hottinger, Harper, New York 1945, and *The Divine Imperative*, tr. Olive Wyon. Westminster Press 1947.

23. Paul Ramsey, *Deeds and Rules in Christian Ethics*, Scribner, New York 1967, pp. 216–217.

24. Fletcher, op. cit., p. 136.

25. It is a curious thing that Fletcher has referred to Immanuel Kant as 'the grandfather of modern ethical absolutizers' (p. 128). This is true in so far as Kant regarded certain formal principles and even certain rules (notably the rule against lying) as absolute. But it is also Kant who was the grandfather of those who, like Fletcher, regard only the will as intrinsically good.

26. Paul L. Lehmann, *Ethics in a Christian Context*, Harper and Row, New York and Evanston 1963, p. 17.

27. Ibid., pp. 131, 159, etc.

28. Ibid., p. 131.

29. Lehmann acknowledges that 'ethics, as Kant has eloquently and elaborately explained, is intrinsically volitional, being concerned with the willing acceptance of a claim' (pp. 75–76).

30. It may be unfortunate semantically that Lehmann elected to make this point by substituting 'is' for 'ought' in the situation of specific choice or action. By insisting upon the terminology 'what I am to do' he suggests to many readers either that a person facing a decision actually has no freedom of choice or that among the available alternatives it does not matter ethically which is chosen. Both of these interpretations would be far from Lehmann's intention in insisting upon an 'indicative' ethic.

31. Lehmann, op. cit., p. 123.

32. Ibid., p. 85.

33. Ibid., p. 159.

34. Ibid., p. 141.

35. Ibid., p. 125.

36. W. A. Visser 't Hooft and J. H. Oldham, *The Church and Its Function in Society*, Willett Clark, Chicago 1937, p. 210.

37. John C. Bennett, *Christian Ethics and Social Policy*, Scribner, New York 1946, p. 77.

38. Ibid., pp. 76–77.

39. In later writing, Bennett has distinguished between 'normative' and 'descriptive' types of middle axioms. The former states an objective to guide policy; the latter describes the relationship between some condition and a normative principle. See his article, 'Principles and the Context', in John C. Bennett, et al., *Storm over Ethics*, United Church Press, Philadelphia 1967.

40. *Christian Ethics and Social Policy*, pp. 120–121.

41. Ramsey, *Basic Christian Ethics*, Scribner, New York 1950. Ramsey acknowledges that his position has changed significantly at this point since this book was written.

42. Ibid., p. 340.

43. Ibid., p. 351.
44. *Deeds and Rules in Christian Ethics*, pp. 123–144. In this essay, Ramsey endeavours to appropriate the insights of Professor John Rawls to the task of Christian social ethics.
45. Ibid., p. 123.
46. Ibid., p. 125.
47. Ibid., p. 127.
48. Ibid., p. 128.
49. Ibid., p. 129.
50. See also, John Rawls, 'Two Concepts of Rules', in *Ethics*, LXXVI, 3 (April 1966), pp. 192–207.
51. *Deeds and Rules in Christian Ethics*, p. 135.
52. Ibid., p. 137.
53. Ibid., p. 128.
54. To be sure, Ramsey's just war principle of discrimination, developed in his book *War and the Christian Conscience: How Shall Modern War Be Conducted Justly?*, Duke University Press, Durham, N. C. 1961, does specify that certain acts in war may be considered immoral regardless of beneficent consequences. The torture or murder of innocent hostages in order to determine the will of an enemy would be such an act, even if entered into from the most loving of motives. But it is doubtful whether Ramsey can make this stick as a general rule apart from an assessment either of consequences (such as, in the long run and on the whole more lovelessness will be set loose among people when such deeds are done regardless of hoped-for gains in the short run) or of the relationship between the act and its motivation. Cf. another kind of criticism of Ramsey's use of the twin principles of discrimination and proportion by Joseph Allen in his article, 'The Relation of Strategy and Morality', in *Ethics*, LXXIII, pp. 167–178. According to Allen, Ramsey's line of argument ultimately 'would produce an ethic with two (or more) irreconcilable ultimate principles – consequences on the one hand and a set of independently established limits on the other. It really argues for an ethic of intuition, one in which no evidence can be given for the intrinsic wrongness of an act except that "any rational man will see" ' (p. 170).
55. See Edgar S. Brightman, *Moral Laws*, Abingdon Press, New York 1933, L. Harold DeWolf, *Responsible Freedom: Guidelines to Christian Action*, Harper and Row 1971, and Walter G. Muelder, *Moral Law in Christian Social Ethics*, John Knox Press, Richmond, Virginia 1966.
56. Walter G. Muelder, op. cit., pp. 152–156.
57. J. H. Yoder, *The Politics of Jesus*, Eerdmans, Grand Rapids, Michigan 1972.
58. Ibid., p. 110.
59. Ibid., p. 192.
60. See particularly Jacques Ellul, *Violence: Reflections from a Christian Perspective*, tr. Cecelia Gual Kings, Seabury Press, New York 1969 and SCM Press 1970.
61. Ibid., pp. 93–115.

2   The Concept of Methodological Presumption

1. Thus Fletcher comments that '. . . when John Bennett pleads, in the spirit of Luther's *pecca fortiter*, that "there are situations in which the best we can do is evil", we have to oppose what he says – much as we admire its spirit. . . . *The situationist holds that whatever is the most loving thing in the situation is the right and good thing.* It is not excusably evil, it is positively good.' *Situation Ethics*, pp. 64–65. In making this kind of statement Fletcher must overlook the distinction between 'evil' and 'sin'. See our discussion of the problem of necessary evil in Chapter 4 below.

2. See Arthur M. Schlesinger, Jr, *A Thousand Days: John F. Kennedy in the White House*, Houghton Mifflin, Boston 1965, p. 296, Robert F. Kennedy, *Thirteen Days: A Memoir of the Cuban Missile Crisis*, W. W. Norton, New York 1969, p. 36, and Kenneth P. O'Donnell and David F. Powers, *'Johnny, We Hardly Knew Ye': Memories of John Fitzgerald Kennedy*, Little, Brown and Co., Boston 1972, pp. 312 ff. and 361 ff.

3. Milton Friedman, *Capitalism and Freedom*, University of Chicago Press 1962. Arguing against governmental provision of the National Parks, Friedman writes that 'if the public wants this kind of an activity enough to pay for it, private enterprises will have every incentive to provide such parks' (p. 31). He reluctantly agrees that it would be impracticable to operate regular highways and roads on a free enterprise basis but thinks that long-distance turnpikes should be privately owned and operated (pp. 30–31). These positions are clearly very extreme. But for our purposes the interesting thing is that this influential conservative economist always requires specific and overwhelming justification for public ownership. In his judgment private ownership should always be the presumptive norm.

4. J. K. Galbraith, *The Affluent Society*, Houghton, Mifflin, Boston 1958. This presumption against expansion of the private sector is even more obvious, of course, in the writings of such socialist theoreticians as Michael Harrington.

5. See our discussion of social strategy in Chapter 8 below.

6. For more than thirty years Ramsey has offered general support for American military and foreign policy positions, including a sturdy defence of the American involvement in Vietnam. (One exception to this overall pattern of support has been his insistence that American use of nuclear weapons should be limited to the disablement of actual enemy forces and not directed against cities. Even here, of course, Ramsey has not opposed the development and potential use of nuclear capability as such.) The comparatively routine support which he has offered for basic American policies contrasts with the considerable fluctuation in his methodological position between the writing of *Basic Christian Ethics* in 1950, with its more situational approach, and the later just war writings,

which come close to the natural law position and in any event involve a more principled methodology. One may therefore question the extent to which his basic methodological position has been the determinative factor in his judgment on military and foreign policy issues – which is to say that his operative methodology has perhaps not been revealed fully in his methodological writings.

7. Paragraph 79.

8. Paragraphs 140–141.

9. Walter Rauschenbusch, *Christianity and the Social Crisis*, Macmillan, New York 1907, pp. 361–2.

10. Report of Section III, 'Social Questions – The Responsible Society in a World Perspective'.

11. The following conditions are usually cited, in one form or another, as criteria for justified war: (1) the cause must be just, (2) war must be duly declared by a legitimate political authority, (3) the war truly must be a last resort, (4) the means of waging war must be fair and just, (5) there must be a reasonable expectation of victory, (6) it must be reasonably predictable that the evil of the war itself will be less than the anticipated and present evil if the war is not undertaken, (7) throughout hostilities, the combatant must maintain a right intention, and (8) the war must be viewed only as means to a better peace.

12. Paul Tillich, *Love, Power, and Justice*, Oxford University Press, New York 1954, p. 49.

13. Paul Ramsey, *The Just War: Force and Political Responsibility*, Scribner, New York 1968, p. 275.

14. Ibid. This concept of a shift in presumption at the point of a war's actual commencing raises problems which need further examination. Ramsey's argument is offered here only as a particularly good illustration of procedural presumption.

3 Positive Moral Presumptions of Christian Faith

1. Christianity is not unique in this respect. Other religions, including Islam, Buddhism, Hinduism, and Marxism, tend also to contain the widest diversity of interpretation and to change mainly through an internal process of re-interpretation. It is only when an adherent discovers that he can no longer re-interpret the religious tradition that he either abandons it or turns his back upon the implications of his own direct life experience by compartmentalizing life. It would be interesting, as a test of these observations, to compare the experience of the authors of *The God that Failed*, all of whom became disillusioned with Marxism, with the experience of the European Marxist philosophers, such as Ernst Bloch, and Milan Machovec, all of whom have continued to grapple with the deeper questions of human existence in the light of Marxist tradition.

2. See, for example, Thomas J. J. Altizer, *The Gospel of Christian*

Atheism, Westminster Press, Philadelphia 1966, and William Hamilton, *The New Essence of Christianity*, Association Press, New York 1961. These writings can be compared with the franker abandonment of theological language altogether in the attempt to construct a humanistic ethics without any presupposition of God, in Paul Kurtz (ed.), *Moral Problems in Contemporary Society: Essays in Humanistic Ethics*, Prentice-Hall, Englewood Cliffs, N. J. 1969. 'Value,' to Kurtz, 'is relative to man and to what human beings find to be worthwhile in experience.' According to this humanistic interpretation, 'human existence is probably a random occurrence existing between two oblivions ... death is inevitable ... there is a tragic aspect to our lives, and ... all moral values are our own creations' (p. 4).

3. I suspect that the difficulty of speaking of God in ethics today has three important roots, all based on misunderstanding or naiveté: (1) There is first the belief that God means some definite thing which limits the creative moral freedom of any person foolish enough to believe in it. (2) There is the notion that God, to be validated epistemologically, must be verified with self-evident clarity in phenomenal experience. (3) There is the optimistic assumption that creative moral freedom is a possibility in a universe in which moral freedom does not pertain to the essence of being. These points need to be considered carefully. The first evidently presupposes a tyrannical or manipulative view of God – ironically, the view of God against which St Paul himself rebelled in distinguishing between 'law' and 'grace' (Romans, Galatians). On a purely human plane, it is clear that interpersonal relationships limit our creativity or our freedom only in so far as one party exercises some kind of tyranny over the other. But when human beings fully affirm each other and experience life together, the effect is not one of limiting but rather one of expanding the boundlessness of human creative freedom. Paul's claim, which has been reaffirmed by many Christians, is that God – far from limiting our freedom – is, when understood in a Christian context, the *source* of it. A Christian understanding of God is personal. The meaning of Paul's conception of 'justification' is that God does not relate to man as a doer of specified things commanded; rather, God accepts man first as a free being: 'So through God you are no longer a slave but a son, and if a son then an heir' (Galatians 4.7). God *affirms* man, *as* man, which means as a free, creative being. Such a statement grates upon many contemporary ears, not because of the understanding of man, but because the conception of God imposed by language must be somewhat anthropomorphic in order to be altogether personal. One must, as it were, continually revalidate the word by remarking that God is a symbol for a personal view of ultimate reality. Of course God is infinitely more than man or than any language we can use to describe him. But those who find difficulty in 'God-talk' ought to ask the reverse question whether it is really comprehensible that man could be infinitely more than that which accounts for his being.

A response to the second difficulty is here anticipated. Verification of

God in phenomenal terms is impossible by definition. For God to be real, he must be the *basis* of nature; he cannot be located *within* nature in the sense that he is an object alongside other objects. God pertains to the whole of being, not to some aspect of being. The answer to the question of the nature of being must, for all of us, be a kind of conjecture. At bottom it is a faith claim. Such a faith claim inevitably regards some limited aspect of experience as providing a decisive clue as to the nature of all of being. (A rational person will apply epistemological tests of consistency, coherence, and parsimony, but it is not finally possible for anyone to experience the whole of reality personally.) Thus Paul's affirmation that 'God was in Christ reconciling the world to himself' (II Corinthians 5.19a) and the identification in Colossians of Christ as 'the image of the invisible God' (1.15) and the affirmation by the author of the Fourth Gospel that 'the Word became flesh and dwelt among us' (John 1.14a) involve Christian faith claims to the effect that the life of Jesus Christ fundamentally reveals the character of reality. Paul Tillich's concept of God as 'being-itself' may be criticized as ambiguous and possibly reductionist, but there should be no question that he has correctly located God for modern man at the point of the ontological question. God either pertains to the whole of being, or God is indeed superfluous. Again, the question is what is the nature of the whole of reality. The Christian's faith in God is a kind of answer. So is Kurtz's view that 'Nature . . . is blind to human purposes and indifferent to human ideals'. *Moral Problems in Contemporary Society*, p. 3. The Christian's faith is a moral faith, for the God who is understood by it is in personal relationship with human persons.

The third point thus arises as to whether, indeed, moral freedom is even possible in a universe in which moral freedom does not itself pertain to the essence of being. In a purely impersonal universe, in which man's transcendent freedom is the lone exception to the otherwise fixed (or at least unconscious) causal relationships, it is difficult to see human life as more than happenstance and tragedy. This may indeed be the human predicament. Kurtz, and many others, believe so. There is no way to *prove* the contrary. But neither can it be said that the more optimistic view of human life and destiny is irrational.

4. This, too, is not to be identified with major figures, such as Gustavo Gutierrez or Rosemary Ruether, both of whom seek to preserve a transcendent dimension to our relationship with the conditions of worldly experience without surrendering to individualism or otherworldliness. See Gustavo Gutierrez, *A Theology of Liberation: History, Politics and Salvation*, tr. Sister Caridad Inda and John Eagleson, Orbis Books, Maryknoll, New York 1973 and SCM Press 1974, and Ruether, *Liberation Theology: Human Hope Confronts Christian History and American Power*, Paulist Press, New York 1972.

5. Dietrich Bonhoeffer, *Ethics*, tr. Neville Horton Smith, Macmillan, New York and SCM Press 1955, p. 133.

6. Ibid., p. 134.

7. Ibid., p. 137.

8. Ibid.

9. These mandates, which bear a striking resemblance to the more traditional Lutheran concept of 'orders', are listed by Bonhoeffer as the church, marriage and the family, culture, and government. Ibid., pp. 288 ff.

10. Karl Barth, *Church Dogmatics*, ed. G. W. Bromiley and T. F. Torrance, III/1, T. and T. Clark, Edinburgh 1958.

11. Ibid., p. 46.

12. Ibid., p. 97.

13. This point is underscored by Paul Ramsey, *The Patient as Person*, Yale University Press, New Haven 1970, p. 151, although Ramsey strongly opposes actual euthanasia. Joseph Fletcher's *Morals and Medicine*, Princeton University Press 1954 remains the most vigorous attempt to support direct euthanasia on Christian theological grounds, although he also places a substantial burden of proof against it.

14. *Crisis in Eden*, pp. 83 ff.

15. Erich Fromm, *May Man Prevail? An Inquiry into the Facts and Fictions of Foreign Policy*, Doubleday, Garden City, New York 1961, p. 196.

16. Bertrand Russell, *Why I am not a Christian, and Other Essays* (New York: Simon and Schuster 1957). This is from the essay, 'A Free Man's Worship', originally published in 1903, p. 115.

17. One biographer, however, quotes him as saying 'I wanted to save a half million boys on our side and as many on the other side. I never lost any sleep over my decision.' Alfred Steinberg, *The Man from Missouri: The Life and Times of Harry S. Truman*, Putnam, New York 1962, p. 259.

18. Cf. Philip Wogaman, *Protestant Faith and Religious Liberty*, Abingdon Press, Nashville 1967, for a more extended discussion of the significance of religious freedom.

19. Americans who think of their own country as an ideal exemplar of respect for freedom usually are thinking of the dominant mainstream of respectable opinion, with which they associate themselves. Freedom has certainly been accorded the expression of mainstream views. But such Americans often forget that important test cases before the US Supreme Court have usually involved the views and practices of less popular sectarian groups such as Jehovah's Witnesses and the Communist Party.

20. L. Harold DeWolf, *Responsible Freedom*, pp. 102–110.

21. Paul Lehmann, *Ethics in a Christian Context*, pp. 57 ff.

22. Joseph Haroutunian, *God with Us: A Theology of Transpersonal Life*, Westminster Press 1965, p. 17.

23. Report of Section V on Intergroup Relations: The Churches Amid Racial and Ethnic Tensions, Second Assembly, World Council of Churches (Evanston, 1954) in *The Evanston Report*, Harper and Brothers, New York 1955, p. 153.

24. 'Race' may be defined as a social category based upon socially perceived physical differences. The net consensus after much scientific study of 'race' is that the term says much more about sociology than biology. Any single physical characteristic (skin colouration, hair, nose, stature, etc.) taken to mark the members of what are socially referred to as 'races' can be replicated within other 'racial' groups, and members of 'races' can be found who do not have this or that of the specified physical characteristic. Intellectual, moral, and emotional traits alleged to be characteristic of certain 'racial' groups are, if real to any extent, social and cultural in origin. From a moral standpoint, therefore, it is a very risky proposition to treat race ontologically. For a useful survey of the basic biological and socio-cultural factors in race, see the UNESCO volume, *The Race Question in Modern Science*, William Morrow and Co., New York 1956.

25. It is to be remembered that not all separatism is, strictly speaking, racial. There exist among black Americans a whole fabric of symbols and meanings expressing the common experience of oppression. People who have experienced oppression together have something in common as a basis for relationship which can hardly be present in their relationships with those who have not had this experience. Intense common experience is an authentic basis for friendship which is not exclusionary in principle. It becomes exclusionary when other kinds of deep human relationship, not founded in the particular common experience, are resisted. In racial relations it is very important for persons of groups with a history of repressing others to be brought into a deep human understanding of what that repression has meant to its victims.

26. This is a point which Martin Luther King Jr and the Southern Christian Leadership Conference understood very well. Far from retreating from relationships, this movement encouraged black people to assert new forms of moral leadership *in* the old relationships, thus transforming them.

27. Ironically, the newer nations have by and large tended to take the United Nations more seriously than have the great powers. The failure of the United States to accord a strong enough presumption for the United Nations in the formulation of its foreign policy during the late 1950s and early 1960s may have resulted in the loss of a golden opportunity to use the new nationalism of Asia, Africa, and Latin America as a positive resource in forging stronger international political institutions.

28. See W. T. Blackstone, 'On the Meaning and Justification of Equality Principle', *The Concept of Equality*, ed. W. T. Blackstone, Burgess Publishing Co., Minneapolis 1969, pp. 115 ff.

29. S. I. Benn and R. S. Peters are right in asserting that equality is not necessarily implied by belief in one God as Father of all humankind: 'This cannot be a rational demonstration – common divine paternity no more entails the principle of equal consideration than common human paternity entails an equal patrimony.' At the same time, these writers are right in treating human equality as a root moral question on the level

where issues are decided by a moral choice. A moral choice in favour of human equality is, however, profoundly supported by faith in a God who *does* love his human children equally. See S. I. Benn and R. S. Peters, 'Justice and Equality', in ibid., p. 63.

30. Karl Barth became convinced that the utter loss of any sinner in death or damnation is inconsistent with the sweep of divine grace in the long run. While this view is in obvious tension with a great deal of New Testament material, such as the parable of the last judgment in Matthew 25, the latter can, of course, be treated as metaphorical.

31. G. F. Hegel, *The Phenomenology of Mind*, tr. J. B. Baillie, 2nd rev. ed., London 1949, pp. 229–240. Suggested by Andrew J. Reck, 'The Metaphysics of Equality' in Blackstone, ed., op. cit., p. 138.

32. Ralf Dahrendorf, 'On the Origin of Social Inequality', in Blackstone, ed., op. cit., pp. 106, 108.

33. The alienative effects of wealth and power are obvious enough and have been the object of literature since man became literate. The similar effects of social prestige are not so obvious. Nevertheless, the deference from others that is implied by prestige may be even more dangerous. Entering into every relationship between persons of high prestige and those who defer to them there is the implication that the opinions, tastes, etc., of the former are alone worthy of consideration. Authentic interpersonal communication is thus greatly impeded. The pattern of racial inequality in American life made genuine relationship between whites and blacks almost impossible for this reason. The higher prestige of the white and the requirement that black people show deference through ritualized patterns of speech and behaviour effectively destroyed mutuality at any deep level. Consequently, both white and black Americans were diminished as persons. An important part of the 'loneliness' of which prominent people sometimes ambivalently complain is exactly this. How could one help being lonely if there were no one from whom one could expect genuine, honest response as a fellow human being? Still, prestige is a fascinating goal. It fascinates one with the illusory promise that 'up there' (in status terms) one will find that fuller response from one's fellows which is involved in the quest for human fulfilment.

34. John Rawls, *A Theory of Justice*, Harvard University Press, Cambridge, Mass. 1972, pp. 14–15.

35. See Philip Wogaman, *Guaranteed Annual Income: The Moral Issues*, Abingdon Press, Nashville 1968, pp. 71–74.

4 Negative Moral Presumptions

1. John Dillenberger, *God Hidden and Revealed: The Interpretation of Luther's Deus Absconditus and its Significance for Religious Thought*, Muhlenberg Press, Philadelphia 1953, p. xvi.

2. See particularly Reinhold Niebuhr, *The Nature and Destiny of Man*, Vol. I, Scribner 1941.

3. Harry F. Ward, *In Place of Profit: Social Incentives in the Soviet Union*, Scribner 1933.

4. Reinhold Niebuhr at one point went so far as to argue that Marxist Communism poses greater danger even than Nazism, since the latter lacked the smokescreen of universal utopian idealism which has masked the former's unscrupulous policies: 'The important point is that the ruthless power operates behind a screen of pretended ideal ends, a situation which is both more dangerous and more evil than pure cynical defiance of moral ends.' *Christian Realism and Political Problems*, Scribner 1953, pp. 37–38. I am unwilling to go this far because Marxism does avoid the barbarities of racism, because it does have some openness to new truth via its conception of science (although its social science remains highly dogmatic), and because its attitude toward ultimate human freedom does have some ambiguous possibilities. Some Marxist philosophers, including Milan Machovec and Cajo Petrovic, have demonstrated that there are more flexible interpretations of Marxism which can arise, with however much difficulty, even within Marxist societies.

5. Robert S. Lecky and H. Elliott Wright (eds), *Black Manifesto: Religion, Racism and Reparations*, Sheed and Ward, New York 1969, pp. 114 ff.

6. Quoted by Mark Shermin, *The Extremists*, Seabury Press, p. 110.

7. Fred Schwarz, *You Can Trust the Communists (to be Communists)*, Prentice-Hall, Englewood Cliffs 1960, p. 2: '... you can trust the Communists. They are extremely trustworthy. You can trust a cancer cell to obey the laws of its lawless growth. You can trust an armed bank robber to take the money and try to escape. Similarly, you can trust the Communists to act in accordance with the laws of their being.'

8. Gail Kennedy (ed.), *Democracy and the Gospel of Wealth*, Heath, Boston 1949, p. xii.

9. Walter Rauschenbusch, *Christianity and the Social Crisis*, pp. 361–2.

10. Saul D. Alinsky, *Reveille for Radicals*, University of Chicago Press 1945.

11. *The Stoic Philosophy of Seneca*, tr. Moses Hadas, Peter Smith, Gloucester, Mass. 1965, p. 236.

12. Ibid. p. 227.

13. Ibid., p. 236.

14. 'A good man would be under compulsion to wage no wars at all, if there were not such things as just wars. A just war, moreover, is justified only by the injustice of an aggressor; and that injustice ought to be a source of grief to any good man, because it is human injustice.' Augustine, *City of God*, Book XIX, Chapter 7. See also Chapter 12.

15. Leo Tolstoy, *My Religion*, Crowell and Co., New York 1885.

16. See especially Leo Tolstoy, *The Kingdom of God is Within You*, tr. Leo Wiener, Farrar, Straus and Cudahy, New York 1961 [1905].

17. Jacques Ellul, *Violence: Reflections from a Christian Perspective*.

18. Ibid., pp. 93 ff.

19. See especially *The Politics of Jesus*, loc. cit. and *Karl Barth and the Problem of War*, Abingdon Press, Nashville 1970.
20. *The Politics of Jesus*, p. 241.
21. Ibid., p. 236.
22. Ibid.
23. Ibid., p. 239.
24. Ibid., p. 112.
25. Ibid., p. 245.
26. *Karl Barth and the Problem of War*.
27. Ibid., pp. 73–74.
28. Ellul, op. cit., p. 167.
29. See 'Notes for Officers', in *Tolstoy's Writings on Civil Disobedience and Non-Violence*, Bergman, New York 1967, p. 36.
30. Karl Barth, *Church Dogmatics*, III/4, p. 455.

5 Polar Moral Presumptions

1. L. Harold DeWolf, p. 176.
2. Edward LeRoy Long, Jr, *A Survey of Christian Ethics*. See especially Section IV.
3. *Nichomachean Ethics*, tr. W. D. Ross, Book II, Chapter 9.
4. George J. Stigler, 'The Proper Goals of Economic Policy', in *Journal of Business* (July 1958), p. 714.
5. Benito Mussolini, *The Political and Social Doctrine of Fascism*, tr. Jane Soames, Hogarth Press, London 1933. Reprinted in John Somerville and Ronald E. Santoni, (eds), *Social and Political Philosophy*, Doubleday Anchor, Garden City, New York 1963, p. 426.
6. Karl Barth, *Christ and Adam*, tr. T. A. Small, Harper and Brothers, New York 1956, p. 91.
7. Friedman, *Capitalism and Freedom*.
8. H. Richard Niebuhr, *The Responsible Self*, pp. 61, 68.
9. In another context, I have argued that there is a form of religious liberty which must be considered absolute: namely, freedom from any requirement to profess beliefs which one does not hold or to engage in overt forms of worship which one does not accept. I continue to believe that no case can be made for abrogating that freedom on grounds of social responsibility, for what such denial of freedom actually means is the obliteration of the freedom side of the polarity altogether. We cannot say quite the same thing in respect to freedom of expression of ideas, although I continue to believe that that freedom should be treated as a 'near absolute'. The burden of proof should rest heavily against any restriction of freedom of expression, although that burden could possibly be met in cases where one person's exercise of the freedom seriously undermines that of others or where what the US Supreme Court once described as 'verbal actions' are involved (such as crying 'fire'! in a crowded theatre or inciting a mob to violent action). For further discussion of forms and

limitations upon freedom see my *Protestant Faith and Religious Liberty*, pp. 182–190.

10. Henry David Thoreau, 'On the Duty of Civil Disobedience', in Somerville and Santoni (eds), op. cit., p. 282.

11. Pope John XXIII suggested the need for invoking a higher level of collectivity in his encyclical *Pacem in Terris:* 'It can be said, therefore, that at this historical moment the present system of organization and the way its principle of authority operates on a world basis no longer correspond to the objective requirements of the universal common good.' Paragraph 135.

12. Note, for example, Milton Kotler's comment in a work on neighbourhood government: 'In short, our knowledge has been misguided in the direction of globalism. World power, not local liberty, captivated our imaginations for so long that it has distracted us from practical thought and civic emotions. For who really cares about the globe! That issue was settled when we discovered it was round.' *Neighborhood Government: The Local Foundations of Political Life*, Bobbs-Merrill, Indianapolis and New York 1969, p. xii. Cf. Charles Hampden-Turner, *From Poverty to Dignity: A Strategy for Poor Americans*, Doubleday, Garden City, New York 1974, which stresses development of 'Community Development Corporations', local institutions, as the best way to overcome poverty.

13. *Christianity and the Social Crisis*, p. 90.

14. *Christianizing the Social Order*, Macmillan, New York 1912, pp. 128 ff.

15. Quoted by John K. Roth, *Freedom and the Moral Life: The Ethics of William James*, Westminster Press 1969, p. 70.

16. Quoted by F. Ernest Johnson, *A Vital Encounter: Christianity and Communism*, Abingdon Press, Nashville 1962, pp. 31–32.

6 Presumptions of Human Authority

1. One of the best summaries of the insights of reference group theory remains Robert K. Merton, *Social Theory and Social Structure*, rev. 3rd ed., The Free Press, Glencoe, Illinois 1957, pp. 225–386. See also Eleanor E. Maccoby, Theodore M. Newcomb, and Eugene L. Hartley (eds), *Readings in Social Psychology*, 3rd ed., Holt and Co., New York 1958, pp. 265–290. Need we remind ourselves that such theory is not merely speculative? It is an intellectually disciplined attempt to account for observed factual experience.

2. W. W. Charters Jr and Theodore M. Newcomb, 'Some Attitudinal Effects of Experimentally Increased Salience of a Membership Group', in Maccoby, Newcomb, and Hartley (eds), op. cit., p. 276.

3. Charles Hampden-Turner, *From Poverty to Dignity*, pp. 23–27.

4. Solomon E. Asch, 'Effects of Group Pressure upon the Modification and Distortion of Judgments', in Maccoby, Newcomb, and Hartley (eds), op. cit., pp. 174–183.

5. Such experiments, which were carried out at Stanford University and elsewhere, also raised serious moral questions concerning the ethics of such an experimental programme.

6. Margaret Mead, *Culture and Commitment: A Study of the Generation Gap*, Doubleday, Garden City, New York 1970.

7. Ibid., p. 78.

8. What Max Weber refers to as 'charismatic authority' should possibly be excluded, although it should be remembered that that form of authority includes elements of rationality along with the non-rational persuasiveness of the leader. Charismatic authority can be either Christian or the furthest thing from it, but our response to it is so largely intuitive that it is difficult to anticipate its emergence intelligently. Without totally excluding this form of human authority and without discounting either its inevitability or desirability in human society (and without forgetting that all forms of authority can be expressed with a charismatic dimension), our own discussion of forms of human moral authority will be confined to those which can be defined and anticipated rationally.

9. *Ethics in a Christian Context*, esp. pp. 45–101.

10. I do not wish to overstate this point. Sub-Christian valuations reflecting racism, nationalism, and class interests have certainly intruded into the vast corpus of denominational and ecumenical pronouncements at many points. Nevertheless, the challenge to transcend such valuations is also evident. One of the best illustrations is in the statements on racial justice made during the decade of the 1950s. By that time a Christian theological consensus against racism had prevailed in virtually every country and denomination, but this consensus had yet to affect social practice at local levels. Christian leadership in such denominations of the American South as the Southern Baptist Convention, the Presbyterian Church in the US, and the Methodist Church, when called upon to formulate the mind of the church on the issue, frequently took a line that they were unable to take in the direct local exercise of leadership. All three of these denominations adopted statements by convincing majorities during the 1950s which clearly marked racial prejudice and discrimination off as evils to be avoided by faithful Christians.

11. Quoted by Hans Küng, *Infallible? An Inquiry*, tr. Edward Quinn, Doubleday. Garden City, New York 1971, p. 98.

12. Ibid., pp. 98–99.

13. In the dogma of the Assumption of Mary, defined by Pope Pius XII in 1954.

14. *Lumen Gentium*, Section 25.

15. Pope John XXIII is alleged to have remarked that 'I'm not infallible; I'm infallible only when I speak *ex cathedra*. But I'll never speak *ex cathedra*.' Quoted by Hans Küng, op. cit., p. 87.

16. Edward Schillebeeckx, 'The Problem of the Infallibility of the Church's Office: A Theological Reflection', in Schillebeeckx and Bas van Iersel (eds), *Truth and Certainty*, tr. David Smith, Herder and Herder, New York 1973, p. 93.

17. Küng, op. cit., pp. 181–185.

18. Ibid., pp. 182–183.

19. *Truth and Certainty*, p. 93.

20. Charles E. Curran, *Contemporary Problems in Moral Theology*, Fides Publishers, Notre Dame, Ind. 1970, p. 264.

21. Ibid., p. 265.

22. Of course authority is not real unless it is accepted as valid. This point is implied by the excellent definition of authority in Robert M. MacIver, *The Web of Government*, rev. ed., The Free Press, New York 1965: 'By authority we mean the established *right*, within any social order, to determine policies, to pronounce judgments on relevant issues, and to settle controversies, or, more broadly, to act as leader or guide to other men. When we speak of *an* authority we mean a person or body of persons possessed of this right. The accent is primarily on right, not power. Power alone has no legitimacy, no mandate, no office. Even the most ruthless tyrant gets nowhere unless he can clothe himself with authority.' (p. 63). The 'right' which establishes authority may or may not be grounded in God or ultimate truth, but in any event it will not function as authority socially unless it is a right which is recognized by the people. In a perceptive study of the psychology of authority, William W. Meissner makes this same point: 'Authority, then, can be defined as a dynamic and reciprocal relationship between two or more persons in which one claims to be a bearer of authority, and at least one accepts the claim of the bearer to be authoritative in some area of his own existence.' *The Assault on Authority: Dialogue or Dilemma*, Orbis Books, Maryknoll, New York 1971, p. 32. Meissner emphasizes the common identification of all persons within this relationship to the group: 'Both superior and subject find common ground in their respective identification with the group. Through that identification they become sharers in a more or less common value-orientation.' (p. 61). This means that the subject must himself regard the exercise of authority as being in harmony with his own fundamental values: 'The individual generally perceives the command as obliging to obedience with moral force only when the command is congruent with accepted role-expectations and when the matter of the command is consistent with the individual's internalized value-system.' (p. 81). These points suggest that at the deeper levels of group life, appeals based on authority cannot be effective unless they express to some extent what is already written in the consciousness of those to whom the appeals are made.

23. Alexander Miller, *The Renewal of Man*, Doubleday, Garden City, New York 1955, section quoted in Harmon L. Smith and Louis W. Hodges, *The Christian and His Decisions: An Introduction to Christian Ethics*, Abingdon Press, Nashville 1969, p. 154.

24. I do not mean to suggest that all Christians in any previous generation supported such outrages, but only that enough did to give great traditional weight to them.

25. Paul Ramsey, *Who Speaks for the Church?*, Abingdon Press,

Nashville 1967.
26. Ibid., pp. 135–136.
27. David Halberstam, *The Best and the Brightest*, Random House, New York 1972.
28. *Who Speaks for the Church?*, p. 138.
29. Ibid.
30. Daniel D. McCracken, 'Ethical Problems of the Expert Witness in National Decision Making Involving the Assessment of Technology', unpublished BD thesis, Union Theological Seminary, New York 1970, pp. 42–50.
31. Quoted by Sebastian de Grazia, *The Political Community: A Study of Anomie*, University of Chicago Press 1948, p. 189.
32. Michael Novak, *The Experience of Nothingness*, Harper and Row, New York 1970, p. 6.
33. Letter to Bishop Mandell Creighton, 5 April 1887.
34. See Chapter 2 above.
35. Cf. Edward H. Madden, *Civil Disobedience and Moral Law in Nineteenth-Century American Philosophy*, University of Washington Press, Seattle 1968, especially Chapter 6.

7 Ideological Presumptions

1. The terms 'ideology' and 'utopia' are distinguished by Karl Mannheim, *Ideology and Utopia: An Introduction to the Sociology of Knowledge* (New York: Harcourt, Brace and World, 1936), trs. Louis Wirth and Edward Shils, on the basis of their supportive or shattering effects on the *status quo*. In a sense, the two terms, even as employed by Mannheim, point toward the same ethical reality: social ideals which transcend any particular situation. In this chapter, the term ideology will include what is usually meant by the term utopia. The tendency of ideological consciousness is to treat particular forms of social organization as ideal, whether these be past, present, or potential.
2. Jan Milic Lochman, *Church in a Marxist Society: A Czechoslovak View*, Harper and Row, New York and SCM Press 1970, pp. 58–9.
3. Ibid., pp. 152–153.
4. Ibid., p. 145.
5. Ibid., p. 106.
6. See in particular Gustavo Gutierrez, *A Theology of Liberation*.
7. In a volume written in the midst of the Cold War era, Charles C. West criticized Josef Hromadka and Hungarian church leaders for 'a longing for a *kulturchristliche* unity of religion with social power' such as was also typical of various Western anti-Communists (including John Foster Dulles). 'In the last analysis', he writes, these representatives of Christian pro- and anti-Communism 'think in terms of a faith which is less than the Christian faith, a faith in culture, society, and politics informed by a unifying religion, which will meet Communism as friend

or enemy, on its own level'. *Communism and the Theologians: Study of an Encounter*, SCM Press and Westminster Press 1958, p. 77. West has since substantially revised his judgment of Hromadka's theology and role during those years, but this writing from that era is an intriguing example of how theology can lead to loss of a sense of responsibility for the overall shape of society. If Christian symbols, etc., are to be used as a 'unifying religion' to provide legitimation and cohesion for a social order based upon values which are deeply alien to Christian faith then, of course, this must be resisted. But is there not a sense in which Christians *must* seek a 'unity of religion with social power'?

8. Christopher Dawson, *The Historical Reality of Christian Culture: A Way to the Renewal of Human Life*, Harper and Brothers, New York 1960, p. 36.

9. Ibid., p. 112.

10. Emil Brunner, *Christianity and Civilization*, Scribner 1949, Vol. II, p. 131.

11. Ibid., p. 132. Brunner did express optimism that 'the lowest point of secularization seems to be behind us' p. 139.

12. Yoder, *The Politics of Jesus*, p. 246.

13. Ibid., p. 248.

14. Martin Luther, 'Temporal Authority: To What Extent It Should Be Obeyed', in *Luther's Works*, XLV, Muhlenberg Press, Philadelphia 1962, p. 91. Luther's viewpoint can be described as 'strangely compatible' with Yoder's in the sense that both divorce the gospel itself and the evangelical ethic from the world of actual governing responsibility and both see the gospel working in the world, not in separation from it. The compatibility is 'strange' however in that Luther strongly urges a Christian sense of responsibility in that other realm of political power while Yoder (having concluded with Luther that one cannot govern without doing evil things) insists that Christians remain over against that other realm, in judgment against it.

15. *Christianizing the Social Order*, p. 127.

16. T. S. Eliot, *Christianity and Culture*, Harcourt Brace, New York [1949] 1960, pp. 21–22. See also Eliot, *The Idea of a Christian Society,* Faber and Faber, London 1939.

17. His position has a curious resemblance to that of Paul Ramsey in the latter's attempt to combine principles of 'discrimination' and 'proportion' in just war doctrine. The principle of proportion is concerned with consequences or, we might say, the relevance of our actions to the achievement of desirable results. The principle of discrimination is concerned with the use of none other than morally permissible means. The latter is essentially a sectarian response, the former a 'church-type' one. But, taking his work as a whole, Ramsey's principle of discrimination (his sectarianism) tends to be overpowered by his realism regarding results, while with Yoder the reverse seems to be the case.

18. Cf. Chapter 4 above.

19. *The Politics of Jesus*, p. 250.

20. It is important to note that the state is not, by definition, simply coercive. R. M. MacIver's analysis of the state in *The Web of Government* emphasizes throughout that civil society is an infinitely complex social phenomenon through which most action is voluntary. Talcott Parsons speaks of political power as 'a mobilization of the total relational context as a facility relative to the goal in question'. *The Social System*, The Free Press, Glencoe, Illinois 1951, p. 126. We can think of the state as being a function of society as a whole: it is when society as a whole, with all of its infinitely complex patterns of private relationships, functions as a whole.

21. Political power needs to be understood more carefully as the power of influence. Franz Neumann, *The Democratic and the Authoritarian State*, The Free Press of Glencoe, New York 1957 [1950], distinguishes between 'control of nature' and 'control of man', and reminds us that the latter alone is properly termed political. Power over nature is intellectual and physical and usually measurable. Political power is essentially a matter of influence. Accordingly, anything that affects or influences the will of human beings is potentially political. The consolidation of the power of influence through the state involves both coercive aspects (it being remembered that coercion is a use of the power over nature to influence the will of man) and voluntary aspects flowing out of our desire to further the objectives of the state or our recognition that the state's law is morally binding upon us. Those who control the mechanisms of state – the government – are in a position to decide what it is that people must do if they are to avoid the state's coercion or what they must do if they are to fulfil the moral understandings associated with obedience to the state in that particular society.

22. I Samuel 8.10–18.

23. Most twentieth-century fascism seems to have populist rootage, although it is often a populism perverted by popular prejudices, inflamed by demagogism, and manipulated by business interests. That is the characteristic formula of Italian fascism, German Nazism, Spanish Falangism, and Argentinian Peronismo, and it has also been characteristic of the less successful fascist-type movements in the Western democracies. The phenomenon of 'working class totalitarianism' has been explored with great insight by Seymour Martin Lipset, *Political Man: The Social Bases of Politics*, Doubleday Anchor, Garden City, New York 1960, which reviews studies of the populist foundations of some fascist tendencies in modern politics.

24. Benito Mussolini, in *Social and Political Philosophy*, p. 437.

25. This is truer of Tolstoyan anarchism than it is of Marxism. As a pacifist, Tolstoy insisted that positive methods of non-violence (presupposing the goodness of man in the present as well as in the future society) will be most efficacious in overcoming repressive institutions.

26. Jacques Maritain, *Man and the State*, University of Chicago Press 1951, pp. 38, 44.

27. Quoted by George H. Sabine, *A History of Political Theory*,

Holt, Rinehart and Winston, New York, 3rd ed., 1961, p. 396.

28. Where kings or priestly oligarchies or charismatic leaders are believed to have a spiritual power conferred by God which must, however, be recognized by the people to be effective, some form of popular sovereignty is actually involved.

29. Amsterdam Assembly, *The Church and the Disorder of Society*, Harper and Brothers, New York 1948, p. 200.

30. Max Weber's well-known *Protestant Ethic and the Spirit of Capitalism* remains the most discerning analysis of the relationship between Protestant (particularly Calvinist) Christianity and the peculiar forms of capitalism which developed in Western Europe and North America, although aspects of that study have been questioned by other writers. In referring to the 'Protestant ethic' it must be remembered that it is in large measure alien to the real implications of Protestant Christian theology. It should also be remembered that even Weber did not believe that Protestantism 'caused' capitalism to develop. Still, in however distorted a form, Protestant Christianity seriously affected the form of emerging Western capitalism and, in particular, its ideology.

31. John C. Bennett, *Christianity and Communism Today*, Association Press, New York 1962, pp. 140–141.

32. Ibid., p. 142. Bennett adds to these 'the problem of recurring depressions which involve mass unemployment'.

33. Joseph A. Schumpeter, *Capitalism, Socialism and Democracy*, Harper and Row, New York, 3rd ed., 1950, p. 415.

34. Theobald refers to a system in which individuals are permitted to create things, such as craft items or new products or art, for sale on the open market in a society with a guaranteed annual income. In the past few years there has been a remarkable development of such activity in Western Countries, particularly among young people. See Robert Theobald, *Free Men and Free Markets*, Doubleday Anchor, Garden City, New York 1965, p. 165. Theobald develops his proposal in the overall context of a form of welfare capitalism.

35. I have discussed the latter at some length in my book, *Guaranteed Annual Income: The Moral Issues*, Abingdon Press, Nashville 1968. That volume also treats a number of these issues of economic ideology more fully than space permits here.

36. See, e.g., Jacques Ellul, *The Technological Society*, tr. John Wilkinson, Alfred A. Knopf, New York 1964 [1954].

37. E. F. Schumacher, *Small is Beautiful: A Study of Economics as if People Mattered*, Abacus, London 1973.

8 *Moral Judgment and Social Strategy*

1. 'The Conspiracy of Ivory Tower Intellectuals', in Arthur P. Mendel (ed.), *Essential Works of Marxism*, Bantam Books, New York 1961, p. 348.

2. Thurman W. Arnold, *The Folklore of Capitalism*, Yale University Press, New Haven 1937, pp. 13–14. It can be argued that such a criticism is not fully warranted. I doubt whether it fairly characterizes the socialist leader's own motives. Moreover, a part of the folklore of American liberal political history is that many of Thomas' proposals found their way, in time, into the party platforms of the major parties and thence into respectability and enactment. Nevertheless, it cannot be maintained seriously that Thomas was an effective political strategist, and the main thrust of Arnold's criticism seems to me to be fully justified several decades after it was made.

3. Walter G. Muelder, *Foundations of the Responsible Society*, Abingdon Press, Nashville 1959, pp. 39 ff.

4. Wilbert E. Moore, *Social Change*, Prentice-Hall, Englewood Cliffs 1963, p. 24. Cf. Talcott Parsons and Edward A. Shils (eds), *Toward a General Theory of Action*, Harper and Row, New York 1951, for a discussion of the theory of social systems by a number of social scientists.

5. I am sympathetic with most of the objectives of many of the theologians of revolution, but a broad reading of this literature suggests a lack of balance at this point. It is almost as though the Christian should feel ashamed to speak of the gospel of reconciling love so long as any injustice or physical suffering remains on earth, lest the gospel be misunderstood as a smokescreen for complacency. Have we forgotten that apart from reconciling love, all else is dust and ashes and we do not even have sufficient reason and credibility in our revolutionary actions? On the other hand, it is a more typical failing in popular Christianity of the Billy Graham variety to stress the spiritual gospel while neglecting the objective conditions in the absence of which the gospel is empty and unfulfilled. One recalls Graham's own celebrated remark that he was a New Testament evangelist, not an Old Testament prophet – as if there could really be such a thing as a New Testament evangelist without an Old Testament prophetic component. The Christian's presumption must certainly be against either form of one-sidedness.

6. It should be added that a further objective of this and similar events was the attempt to forge a new movement. A movement, as such, can be understood in both instrumental and intrinsic terms. It is instrumental in the sense that it serves the goals of the cause to which it is directed (in this case, civil rights). It is intrinsic in the sense that the quality of fellowship and restoration of personal dignity within the movement already transcend the tangible, intrumental conditions of human existence. Great movements thus have a kind of religious quality, even though they may not be based upon explicitly religious commitments. But as a movement directed toward transcendent ends, it knows that these intrinsic qualities must be undergirded by appropriate new social, economic, and political conditions in order for it to have any lasting significance.

7. These twin objectives of the church are suggested by the line from the Message of the First Assembly of the World Council of Churches (Amsterdam 1948): 'We have to make of the Church in every place a voice

for those who have no voice, and a home where every man will be at home.'

8. See, e.g., John P. Dean and Alex Rosen, *A Manual of Intergroup Relations*, University of Chicago Press 1955.

9. James B. McKee, 'Community Power and Strategies in Race Relations: Some Critical Observations', *Social Problems* 6, Winter 1958–59, p. 202.

10. No value judgment is intended here. It is arguable, as a value proposition, that since both peace in Vietnam and party reform were of great importance, it was morally preferable for McCarthy and McGovern to lose while emphasizing both rather than to win while sacrificing one to the other. But there is not much evidence that either of these campaigns was sufficiently clear about all this strategically.

11. Robert Merton, *Social Theory and Social Structure*, pp. 19–84.

12. Task Force on Violent Aspects of Protest and Confrontation, National Commission on the Cause and Prevention of Violence, Jerome H. Skolnick, Director, *The Politics of Protest*, Simon and Schuster, New York 1969, pp. 107–108. See also various articles in Priscilla Long (ed.), *The New Left: A Collection of Essays*, Porter Sargent, Boston 1969.

13. A striking illustration of how strategies can either enlarge or constrict a potential base of power was afforded by the contrast between the Vietnam Moratorium of 15 October 1969 and the New Mobilization of 15 November 1969, both anti-war events. The former, under the leadership of young people committed to a reformist perspective, snowballed dramatically into a major national event, with large numbers of public officials and leading private citizens participating in several major cities. The event substantially increased public pressure against the Administration's Vietnam policies. The New Mobilization, under the leadership of a coalition of organizations, some of which consciously sought greater polarization, succeeded in massing an immense crowd of protestors in Washington, D.C. But these were mostly young people, and the net effect of the event and its largely revolutionary rhetoric was to constrict, rather than enlarge, the movement's base of power. These observations are based upon close personal contact with both events.

14. Robert M. MacIver, *The More Perfect Union*, Macmillan, New York 1948, pp. 52–61.

15. See Walter Laqueur, 'A Look Back at the Weimar Republic – The Cry Was "Down with Das System"', *The New York Times Magazine*, 23 August 1970, pp. 12 ff., for interesting reflections on the period.

16. George D. Beam, *Usual Politics: A Critique and Some Suggestions for an Alternative*, Holt, Rinehart and Winston, New York 1970, pp. 191–192.

17. See, e.g., Phillip I. Blumberg, 'Introduction to the Politicalization of the Corporation', *The Record* of the Association of the Bar of the City of New York, Vol. 26, No. 5 (May 1971) for an informed discussion of attempts to involve corporations more directly in solving social problems.

18. The demand of James Foreman's 'Black Manifesto' in 1969 for $2 billion in reparations from American churches was and seemed utterly

beyond possible expectation; but that amount was still less than one per cent of the Federal budget. Moreover, as the Synagogue Council of America noted in a statement responding to the Manifesto, 'it is clear that even if these demands were met in full, these inequities and injustices would not be rectified'. The Council urged that 'a far more reliable guide for priorities is to be found in the Kerner Commission Report, the "Freedom Budget" of the A. Philip Randolph Institute and in the National Urban League's "Domestic Marshall Plan",' each of which, it may be noted, places primary reliance upon governmental action. The net effect of the Manifesto was to become – both for its advocates and for its opponents – a diversion at a time when there was need for increased church efforts to involve government in the problems of black economic empowerment. See Robert S. Lecky and H. Elliott Wright (eds), *Black Manifesto: Religion, Racism and Reparations*, p. 141. Another illustration of a tendency to avoid strategies oriented towards government was provided by a special committee at the US Conference on 'The Church and Society' in 1967. The committee was created by the Conference to formulate, for the churches, a strategy of response to the urban crisis. The strategic suggestions offered by the group had mainly to do with the churches' own education and action programmes, investment of church money, etc. Only as an afterthought, and at the insistence of one or two members, was it added that Christians should 'demand and mobilize support for legislation that will attack the problem of redistribution of power and income'. *Report of the US Conference on Church and Society*, National Council of Churches, New York 1968, pp. 89–90. This document should be compared with the report of the Kerner Commission, in preparation at the same time, which emphasized greater governmental involvement in dealing with the problems of the cities.

19. Cf. Saul D. Alinsky, *Reveille for Radicals*.
20. George D. Beam, *Usual Politics*, pp. 115–116.

Index

Index

Index

269

Index

Race relations, 140, 148f., 250f., 255
Racism, 90ff., 112, 255
Ramsey, Paul, 16, 23ff., 31f., 45f., 53f., 170, 172f., 180, 243f., 246, 249, 256f.
Rand, Ayn, 88
Rasmussen, Larry L., x
Rauschenbusch, Walter, 48, 66, 115, 145, 190, 235, 246, 252
Rawls, John, 25, 100, 244, 251
Reference groups, 153ff., 154
Reformism, 225f., 262
Relativism (see also Situation ethics), 9ff., 61ff.
Responsible society (see also World Council of Churches), 201
Revolution, 34, 143, 149, 204, 217, 225f., 228ff., 236, 238, 262
Revolution, theology of, 66
Rosen, Alex, 262
Rousseau, Jean Jacques, 200
Ruether, Rosemary, 248
Rules of Practice, 25f., 31
Russell, Bertrand, 81, 249

Schillebeeckx, Edward, 163, 255
Schumacher, E. F., 214, 260
Schumpeter, Joseph A., 209, 260
Schwarz, Fred, 112, 252
Secular theology, 12f.
Seneca, 118
Sermon on the Mount, 119
Sex (see also Marriage), 8, 45, 77f., 89f., 96, 108, 168
Shermin, Mark, 252
Sin, 72, 80, 95, 106, 108ff., 116, 119f., 238
Situation ethics, 14ff., 27, 28ff.
Smith, Adam, 206f.
Smith, Harmon L., 256
Social Gospel, 66, 182
Social sciences, 9, 31f.

Socialism (see also Marxism), 8, 184, 205, 209ff.
Spiritual life, 64f.
Spiritualism, 71, 128
State (see also Government), 176ff., 197ff., 233ff.
Stigler, George J., 136f., 253
Stoicism, 117f., 200
Subsidiarity, doctrine of, 46f., 142ff.
Suicide, 73ff.
Summary rules, 15f., 24f., 51

Technology, 8, 34, 169, 214f.
Tennyson, Alfred, Lord, 10
Theobald, Robert, 212, 260
Thomas, Norman, 216, 261
Thoreau, Henry David, 142, 254
Tillich, Paul, 11, 51, 242, 246, 248
Tolstoy, Leo, 119ff., 252, 259f.
Troeltsch, Ernst, 33, 191

United Nations, 22, 250
Universalism, 251

Vahanian, Gabriel, 14, 242
Vatican Council, first, 161
Vatican Council, second, 7, 162
Vietnam War, 171f., 225, 232, 262
Violence (see also War), 34f., 85, 121f., 217, 226, 237f.
Visser 't Hooft, W. A., 243

War (see also Violence), 46, 51, 79, 117, 180
Ward, Harry F., 111, 251
Ward, W. G., 161
Weber, Max, 255, 260
Wesley, John, 109, 207
West, Charles C., 257f.
World Council of Churches, 48f., 91, 115, 170, 172, 201, 262

Yoder, John Howard, 33ff., 124ff., 187ff., 191, 193, 244, 258f.